THE DEVELOPMENT OF EDUCATIONAL
ADMINISTRATION IN ENGLAND AND WALES

THE
DEVELOPMENT
OF
EDUCATIONAL ADMINISTRATION
IN
ENGLAND AND WALES

P. H. J. H. GOSDEN

Department of Education, University of Leeds

BASIL BLACKWELL OXFORD

First printed in 1966

Printed in Great Britain for BASIL BLACKWELL & MOTT, LTD.
by A. R. MOWBRAY & Co. LIMITED in the City of Oxford
and bound at the KEMP HALL BINDERY

CONTENTS

ACKNOWLEDGMENTS

THE preparation of this study has left me indebted to many for assistance in tracing material. My thanks are due especially to members of the staffs of the University and Institute of Education Libraries at Leeds and to Miss Downie and her staff at the library of the Department of Education and Science for their patience in meeting my requests from time to time during the last few years. I would like to thank the Editor of the *British Journal of Educational Studies* for permission to include in chapter five some material concerning the establishment of the Board of Education which has previously appeared in that Journal. I also wish to acknowledge the assistance which is being given by the University of Leeds towards the publication of this work.

P. H. J. H. GOSDEN
Department of Education, University of Leeds

November, 1965.

ABBREVIATIONS

Minute — Minute of the Committee of Council for Education.

Newcastle Cssn — Royal Commission to Inquire into the State of Popular Education in England.
Chairman: Duke of Newcastle.

S.I.C. — Schools Inquiry Commission.
Chairman: Lord Taunton.

Cross Cssn — Royal Commission to Inquire into the working of the Elementary Education Acts in England and Wales.
Chairman: R. A. Cross.

Bryce Cssn — Royal Commission on Secondary Education.
Chairman: J. Bryce.

P.R.O. — Public Record Office.

INTRODUCTION

THIS book is not a history of education; its aim is the much more limited one of examining the way in which the present central and local agencies for the administration of the educational system have come to be as they are. The main elements in the present administrative organization came into existence in the years around the turn of the century, the Board of Education at the centre and the local authorities immediately responsible for the schools in town and country. During the last half century there has been a great increase in the amount of work falling on the central and local administrations, their powers have been modified as their responsibilities have widened, but the essential structure has not been changed. For this reason I have laid emphasis in this book on the developments in the last years of the nineteenth and the first years of the twentieth centuries.

The growth of these administrative agencies formed part of the extension of the machinery of government which a wider conception of the role of the state made necessary. It is easy to look back at the nineteenth century and to criticize the limited and occasionally fumbling approach shown by statesmen to the problems of administering the schools. The need to encourage the spread of elementary schooling, to encourage the study of those sciences and arts which were of value to industry and to reform the endowed grammar schools all appeared to be quite separate issues, each needing its own government office to deal with it; the idea of education as a comprehensive community service had not gained acceptance.

The difficulty of creating a complete system of elementary schooling without the aid of some local authority was such that in 1870 school boards began to be set up. They are a useful example of authorities directly elected solely for educational purposes. Where they governed large enough areas, they were successful, sometimes outstandingly so; it can be argued that education in this country would have been better served had its local administration been entrusted to such *ad hoc* authorities after 1902 instead of coming within the orbit of multipurpose local government bodies.

One of the main functions of the administration is to ensure an adequate supply of school buildings, teachers, books and so on; this is a function which can only be discharged through the provision of finance, and it is possible to look on the system of educational administration as a system created for bringing finance to the schools. In these terms the growth of the administration may be measured from the first grant of £20,000 in 1833, distributed directly by the Treasury, to the £1,166,800,000 spent by public education authorities of England and Wales in the fiscal year 1963–64.

Experience has shown that the source of the financial supply has an important bearing on the relative amount of influence exercised by the central and local agencies and there can be little doubt of the need for locally raised finance if the locality is to have much influence over the policy which it is to implement. Since the beginning of this century the state has usually provided a half or slightly more of the total needed and the rest has been found from local sources.

Public Expenditure on Education, 1900–1938

	Total	From government grants per cent	From rates, etc. per cent
1900–01	£16,200,000	56·4	43·6
1910–11	£27,537,000	48·5	51·5
1920–21	£70,541,000	56·1	43·9
1930–31	£82,323,000	53·2	46·8
1937–38	£92,369,000	49·5	50·5

In the decade preceding the Local Government Act of 1958 about 60 per cent of expenditure was met from government grant. The introduction of the block grant under that Act to cover the main local government services has made any accurate division of educational expenditure impossible in more recent years.

The papers dating from the early years of the Board of Education have been sorted and are now available at the Public Records Office; without access to these it would have been impossible to undertake much of this study. Unfortunately the operation of the Records Act continues to render impracticable a close and fully informed study of the internal working of the central administrative agency in recent years.

THE DEVELOPMENT OF EDUCATIONAL ADMINISTRATION IN ENGLAND AND WALES

Chapter 1

THE COMMITTEE OF COUNCIL FOR EDUCATION TO 1856

ONE of the effects of the contest between the religious parties for control of the schools of this country in the nineteenth century was to make statesmen extremely cautious in their approach to the question of elementary education. This can be seen in the long delay before any state aid was given to the schools, in the form which the aid eventually took and in the extraordinary administrative system that was evolved to deal with primary education.

The first grants to assist in building elementary schools were offered in 1833, but no special machinery was set up to administer these funds before 1839. The limited nature of this first incursion into educational finance may be seen from the wording of the vote 'That a sum, not exceeding twenty thousand pounds, be granted to His Majesty, to be issued in aid of private subscriptions for the erection of school houses for the education of the poorer classes in Great Britain, to the 31st day of March, 1834'. The grants were paid directly to promoters of schools by the Treasury which laid down the conditions applicants had to meet in a Minute of 30th August, 1833. The main requirements were that the whole of the sum must actually be spent on erecting the school itself—none could be spent on a teacher's house—no grant was to be made until the promoters had received at least one half of the total cost from voluntary contributions, applicants were to submit their accounts to audit, no application would be entertained which was not recommended by the National Society or by the British and Foreign School Society and the most populous places were to be given preference in the allocation of grants. An immediate result was to give a great stimulus to local effort so that far more applications were received than could be satisfied from the total sum available. In these circumstances the Treasury gave priority to the claims of those promoting large schools providing more than four hundred places.

The administration of these grants was extremely loose. The Treasury had no officers to inquire fully into the applications which it received, and relied on the reports supporting applications from the National Society and from the British and Foreign Schools Society

1

who really became the agents for discovering whether applicants for grant were proposing to meet real needs and whether they were likely to do so in an efficient manner. The schools were not constructed to any approved plans, nor was any particular form of trust deed indicated. The Treasury laid down no conditions to ensure either that the fabric would be maintained or that the instruction would be sound.

The need both to increase the grant and to enforce more stringent conditions for its disbursement lay behind the decision to appoint a Committee of the Privy Council for Education. The establishment of this Committee did not need an Act of Parliament, being effected by an Order in Council. In this way it was possible to proceed without stirring the rival religious parties too vigorously. Moreover, the accepted manner of dealing with fresh executive functions was by setting up a Committee of the Privy Council. The recognized functions of government at the beginning of the nineteenth century did not extend far beyond questions of peace and war, foreign relations, and justice. The century saw a vast extension of those functions in such fields as trade, local government and agriculture as well as education; it saw, in fact, a revolution in the concept of the work of government of which the establishment and growth of an Education Department was but a part.

The Committee of the Privy Council for Education was set up on 10th April, 1839, and consisted of four members, the Lord President of the Council, the Lord Privy Seal, the Chancellor of the Exchequer and the Home Secretary. The Lord President and the Lord Privy Seal normally served on all such committees, the Chancellor of the Exchequer had an obvious interest in the distribution of grants, while the Home Secretary was concerned with domestic matters generally. Dr. Kay (later Kay-Shuttleworth) was appointed as secretary to the Committee; he first made a reputation by his study of housing conditions and public health in Manchester, later he had joined the Poor Law Commission and had taken a special interest in pauper education. As Secretary to the Committee for Education, he soon showed what a wise choice the Committee had made in appointing him.

The Committee met in the Privy Council Office at Whitehall probably about once a month. Its decisions were published as Minutes of the Committee of Council on Education. Correspondence was conducted by the Secretary in the name of the 'Lords of the Committee' and until the establishment of the Board of Education at the end of the century, all letters from members of the staff of the central office were phrased to express their Lordships' wishes. 'My Lords desire it to be known that . . .' or 'My Lords regret that . . .' were customary openings to letters originating with civil servants at the Education Office. The Lord President attended daily at the Office of the Privy Council to deal with business arising in any of its departments and the Secretary took controversial or doubtful matters to him for a decision, dealing with routine matters himself.

The establishment of a Committee and the appointment of a Secretary made it possible for the state to evolve a policy which it could enforce by making grants available for particular objects and conditional on the fulfilment of certain requirements. Changes in the conditions on which the only existing grants—those for building— were made came in June, 1839, when two important alterations were announced. In the first place the Committee made it clear that it was willing to make grants to schools which stood outside of the two great societies and secondly 'that the rules hitherto adopted of making a grant to those places where the largest proportion is subscribed be not invariably adhered to, should application be made from very poor and populous districts, where subscriptions to a sufficient amount cannot be obtained'.[1] In September a Minute was published setting out Regulations for the Grant of Parliamentary Moneys[2] which stated that, among other things, the Committee would need to be satisfied that the proposed school would be 'efficiently and permanently supported', that the building would provide at least six square feet for each child and that the school would be open to inspection. Two months later a standard application form for building grants was issued, much of which was concerned with seeking particulars of the construction of the proposed building.[3]

At the end of the year a circular was issued setting out the circumstances in which applications for aid to meet current expenses in running schools might be made.[4] Such grants were to be regarded as exceptional for 'My Lords are of opinion that Schools will be most extensively used when supported by the exertions of the school committees and other benevolent individuals by whom they have been founded. The grant of money voted by Parliament is intended to encourage, not to supersede or impair, such local exertions; applications for aid to defray the annual expenses of a school can therefore only be admitted in consequence of difficulties of a peculiar character rendering the case an exception to general rules.' There were three conditions to be met for this aid, firstly, a great local educational deficiency, secondly, the inhabitants must have done their utmost without aid, and, finally, it had to be shown that temporary aid would ensure the lasting prosperity of a school.

In 1840 the Committee issued a series of plans with specifications for new school buildings in order 'to diffuse an acquaintance with the arrangements which have been sanctioned by extensive experience, as best adapted to different systems of instruction'.[5] The Committee offered the assistance of their counsel on such legal matters as the titles to sites, trust deeds and building contracts. Later in the year, specimen forms of conveyance were published. Copies of these specimen conveyance forms and of model plans were sent to all applicants for building grants.

Perhaps the most important development brought about on the setting up of the Committee of Council was the formulation of a policy for the training of teachers. One of the first moves made by the Committee was to attempt to establish a State Normal School, but this proposal had to be withdrawn in the face of bitter opposition from the rival religious communions. Having frustrated the plan for state training facilities, the various churches began to set up their own training colleges. The Committee of Council encouraged these projects by offering grants towards the erection of suitable buildings from 1843. The most important step in this field was taken in 1846 when the Dutch system of apprenticing future school teachers was introduced. Queen's Scholarships of £20 or £25 tenable at a normal school were offered to those who had successfully completed their apprenticeships and passed the appropriate examinations. Special annual grants were offered to schoolmasters who had completed courses of training in normal schools to augment their salaries. The apprentices received stipends from the Committee of Council rising from £10 in the first year to £20 in the fifth and last year.[6] Kay-Shuttleworth estimated that in 1852 about four-fifths of the total cost of a place in a training college was being met from government funds;[7] he forecast that 'The Minute of 1846 will make a complete revolution by filling the training colleges with the Queen's Scholars—the elite of the apprentices, who are themselves the most promising scholars in the elementary schools of Great Britain'.

The Order in Council of 3rd June, 1839, made it clear that the Committee would in future appoint officials to visit all schools in respect of which grants were paid to see that the conditions attached to them were fulfilled.[8] In December the first two inspectors of schools were appointed. There was a great deal of opposition from the Church of England to the appointment of government inspectors, and after negotiations the so-called Concordat of 1840 was issued in the form of a Minute.[9] This included provisions which really gave a right of veto over the appointment of inspectors of Church schools to the two Archbishops since 'no person be appointed without their concurrence'. Moreover 'the inspectors of such schools shall be appointed during pleasure, and that it shall be within the power of each Archbishop, at all times, with regard to his own province, to withdraw his concurrence in such appointment, whereupon the authority of the inspector shall cease, and a fresh appointment take place'. It proved necessary to make similar agreements with the other religious denominations shortly after.

The instructions issued to the inspectors from time to time give a reasonably full picture of their activites. In 1840 their duties fell into three categories.[10] Firstly they were to inquire into applications for grants to build or to support schools, checking such particulars as the size of the populations to be served, the number of children involved and the schoolmaster's salary. Secondly, it was their duty to inspect schools which had been aided by grants from public funds. Here they were to report on the condition of the building, arrangement of classes, school organization and discipline, the means of instruction and its efficiency, also 'whether the master has an opportunity of becoming a companion to the children in their hours of relaxation'. In their inspection of schools, inspectors were especially to collaborate with the promoters and to avoid undermining their authority. Thirdly, they were to undertake inquiries into the general condition of elementary education in particular districts as instructed from time to time.

The amount of work falling on the inspectors increased rapidly as the influence of the Committee of Council became more widespread. In 1846 the Minutes pointed out that while each grant-aided school should be visited annually, it was not possible with the limited number of inspectors to visit each school more often than once every two years. In 1850 the first two assistant inspectors were appointed, these men worked under the guidance of the full inspectors in charge of districts. By 1852 there were 24 inspectors and 9 assistant inspectors, their salaries and travelling expenses amounting each year to about £26,000. The Minutes of 1846 had added greatly to their duties, indeed, Kay-Shuttleworth wrote that 'The time of the inspectors is now almost absorbed by the administration of the Minutes of 1846 and their personal influence concentrated on the schools which partake of the benefits of those Minutes'.[11]

The work of the inspectors was complicated by their denominational form of organization. By the end of the 1850s there were seven different sets of inspectors in England and Scotland, of which four covered the whole of England—namely those of the Church of England, the British and Foreign Society, the Roman Catholic Church and the workhouse schools. One consequence of this arrangement was that each inspector had to spend more time and money on travel than he would otherwise have had to do. Another was that the administration became much more complicated for all accounts in the Education Department had to be kept in this sevenfold division of denominations thereby adding greatly to the amount of labour involved.[12]

The principal check made by the office on the activities and movements of inspectors was through a system of official diaries in which inspectors recorded how they spent their days and which were forwarded weekly to the Secretary for inspection. The inspection of diaries and the maintenance of a close check on the work of inspectors in order to preserve consistency throughout the country in the disbursement of the various grants (usually paid in small sums to individual schoolmasters, pupil teachers and bodies of managers) complicated further the rapidly growing administrative work of the Committee. The staff of the Education Office itself had grown from the one secretary of 1839 to 41 officers by 1854, this figure included the secretary, two assistant secretaries, six examiners, a solicitor, an architect and thirty clerks.[13]

Kay-Shuttleworth resigned from the post of Secretary in 1849, and was succeeded by R. W. Lingen. A great deal of the success of the Committee of Council was due to his efforts in the early years. He wrote of the years of Peel's Ministry (1841–46), 'the principles of a great public policy were in operation, and were silently attracting to themselves, like centres of crystallization, a mass of precedent and authority, which was destined to become irresistible'.[14] In the first few years of its existence, the Committee of Council had developed a system of specific grants designed to forward its policies, and it had built up a central administration and an inspectorate. The annual budget administered by the Committee increased from £30,000 in 1839 to £369,000 in 1855, the last year before the creation of the Education Department proper and of the office of Vice-President.

It was this rapid growth in the activities and therefore in the expenditure of the Committee of Council which led to the appointment of a Vice-President in 1856. Members of the House of Commons had complained that they were without any effective means of contact with an office that was spending more and more.[15] This complaint was justified. The Committee had no statutory authority for extending its activities but relied upon the discretion which the executive is held to possess. Thus the Lord President and his Committee quite legally extended their activities so long as no statute forbade them to do so. Furthermore the government could ask Parliament to vote supply for a non-statutory activity and the procedure connected with this particular vote gave the Commons little opportunity for detailed criticism.

In a Memorandum which he wrote in 1855 on this problem of the representation of the Committee of Council in the House of Commons, the Secretary, Lingen, indicated that such representation as there was might be held to be through the Home Secretary who was a member of the Committee. He pointed out that the Home Secretary was thought to be too busy with his other duties to be familiar with more than the general outlines of the Committee's work and that a real difficulty did exist. He felt that the best step would be to make the Secretary's office a Parliamentary one. 'It would effectively put the Education Department *en rapport* with the House of Commons, and indeed generally with the Legislature. The Parliamentary Secretary would be a sort of junior counsel *ad hoc* to the Home Secretary as his leader in the House of Commons, and departmentally, he would act under the Lord President as chief.'[16]

The administrative system was not statutory because of the religious difficulties which made it almost impossible to get a majority in the House of Commons for any educational measure. Lingen set out clearly the main obstacle in bringing about a closer relationship between the Committee and the House of Commons. He feared that his own scheme might have the effect of breaking up the whole educational system. 'The public with which the Department deals is not a political but a religious one, and a religious one in fragments. Take each fragment by itself, Church, Wesleyan, Roman Catholic, etc., and talk to any one of their leading men and you see in a moment how they dread and shrink from any system which subjects the congregation to any civic and undenominational power; no matter whether that power be the Vestry, Town Council, Board of Guardians, or the

B

House of Commons. "Find us the money and leave us to ourselves" is the prayer of each and all of them. Now this system can be, and has been, carried on by an office not so directly represented in, or communicating with, the House of Commons as to involve a clash between the political and religious systems. I do not think myself that the two could proceed in very close contact on the present footing. The schools are so purely Church, Roman Catholic, Wesleyan, etc., in their character and in their management so little educational, that I think the relations of the government with them require to be manipulated by passionless hands such as belong rather to bureaucracy than to Parliamentary ministries.' The only people prepared to work in the educational field were solely prepared to do so 'as members of religious bodies, and not as simple citizens'. If they were driven out of the business—perhaps as a consequence of political defeat, 'their beating might have much the same effect upon Education in England as the revocation of the Edict of Nantes had upon trade in France, viz., to leave no one ready to go on with the work for the public benefit'.[17]

Apart from the lack of contact between the Education Office and the House of Commons and the difficulties which might beset any attempt at a reorganization of the relationship, the lack of any coordination among the various government agencies which offered aid to education appeared to be an increasingly pressing problem. In 1856 the government tried to deal with both of these issues and introduced measures intended to represent the Education Office in the Commons and to unite the agencies offering grants. An Act was passed[18] to establish the post of Vice-President of the Committee of the Privy Council on Education 'who would be the responsible minister there in all matters connected with education so far as the government were concerned'.[19] By an Order in Council the Science and Art Department was removed from the superintendence of the Board of Trade and placed under the Committee. The Education Department was set up under this title and was to consist of the 'educational establishment of the Privy Council Office' and of the 'establishment for the encouragement of Science and Art'. These were not to merge, but by placing them both under the same political leadership, it was hoped that their activities would be co-ordinated. The Order in Council[20] also brought the inspection of Army and Navy schools within the jurisdiction of the Committee of Council. The Committee itself was enlarged to take account of its new responsibilities; apart from the addition of the

Vice-President, the Secretary of State for War and the First Lord of the Admiralty became members.

The reorganization of 1856 recognized that the essentially temporary Committee of the Privy Council had developed into an executive department of the State. Unfortunately some of the new arrangements did not work as smoothly as had been expected. By 1863 those schools appertaining to the Army, the Navy and the Poor Law authorities had been withdrawn from the jurisdiction of the Department. The position of the Vice-President led to a certain amount of constitutional confusion. Many members of the House of Commons felt that the head of the Education Department should be a member of their House and answerable directly to them, consequently the relative powers of the Lord President—always a peer—and the Vice-President became a matter of contention. The Science and Art Department developed quite independently of the Education Department, the former at South Kensington, the latter in Whitehall. The whole arrangement was to be subject to inquiries by Parliamentary Committees in 1865, 1866 and 1884 and it was only with the reorganization at the beginning of the twentieth century that a satisfactory solution was found.

REFERENCES

[1] Order in Council, 3/6/1839.
[2] Minute, 24/9/1839.
[3] Minute, 20/11/1839.
[4] Circular of December, 1839.
[5] Minutes of Committee of Council, 1839–40.
[6] Minutes of August and December, 1846.
[7] J. Kay-Shuttleworth, Public Education as affected by the Minutes of the Committee of the Privy Council from 1846 to 1852, p. 69.
[8] Ibid., p. 72.
[9] Minute, 15/7/1840.
[10] Instructions for the Inspectors of Schools, Minutes of 1840.
[11] J. Kay-Shuttleworth, op. cit., p. 87.
[12] Newcastle Cssn., 1861, vol. VI, para 500. Evidence of Lingen.
[13] Civil Estimates, 1854–55.
[14] J. Kay-Shuttleworth, op. cit., p. 6.
[15] MS. Confidential Memorandum by Lingen on the Committee of Council on Education in the House of Commons, 6/6/1855.
[16] Ibid., para. 7.
[17] Ibid., para. 8.
[18] 19 & 20 Vic., c. 116.
[19] Sir George Grey, Hansard, 17th July, 1856, col. 991.
[20] Order in Council, 25/2/1856.

CHAPTER 2

THE COMMITTEE OF COUNCIL FOR EDUCATION
1856–1899

APART from including elementary schools administered by other government departments within the surveillance of the Inspectorate, the reorganization of the Committee of Council and the establishment of the Education Department had little immediate effect on the actual work of the state in this field. There was a good deal of dissatisfaction with the existing condition of elementary education as it had grown up under the voluntary system. A great sum of money had been spent by the State since 1839, yet many children remained unscathed by the educative influences thus encouraged. The whole question of whether the Voluntary system had shown itself capable of developing to meet the need or whether a solution should be sought in other directions needed to be settled. The House of Commons agreed to a motion proposed by Sir John Pakington urging that a Commission be appointed to inquire into the problem of elementary education; the consequence was the appointment of a Commission under the chairmanship of the Duke of Newcastle which reported in 1861.

The evidence which the Commission heard throws a great deal of light on the administrative structure which had grown up. The Commission found that 'The general nature of the administration of the Privy Council grants may be most easily understood by viewing the Committee of Council for Education in the light of a Society, like the National or British and Foreign Schools Societies, assisting local efforts to promote Education, without reference to the religious denominations by which they may be made, but supported by general taxation instead of voluntary contributions'.[1]

The method of working by offering grants while the initiative in building and running schools was left to others meant that the Committee of Council's control over its own expenditure was limited. 'The only control possible must be exercised in the framing of their Minutes; they frame certain conditions, having regard in those conditions, as far as they can judge a priori, to the needs of the country. Having laid down these conditions in a Minute, the Minute constitutes a general offer, and those who fulfil those conditions may afterwards

10

claim the grant. If it should be found that the conditions are inexpedient the Committee does not undertake to vary those conditions as between locality A and locality B; but their Lordships must, if they make any change at all, alter their Minute which constitutes the general offer.'[2]

The limited nature of the Department's control over its own expenditure is illustrated to some extent by this account of the procedure adopted in dealing with new claims for grants. 'Almost every grant begins in this way: someone writes up from a parish to say, "We have got a school here under such and such circumstances; what aid can we get?" In answer to that, a printed form of questions is sent down requiring certain particulars regarding the school, whom it belongs to, who manages it, what its tenure is, what buildings it has got, its income and expenditure; and then winding up at the end by saying, "Do you want a grant for books? Do you want a grant for a certificated teacher? If you do, what is his name? Do you want a grant for pupil teachers, and, if so, how many children have you got in the school? Do you want a capitation grant?" They answer "Yes" or "No", or as the case may require, to all these particulars, and upon that, suitable instructions are sent to them. That is the commencement of almost every application for grant in aid. It originates from someone on the spot who has more or less information that aid is to be got from the government, and writes to the Committee of Council about it.'[3]

In these circumstances it was often difficult to make accurate estimates of the Department's requirements for submission to the Treasury and Parliament. This was especially true in the case of capitation grants and to some extent in building grants; the others could often be estimated more accurately. The number of pupil teachers and certificated masters was known and while a few would fall out each year a few others would come in and a rough balance would be achieved. The problem of estimating the likely increase in the funds required for a particular grant was worst in those years when a more liberal rate of aid was offered. At such times not only did the expenditure become greater upon the same number of applications, but more applications would be made. This had been particularly noticeable in the case of the building grant where the rate had been more than doubled at one time with the result that the actual number of applications was much increased for a number of years.[4]

Capitation grants had only been introduced in 1853 when Russell had introduced a bill to give towns with a population of more than

5,000 power to supplement educational expenditure from the rates. Rural areas were thought not to be able to afford such a levy and for them the government proposed that there should be a capitation grant from the Committee of Council, this was to amount to 4s. to 6s. per boy, and 3s. to 5s. per girl. The conditions attached to this grant were that the inspector should certify average attendance to be at least 75 per cent of the possible number of attendances, that the school should already have an income of at least 14s. each in boys' and 12s. each in girls' schools and that the teacher in charge of the school should be certificated or registered. Russell's bill failed to pass, consequently schools in rural areas now received this aid while those in the towns were no better off. This anomaly was ended in 1856 with the extension to the towns of capitation grants.

The procedure attached to the administration of this grant was that the managers applied on the prescribed form and if the answers were satisfactory, the inspector for the denomination and area in question was asked to visit the school. He would visit the school, having notified the managers of the date of his visit in advance so that they might meet him. He would then write to the examiners at the office setting out his views on the payment of the grant and any other observations on the school he might care to make. The office then communicated with the managers telling them of the inspector's decision and passing on any comments that he might have made. Because of the conditions on which they were paid, the estimate for capitation grants was unusually difficult to make, there was no certainty as to how many schools and scholars would fulfil the conditions in any year. The Secretary of the Department admitted that 'I can only guess it from the number of schools which fall under inspection and from the average number, in past years, of capitation scholars to the rest'.[5] The separate calculation and payment of this grant to each school which satisfied the requirements for this form of aid added greatly to the clerical work of the Education Department.

The grant which gave the Department most scope for the exercise of administrative discretion was probably that for building. The Department tried to ensure that any school which received this aid was built in such a way that one teacher could manage as many as 150 children if necessary since his only assistants would, at best, probably be no more than pupil teachers; in these circumstances the shape and arrangement of the building was a matter of great concern to the Committee of Council. When the number of places to be provided was settled, the central office sent to the sponsors a model plan and specification which stated the quantity of materials that would suffice. The sponsors could vary the specification and plan to some extent, but the final plans had to be submitted to the Committee of Council to be examined by the official architect and get his approval before any building actually began, The office frequently had to object to the plans submitted by sponsors on the grounds of expense and to insist upon reductions before agreeing to the payment of a grant.[6]

After 1859 another factor which began to play an important part in the decision to give or to withhold a building grant was the question of putting a 'conscience clause' in the trust deeds of new schools. The purpose of these clauses was to permit those who were not members of the congregation which ran the school to withdraw from lessons in religious instruction. The use of such clauses was bitterly opposed by the Church, which provided most of the schools. These clauses came to be considered more closely by the Department as a means of checking expenditure during the time that Adderley was Vice-President in Lord Derby's ministry from 1858 to 1859. There was a feeling in Parliament that the education estimates were growing too rapidly, the estimate for 1858 was for £663,435, that for 1859 for £836,920. For this reason it was decided to try to avoid giving grants for two schools in any place where one would serve and so the conscience clause was applied.[7] A few years later under Lowe this policy was to be taken a great deal further, for instead of being occasionally applied to avoid duplication, it became virtually a rule to insist upon it. He claimed that his main object had been to save the public purse and avoid giving the building grant altogether; the cases where promoters of schools yielded and accepted the conscience clause were 'wonderfully few altogether'.[8]

Apart from difficulties in estimating and controlling expenditure accurately, the way in which the grant system was organized had come to place a well-nigh unbearable strain on the administrative organization of the Education Department. The Department was trying to appropriate grants to certain purposes within each school, not simply to hand over a lump sum to the managers annually. Naturally the machinery to ensure such appropriations had to be complicated. In his evidence to the Newcastle Commission, Lingen said, 'If you may have a school in any one of the 52 counties of England and Wales, and if it may belong to either of four different denominations, and if the money which you send down to it may be for four or five different objects each of which has its own conditions and is subject to its own questions, a system of that sort is, of course, one enormous complication. Vice-Presidents who have seen other departments on a large scale would state to you that the internal complication of the system is far greater than they have seen anywhere else. I think that if you were to follow out the present system with its local and denominational sub-division, and with its detailed appropriations, it would break down at its centre, unless you provided a much greater establishment than I think either Parliament or the country would be willing in the long run to agree to. The only way in which you could extend the system would be by simplifying the payments; and simplification really means either not appropriating the money or not following out the appropriation as strictly as you do now. For these reasons I think that the present system is not capable of extension to the whole country.'[9] The administrative work while petty in that comparatively small sums of money were involved in each payment yet was really responsible in that the questions involved in these payments stirred people's deepest feelings very easily. Thus the staff who dealt with the administrative work at the Education Office had to be men of considerable discretion.

The Newcastle Commission found the expense and its tendency to increase to be one of the main defects in a system which had in many ways achieved a great deal. It was particularly alarmed by the capitation grant which had shown very rapid growth. In 1854 this grant had amounted to £5,957, two years later to £20,079, and in 1869 to £61,183, and the Commission found that repeated attempts were being made to get it increased still further. The Commission feared it would soon amount to £300,000 or even more each year.[10] But while expenditure was increasing at this rate, there were thought to be important defects in the system in that the poorer areas were unable to raise the necessary voluntary subscriptions to qualify for grant aid— it was found that only one of the 280 parishes with populations of less than 600 in Somerset had received aid—and the younger and weaker pupils in the aided schools were said to be neglected in favour of the older and brighter. The Commissioners recommendations were, therefore, aimed at remedying these defects and at checking the complication of business in the central office of the Education Department while encouraging greater local interest in the schools.

The recommendations of the Commission brought about important modifications in the administrative system. The most radical suggestion in this regard was that county boards for education should be established with power to levy rates, thus bringing assistance to schools in poorer areas. Whatever its significance as a pointer to later developments, at the time this suggestion was rejected by the government which felt that to place a legal burden on the localities without giving them corresponding control over the schools was unjust. If the system was to remain denominational—as the Commission agreed it should—then control could certainly not pass to county boards. Lowe, in rejecting this particular proposal, pointed out that it merely distributed public expense in a different way without ensuring its more effective use; he found the appropriate classical parallel in the story of Liston who fined himself by taking money out of one pocket and putting it in the other.

Of the two principal administrative changes which arose from the Report, the most widely known is the re-costing of the grants which were offered in order to give effect to the Commission's conclusion that the only way to secure the efficiency of the teaching of every individual scholar 'is to institute a searching examination by competent authority of every child in every school to which grants are to be paid, with the view of ascertaining whether the indispensable elements of knowledge are thoroughly acquired and to make the prospects and position of the teacher dependent to a considerable extent on the results of this examination'.[11] Grants payable to certificated teachers to augment their salaries were abolished and so was the capitation grant in its existing form, and in their place a grant was offered in respect of each child who attained the 'standard' required by individual examination in reading, writing and arithmetic. The new grant would only be payable in respect of children who had made a minimum number of attendances at a school held in approved premises and in the charge of a certificated teacher.

In order to prevent the administrative arrangements at the central office from becoming even more complex, payments to teachers personally were to cease and all payments were in future to be made to the managers of schools. This arrangement was intended to increase the responsibility of managers for their schools and this it achieved in that it ended the direct relationship between teachers and the State. No longer was the teacher to occupy the position of being almost a servant of the State; although he would continue to hold the Department's certificate, he was to be entirely the employee of the managers, to make with them the best terms that he could. It was agreed that the managers would be willing to pay well so as to secure a good teacher who would earn them a large grant; the reality was somewhat at variance with this, at least in the early years, for teachers' salaries fell considerably.

These new arrangements were set out in the Revised Code of 1862. The first Code had been drawn up in 1860 in the form of a House of Commons return.[12] Hitherto the Education Department had always worked through issuing Minutes on particular points, the Code was simply an attempt to bring together such Minutes or parts of Minutes as were still in force so as to give a complete picture of the state's service to elementary education in 1860. Parliamentary papers had been issued a few years previously listing the Minutes in chronological order without attempting to codify them. The Code was henceforth to be issued annually and to be laid before both Houses of Parliament. Although the Codes of the last forty years of the nineteenth century were not a direct result of the work of the Newcastle Commission, they were certainly an indirect result for they really originated with the attempt to view the state's work in this field as a whole. The Codes were really an administrative innovation, their legal basis rested on that of the individual Minutes which they contained. The Minutes were in theory resolutions of the Committee of the Privy Council on Education; in fact they were often issued without any meeting of that Committee taking place. In the early days of the Committee, when some problem or issue arose calling for a new Minute, the Secretary would draft it and take his draft to the Lord President. This would be circulated to members of the Committee who would comment on it and propose any amendments they felt were necessary; eventually a formal meeting would be held and the final draft of the Minute would be approved, this would then be laid on the table of the House of Commons. By the 1860s the only factor certain in this procedure was that the Minutes were first prepared by the Secretary at the behest of the Lord President. Legally the Final Act by which a Minute was created was still the act of the Committee of Council, but Lingen admitted to a Select Committee of the Commons in 1865 that the members did not always attend the office to consult upon the Minute.[13]

In 1864 the Department introduced for the first time a form of administrative direction known as the supplementary rule. Supplementary rules were intended as directions to persons who had to act on the Minutes 'as to much that is not expressed in the Minutes themselves'. The supplementary rules were not drawn up even in theory by the Committee of Council but were simply devised by the Secretary and Vice-President acting together. These rules were really only the Department's interpretation of its own Minutes and in law had no more significance than that might warrant, but in practice they were of considerable importance.

The Code was given much greater weight as a result of the passing of the Elementary Education Act of 1870. The general effect of this Act on the administrative system of the Education Department was to extend its functions and powers beyond those hitherto associated with it as an agency for the distribution of grants. The great power which the Act gave to those who drew up the Code each year may have been unintentional in that Parliament probably did not foresee its possible applications, but the position is well brought out by this dialogue from the evidence given by Cumin—then Secretary to the Department—before the Cross Commission which was inquiring into the working of the Elementary Education Acts.

Canon Gregory: 'In your view there is nothing whatever to hinder the Department from sanctioning any subject being introduced into elementary education?—(Cumin) That is the Code; the Code says so. If I may be allowed to refer to them, the words in the Code are these. Article 16, after enumerating the obligatory subjects and the optional subjects, says: "Any other subjects, other than those mentioned in this article, may, if sanctioned by the Department, be taken as a specific subject provided that a graduated scheme of teaching it be submitted to and approved by the inspector".'

Canon Gregory: 'But is not that in the Code and not in the Act of Parliament?—But the Code is in the Act of Parliament.'

Canon Gregory: 'As a matter of fact has not the Code introduced a tyranny at the Education Office to define what elementary education is?—If it is a tyranny it is the Act of Parliament.'

The Chairman: 'Which section of the Act do you refer to which gives this enormous power?—The 7th section provides "that the school shall be conducted in accordance with the conditions required to be fulfilled by an elementary school in order to obtain an annual Parliamentary grant shall be those contained in the Minutes of the Education Department in force for the time being". Consequently every single public elementary school must be conducted on the Code, because the Code is a document contained in the Minutes.'[14]

The Minutes had originally set out the conditions on which the state would give grants to aid elementary schools and the codified sets of minutes issued annually after 1870 defined public elementary schools as those which fulfilled the conditions laid down in the current Code and since School Boards could only establish and run public elementary schools, the Code also expressed the conditions governing the use of the rates.

The annual Code not merely defined the standards, the subjects which might be taught and curricular matters generally, it also contained many other administrative instructions which the Education Department wished to issue to the schools concerning qualification of teachers, building requirements and the like. The various difficulties and complaints that arose in connection with a Code each year were noted so that the Secretary with the Vice-President or Lord President could bear them in mind when determining the next Code. In 1881 a Code Committee was set up by Mundella on his coming into office as Vice-President. This Committee consisted of a number of inspectors whose duty it was to discuss possible changes along with the Vice-President or the Lord President. The Code's particulars were agreed by both the Lord President and the Vice-President, the new Code was then laid on the table of the House for one month and, if no part of it was successfully challenged, it became law.[15]

Apart from greatly enhancing the importance of the Code, the Elementary Education Act of 1870 had the effect of increasing the powers of the Education Department in other directions. These new powers arose out of the creation of School Boards to supply elementary schools where the voluntary provision was deficient. The decision as to whether there was a deficiency in a particular area depended on the Department.[16] The country was divided into school districts, these were usually borough or parish divisions, but the Education Department could modify these areas if it wished, each of these school districts was required to have sufficient places in public elementary schools for the total number of children that might be expected to attend. The Education Department had the duty of obtaining returns from the local authority in each district—from the municipal council in the case of a borough or from the overseers in the case of a parish.[17] These returns were checked by the Department which appointed a special staff of inspectors of returns for this purpose; the Committee of Council's decision in each case was then made known. This decision could be challenged locally by the managers of voluntary schools or by any ten ratepayers; if it were challenged, then a public inquiry was held. Finally, the School Accommodation Notice would be published stating the amount of accommodation needed before the district's condition would be satisfactory.[18] There followed an interval of six months during which the voluntary organizations could make up the deficiency, but if they failed to do so, then the Department had to take steps to set up a school board. In London and some of the larger boroughs, school boards were set up without these preliminaries under sections 12 and 37 of the Act.

Not only did the Education Department have the duty of deciding whether a school board was to be set up, once a board had been elected, it had powers to deal with any board which seemed to be failing in its duty. Any board which failed in its duty to provide elementary school places could be declared in default and the Department could appoint additional members to it or dissolve it and order new elections. Although these strong powers were doubtless intended for use in cases where boards failed to act, they could be used for other purposes such as disciplining a board which flouted the Code for in this matter the Department was really judge in its own case 'If the school board do or permit any act in contravention or fail to comply with the regulations according to which a school provided by them is required by this Act to be conducted, the Education Department may declare the school board to be and such board shall accordingly be deemed to be a board in default. . . . If any dispute arises as to whether the school board have done or permitted any act in contravention of or have failed to comply with the said regulations, the matter shall be referred to the Education Department, whose decision thereon shall be final.'[19]

The full extent of the Department's authority is well illustrated by this passage from Cumin's evidence before the Cross Commission: 'You may say generally that if a local authority neglects its duty you can declare the school board in default, by which I mean that you can cashier the school board, and appoint another body to act for the school board; and not only that, but you may direct the payment of the members of that board to be made out of the rates. There was a case of that kind where a parish would not build a school, and I think the clergyman said, "You cannot do anything with us, because the whole parish is with me, and you will get nobody to serve". So we said, "Well, if you do not build a school and supply the accommodation, we shall be obliged to get the members elsewhere". And so we got a body of people from some 40 miles off, and the school was built and the money was paid.'[20]

The first task of the school boards was to build schools and it was clearly unreasonable to expect the ratepayers to find the capital expenditure involved in one year, therefore the boards were given authority to raise money on the security of the school fund and to repay the capital thus borrowed by instalments. These advances were made by the Public Works Loan Commissioners on comparatively easy terms but before they would grant a loan, the board seeking it had to get the recommendation of the Education Department. In some of the more crowded quarters of the bigger cities it proved impossible to buy land in the open market on which to erect the public elementary schools which were needed. In these cases boards had authority to acquire sites by compulsory purchase. Here, again, boards could only act with the approval of the Department which had to secure a confirming Act from Parliament in each case.[21]

The first school boards were set up towards the end of 1870 and their establishment meant that an element of keen competition came to be introduced into the provision of elementary schools between the voluntary organizations—especially the church—and the rate-supported boards in many districts. The Education Department found itself with the unwelcome duty and power of acting as umpire in some of the disputes which arose. The Elementary Education Act withdrew from the voluntary societies all building grants from the end of 1870 thus one immediate effect of the Act was to bring about a tremendous burst of activity in building voluntary schools in a now-or-never attempt to occupy the field before school boards were set up and the building grant vanished. But even though there was to be no public grant towards building costs, it still remained possible even after the year had elapsed for the churches to build schools provided that they met the whole of the cost themselves. Once the school was built, they could then apply for annual grant aid under the Code; the Department then had to decide whether or not to allow the claim. This question of the supply of 'additional' accommodation which might be needed in areas where the population was growing, was presumably covered by the Act's provision that the school board was to supply such accommodation as was in their opinion necessary.[22] The Department interpreted this as meaning that the school board had a prior right to provide any additional accommodation, and that new voluntary schools could be considered unnecessary in such circumstances and not eligible for an annual grant. As Sir Henry Craik, Secretary to the Scottish Education Department wrote 'as a discouragement to vexatious competition with the rate-established and rate-supported schools, the Department was enabled to refuse the benefit of Parliamentary grant to voluntary schools established after the passing of the Act, if they were convinced that such schools were not necessary for the supply of the district'.[23] Decisions in this field led to a great deal of friction and some members of the Cross Commission showed much determination to find out exactly what were the grounds on which the Department would judge that a denominational school was not necessary for the supply of a district. The Secretary to the Department, Cumin, had a most unhappy time evading, so far as he was able, the questions which members of the Commission put to him. The general impression that his evidence gives is that if a voluntary school was established and kept up its numbers for a year, this was usually accepted as showing that it was sufficiently necessary and suitable to justify grant aid in accordance with the Code. Undoubtedly the Department always tried to avoid having to define a frontier between school board supply and voluntary accommodation, and left these decisions to be taken locally so far as possible, but where feelings were running very high, such decisions had to be taken at the centre.

The system created by the Elementary Education Act of 1870 was completed by the Acts of 1876 and 1880. The first of these permitted the establishment of School Attendance Committees in districts where there were no school boards which had powers similar to those exercised by the boards of making byelaws to enforce school attendance. In 1880 a further Act was passed which imposed a duty on all school boards and attendance committees of framing and enforcing satisfactory laws for compulsory school attendance. The attendance committees were, in effect, sub-committees of the body appointing them since their expenses were to be met by the appointing body. The body responsible for appointing them in the boroughs was the municipal council while in the parishes the Guardians of the Poor Law Union were responsible. The Education Department exercised a general oversight of these arrangements and issued sets of model byelaws. The Act of 1876 also imposed on the Guardians the duty of paying the school fees of children whose parents could not afford to pay. The Education Department did not find its experience of dealing with the Guardians a pleasing one. Mundella said that 'It is only with the greatest possible difficulty now, that with an absolute statutory power, and an obligation upon them (the guardians), we can induce them to appoint school attendance officers and pay them, or even to pay the fees of the poor children that cannot pay for themselves. That is the greatest difficulty that we have in connection with English education.'[24]

The creation of the school boards and the great extension of the elementary school system at public expense after 1870 meant that the Education Department had its powers and responsibilities greatly increased for the last quarter of the nineteenth century. Its powers to control local authorities were enormous. There had been virtually no experience in this country of public local education authorities before 1870, consequently there was no obvious line of demarcation between state control and local responsibility which the legislators could follow. The new local agencies were untried, it would have been extremely rash to have made no provision for the central department to have reserve powers by which it could step in if local boards behaved unjustly or if they broke down and failed altogether in their duties. The Department certainly showed no great eagerness to use its powers unduly. When necessary the threat that it would reduce the grant or refuse its approval for a loan or that it would declare a board in default was usually enough to enforce its will without proceeding to more extreme measures. Any criticism that might be made of the Department at this time would not be that it over-used its powers, but rather that in its concern for the discharge of its day-to-day responsibilities it did not sufficiently consider the longer term implications of its decisions. Thus, by the 1890's the 'elementary' schools were blundering at various points into what was really 'secondary' education and the Department was certainly not without a share of the blame for the extremely confused condition of educational administration in the last decade or so of the nineteenth century.[25]

II

STAFFING AND ORGANIZATION OF THE EDUCATION DEPARTMENT

The expansion in the functions and powers of the Education Department naturally led to important changes in its staffing and organization. The section of the staff whose work changed in nature and grew most rapidly was probably the inspectorate. In the years immediately following the establishment of the Department it was customary for the inspectors—still organized on a denominational basis—to visit annually such schools in their charge as applied for annual grants. Schools which had only received grants for buildings or for books were visited rather less frequently, perhaps once in two years. The establishment for inspectors was really determined by the number of schools which received annual grants such as those for capitation, for the augmentation of the stipends of certificated teachers and for pupil teachers. Here an annual visit was clearly an essential part of the procedure for paying the grants due.[26] The annual inspection at this time was quite a thorough undertaking. The pupil teachers and the registers had to be examined for grant purposes; the state of the premises, teaching apparatus and school organization was commented on in the inspector's report as were the examinations he had made of each class in every subject of inspection. These examinations were essentially examinations of individual pupils. The Newcastle Commission fastened upon this very point as one of weakness in the existing system of inspection '. . . it does not profess to be an examination of individual boys. It is at present . . . directed mainly to the higher classes rather than to the junior ones; and thus regarded as an examination it is insufficient, and especially insufficient with respect to that part of the school which requires most vigilant and assiduous teaching.'[27] Elsewhere the Commission concluded that '. . . inspectors are tempted to attend to the state of the upper, more than of the junior classes in schools, and to estimate the whole school accordingly'.[28]

It was against the background of this Report that the duties of inspectors came to include an annual examination of every child in the school in respect of whom a grant was claimed. The institution of this annual examination in the Revised Code led to a radical change both in the nature and in the amount of work falling upon inspectors. The change in the nature of the work is probably best shown by Matthew Arnold in his Report for 1863. 'Inspection under the old system meant something like the following. The Inspector took a school class by class. (He seldom heard each child in a class read.) . . . The whole life and power of the class, the fitness of its composition, its handling by the teacher, were well tested; the Inspector became well acquainted with them, and was able to make his remarks on them to the head teacher; and a powerful means of correcting, improving and stimulating them was thus given. In the hands of an able Inspector . . . this means was an instrument of great force and value. . . . (In the new system) He hears every child in the group before him read, and so far his examination is more complete than the old system. But he does not question them; he does not as an examiner under the rules of the six

C

standards, go beyond the three matters—reading, writing and arithmetic—and the amount of these three matters which the standards themselves prescribe. . . . The whole school felt, under the old system, that the prime aim and object of the Inspector's visit was, after ensuring the fulfilment of certain sanitary and disciplinary conditions, to test and quicken the intellectual life of the school. The scholars' thoughts were directed to this object, the teachers' thoughts were directed to it, the Inspectors' thoughts were directed to it. At present the centre of interest for the school when the Inspector visits is changed; scholars and teachers have their thoughts directed straight upon the new examination.'[29] The Education Department refused to recognize this change in the nature of inspection. It claimed that the new examination did not replace the individual inspector's judgment of the intellectual and moral value of a school's work, but merely reinforced it. 'If you keep these distinctions steadily in view you will see how little scope of your duties is changed.'[30]

The change in the amount of work falling on the inspectorate as a result of the introduction of the Revised Code was, of course, due to the amount of examining and marking that was now called for. In order to deal with this problem a grade of Inspector's Assistant was created in 1863. The principal task of these Assistants was to mark worked exercises, they were only allowed to examine in the presence of or on a written order from an Inspector. The Assistants were chosen from among heads of elementary schools.

From 1862 the Education Department's Inspectors ceased to inspect workhouse schools. This was due to a conflict of authority for the grants paid to teachers in these schools came from the Local Government Board's vote, yet the certificate of efficiency authorizing the payment was issued on the responsibility of the Education Department. In 1862 the Education Department Inspectors who did this work were transferred to the service of the Local Government Board.[31] The Poor Law authorities resented any comments other than those which were strictly necessary for the grading of the teacher and the assessment of his salary: any comment that the teacher should keep the schoolroom in a more orderly fashion or that the children should be allowed a little more liberty would evoke a complaint from the Local Government Board that the Education Department's Inspector was exceeding his duties and interfering in a matter that was the concern of the Board.[32]

With the changes that followed the introduction of the Revised Code, inspectors might well have felt that the status of their office was being undermined. The changes associated with the new Code were not the only ones which appeared to diminish their status. It had been the custom to hold an annual meeting which was presided over by the Vice-President. This meeting had always taken the form of a series of debates or discussions on topics proposed by the inspectors beforehand. It was usually attended by about two-thirds of the inspectorate. When Adderley was Vice-President during Derby's ministry (1858–59) he prevented those present from voting at the end of their discussion on each question. He considered that these meetings were valuable from two points of view, firstly because inspectors could help one another by consulting together on common problems and, secondly, because he found their experience a valuable guide. On the other hand, he put an end to the practice of voting since he felt that if the majority agreed to a motion which was adverse to the policy being followed by the Department, it would cause embarrassment to the office and place him in a false position.[33]

After the resignation of Adderley, these meetings ceased entirely. At least some inspectors resented this and felt that the administration by the Department was suffering as a consequence of no longer consulting the inspectorate to the extent that it had hitherto. One of their number, E. C. Tufnell, told the Select Committee of 1865 that 'Most of the experienced inspectors have complained to me that they have never been consulted on the most important measures of the Privy Council Office, and as there is no one in the Privy Council Office, either among the clerks, secretaries or examiners who has been an inspector, there is no one who has the same practical acquaintance with the subject which the inspectors necessarily acquire after performing their duties for a year or two'.[34] Tufnell claimed that many parts of the Revised Code would never have been passed if the Department had made any use of the practical information which the inspectors were ready to give it.[35]

The Elementary Education Act of 1870 led to the re-organization of the inspectorate and to a steady increase in its size. The Act put an end to the Concordat of 1840 which required that the inspectorate should be organized on a denominational basis since the inspection of religious instruction was removed from the field of study falling within the competence of inspectors. It became possible now to reduce the amount of time spent in travel by organizing the inspectorate territorially. The whole country was divided up into districts of a suitable size and each inspector became responsible for the inspection of all schools—school board and voluntary—within his district. In 1871 these districts were grouped in divisions with a Senior Inspector in charge of each; there were eight divisions each consisting of from eight to ten districts. These Senior Inspectors were supposed to give especial care to the maintenance of an even standard of judgment among the inspectors working under them.

The maintenance of a universal standard of judgment was a very difficult undertaking. When H. A. Bruce was Vice-President in 1865 he admitted that it was inevitable that inspectors were affected in their judgments by the prevailing standards of the area in which they worked. The standards of those in districts where the schools were backward and weak were almost necessarily lower than those where the schools were better.[36] In spite of this frank admission by the Vice-President, the application of the same standard of judgment to all schools was implicit in the whole system of grants and the organization of the inspectorate after the ending of the Concordat was aimed at attaining that objective. The idea of having Senior Inspectors to co-ordinate the work in eight or ten districts was taken further and made more effective a dozen years later. The Senior Inspectors were re-named Chief Inspectors, every quarter these Chief Inspectors were required to send in a return consisting of a report from each of his subordinates. The reports gave the percentage of passes in the various subjects and the proportion of schools qualifying for the merit grant. If there appeared to be a considerable discrepancy between the pro-portions passing or being recommended for grant in different districts, the Department called for an explanation of this from the Chief Inspector. It was one of the duties of Chief Inspectors to hold con-ferences of their subordinates in order to determine exactly what standard they would require for 'excellent', 'good', and so on, it was then for the individual inspectors to apply the standards which they had agreed. The Secretary stated in 1884 that 'we hope in time to get uniformity throughout the country' adding 'it is extremely difficult'.[37] Some inspectors—justifiably or unjustifiably—acquired the reputation of being unduly severe and schools boards were apt to complain bitterly if they found their schools earning smaller grants than they had expected and an additional burden thrown on the rates as a con-sequence of inspectorial 'unfairness'.

The problem of maintaining uniformity of standards inevitably became more difficult as the number of persons employed to make the necessary judgments increased. There was certainly a fairly rapid and continuous increase in the numbers of inspectors that the Department found it necessary to employ in order to apply the Revised Code to the fast growing number of schools and pupils after 1870. Almost every year the Department had to ask the Treasury to agree to a larger establishment. It asked for one of the largest increases in preparing the estimates for 1871–72. In 1870–71 there was an establishment of 76 inspectors and 26 inspector's assistants, the Department now sought to enlarge this by appointing 16 more inspectors and 50 more inspector's assistants. The Treasury accepted the proposal for the increase in inspector's assistants, but rejected the request for more inspectors, arguing that now the system of denominational inspection had been ended, existing inspectors could be employed more economically and the increase was unjustified; after more correspondence the Treasury eventually consented to the larger establishment of inspectors also.[38] After an increase each year from 1870, when the Department asked the Treasury to authorize 6 more inspectors and 10 inspector's assistants for the year 1880–81, it met with a flat refusal. Sir Francis Sandford, the Secretary, then asked the Treasury to think again, and in reply got a letter asking the Education Department if it foresaw any end to these requests for more inspectors. The Department replied soothingly and pleadingly that it believed the limit of the demand for new inspectors 'has been very nearly reached'. The letter pointed out that 'the fact that the children of more than 17,000,000 of the population cannot legally go to work until they obtain certificates of the result of the individual examination in certain standards makes it impossible to dispense . . . with the yearly examination of the scholars in every school'. The Treasury finally accepted the Department's request.[39] At the time of the Cross Commission there were 12 Chief Inspectors, 120 inspectors, 30 sub-inspectors and 152 inspector's assistants, a total inspectorate of 314,[40] by this time the expansion had slowed down and in 1899, on the eve of the establishment of the Board of Education, the Department's inspectorate numbered 352.[41]

Inspectors were appointed by the Lord President in accordance with the recommendations of the Committee of Inquiry of 1853 presided over by Sir Charles Trevelyan. This Committee thought that future inspectors should be men who had obtained a good honours degree and that they should be appointed while young, since the services they would undertake gave them the opportunity of learning their job while doing it. The Committee recommended that they should begin with moderate salaries, and that as they became more experienced, so should their salaries be increased. Elementary schoolmasters were never recruited to this grade, nor were sub-inspectors or inspector's assistants promoted to it. On the other hand, all the Chief Inspectors were drawn from it. In justification of the policy of restricting entry to the grade of inspector to those with high honours degrees it was pointed out to the Cross Commission that inspectors had often to deal with people of consequence in their districts, and that it would certainly be wrong to think of them merely in respect of their work in the schools. Not all Vice-Presidents were entirely satisfied with this arrangement. A. J. Mundella found that just before he took office eight new inspectors had been appointed, and he decided to appoint no more for a while since he thought that young and inexperienced inspectors were very mischievous to the schools. He preferred to make greater use of inspector's assistants and to promote some of the best of them to a new class which he created to be known as 'sub-inspectors', giving them the full powers of inspectors in regard to the inspection and examination of schools. Mundella told the Select Committee of 1884 that the creation of this class in 1881 had enabled him to meet all requirements for inspectors to date, and that he proposed to increase the class of sub-inspectors still further before creating any new inspectors. All promotions to the grade of sub-inspector were made by the Lord President after consultation with the Vice-President.[42] As vacancies for inspectors occurred, sub-inspectors were appointed so that by increasing the size of each district and by attaching a sub-inspector to the inspector the number of full district inspectors was reduced.[43]

As stated above, inspectors' assistants were recruited from among head teachers of elementary schools. A list was kept at the Department of head teachers who wished to become inspectors' assistants, and heads could apply to have their names put on this list at any time. Of those on the list, preference in selection was given to those with a university degree or to those who were reading for one. The other factors which were considered in deciding which were most suited for appointment were the class applicants obtained when they got their teaching certificates, the reports of the managers of the schools in which they had served and the reports of the inspectors who had examined their schools. When vacancies arose, the Secretary drew up a list of those who seemed best qualified, and they were sent for to be interviewed at the Department. The final decision as to which candidate should be appointed rested with the Lord President.[44]

The expansion in the number of elementary schools and pupils and the wider responsibilities which the Department had to accept after the passing of the Elementary Education Act in 1870 naturally required a considerable increase in the staff employed at the central office, as may be seen from the following tables.

TABLE I

STAFF ESTABLISHMENT OF THE EDUCATION DEPARTMENT OFFICE FOR THE YEAR 1857–58[45]

Number in grade	Grade	Salary (£s) Minimum	Maximum
1	Secretary	—	1,500
2	Assistant Secretaries . .	700	1,000
6	Examiners	300	600
5	Clerks	110	300
39	Assistant Clerks . .	100	300
1	Private Secy. to Vice Pres. .	—	150
1	Architect	—	400
1	Advising Counsel . .	—	300
56	Total	—	—

N.B.—In addition to the clerical staff shown here a number of clerks were hired from time to time to deal with exceptionally heavy business from the Law Stationers Company.

In spite of the great increase in the size of staff and in the amount of work undertaken, the general method of working and the duties of the various grades seems to have changed little in these years from that given in this description by the Secretary in 1865. 'The Council Office is organized in this manner: above the clerks, who are employed merely in copying and drafting letters, there are a certain number of officers called examiners: the letters of the day are divided among those officers, and they make upon them the minutes which the cases seem to require; perhaps three out of four of them require only the despatch of a certain printed form to be minuted upon them; in other cases letters may have to be written; the cases about which those officers doubt are referred to the two assistant secretaries, and if they feel any doubt about them, they send them on to me; the whole of

TABLE 2

STAFF OF THE EDUCATION DEPARTMENT IN 1899[46]

Number in grade	Grade	Salary (£s) Minimum	Maximum
1	Secretary	—	1,800
4	Assistant Secretaries . .	900	1,200
1	Assistant Secretary . .	900	1,000
8	Senior Examiners . .	650	800
18	Junior Examiners. . .	250	600
1	Architect	—	850
1	Assistant Examiner for Drawing	250	550
1	Examinations Clerk . .	400	550
17	First Class Clerks. . .	360	500
4	Clerks (2nd Class Staff) . .	300	400
3	Permanent Staff Clerks .	360	400
23	Additional Staff Clerks .	250	350
4	Clerks (2nd Div., Higher grade)	250	350
87	Clerks (2nd Division) .	70	250
58	Assistant Clerks . . .	80	150
26	Assistant Clerks (new class) .	55	150
22	Boy Clerks . . .	14/- a week	18/- a week
279			
5	Office for Special Inquiries and Reports		
284	Total Permanent Staff (excluding Inspectors)		
225	Temporary Clerks, Copyists and Boy Copyists.		
509	Total Staff (excluding Inspectors)		

each day's letters being minuted in this way by the examiners, and their minutes being made into fair drafts of letters come with the original papers before the two assistant secretaries; they, as a rule, sign the day's letters, and they send on to me any about which they have any doubt, and in the same way I take on any letters about which I have any doubt to the Vice-President; once a week, instead of the assistant secretaries signing the letters, I sign the whole of them myself, in order that I may, so far as I can, observe the working of the office; that is the daily practice.'[47]

It may be doubted whether even the most assiduous Secretary could have signed all the letters of one day each week in the later years of the century, but there is no doubt that the main burden of the administrative work throughout fell on the examiners and the assistant secretaries under the general direction of the Secretary. The assistant secretaries were usually chosen from among the examiners who were themselves required to be men with high honours degrees.[48] The title 'examiner' was derived from the duty of examining the various documents sent to the office in order to see that the conditions for the payment of grant were being fulfilled in the schools for which it was being claimed. They naturally supervised the arrangements for the examinations of the various standards that inspectors conducted throughout the country each year, and they were rather more intimately concerned in the examinations for pupil teacherships, Queen's scholarships and teachers' certificates, since all the marked scripts were sent on to them for their inspection so that they could ascertain that there was a reasonably uniform scale of marking. 'This task can only be satisfactorily performed by men who both are, and who are known to be, of high attainments. We are happy to be able to record our opinions that this principle appears to have been fully maintained in the appointments hitherto made to the office of examiner; and we recommend that the standard which has been adopted should on no account be lowered.'[49]

The division of the grade into senior and junior examiners was made after consultation with the Treasury in 1871 as part of a general strengthening of the establishment to meet the pressure of business produced by the Act of the previous year. The Department proposed to increase the number of examiners from 16 to 20, dividing them into 6 senior and 14 junior. The Treasury accepted this proposal but reduced the proposed salary maxima; the Department had sought to replace the existing scale of £300 to £650 by a scale of £650 to £800 for senior examiners, while making the existing scale apply to all junior examiners, the Treasury reduced the maximum for senior examiners by £25 and that for junior examiners by £50.[50]

The constant struggle which an expanding bureaucracy had with ever increasing quantities of paper was reflected in the frequent requests which the Department made to the Treasury to authorize the employment of additional clerical and copying staff. In 1869 the Treasury agreed to a proposal from the Department to create a new class of clerks to be known as 'Boy Clerks'. These were recruited between the ages of fourteen and sixteen, and were paid 12s. per week rising by annual increments of 1s. per week to the age of nineteen when they were discharged. Both the youths and their parents were to sign a declaration indicating that they understood they had no claim to be employed after their nineteenth year.[51] In spite of the temporary nature of the employment, this experiment was a successful means of getting clerks, and the class was to last until the end of the century, the final appointments being made to it in January, 1897.[52] The amount of work produced by the rush of applications for building grants before they were brought to an end by the Act of 1870 was reflected in the need for the Department to open on Sundays during the latter part of that year for which the Treasury authorized overtime payments to the clerks at the rate of 3s. per hour.[53]

With the establishment of entrance examinations under the Civil Service Commission, the Education Department, along with all other government offices, had come to look to the Commissioners for the recruitment of much of its staff. From 1st April, 1871, the Treasury forbade it to hire temporary clerks from the Law Stationers, in future the Civil Service Commissioners must be asked to supply staff to meet exceptional pressure.[54]

In 1873 the Department sent a request to the Treasury for higher salaries for everyone because of the increase in work under the Education Act of 1870. The justification given for the claim was supported by particulars to show by how much the work had increased, for example, the number of documents registered in the office in 1869 was 37,778, in 1872 this had become 72,274. In the year to 31st August, 1869, 7,845 schools with 11,404 departments and 1,328,863 scholars present were inspected, but in the year to 31st August, 1873, 11,095 schools with 15,931 departments and 1,811,590 scholars were inspected. The Treasury was not prepared to meet any advance in salaries on these grounds.[55] In the correspondence between the Education Department and the Treasury concerning this period there were few years when increases in the staff of some sort were not sought, the rate of expansion being greatest in the 1870s.

III

CONSTITUTIONAL ARRANGEMENTS

The enormous increase in the number of elementary schools and pupils which led to the rapid growth in the duties, powers and expenditure of the Education Department caused much dissatisfaction to arise among members of the House of Commons with the constitutional arrangements for the oversight of elementary education. The enlargement of the Committee of Council in 1856[56] did not turn it into an effective governing body. The appointment of a Vice-President to act as spokesman for the Education Department in the Commons in the same way that the Lord President had acted as spokesman in the Lords led to some confusion as to who was the effective head of the Department and as to the relationship of both the Lord President and the Vice-President to the Committee of Council. The evidence gathered by Select Committees of the House of Commons appointed to inquire into this problem in 1865, 1866 and 1884 showed that there were almost as many views of the powers and responsibilities of the two ministers and of the Committee as there were witnesses. The position changed with the passage of time, and the contrast between the evidence given in 1865 with that given in 1884 indicates to some extent differences in practice—but not, of course, in law—that had appeared as a result of the expansion.

In his examination before the Select Committee of 1865, the then Secretary, Lingen, said that the principal change which the new system of 1856 had led to was that the Vice-President gave much more constant attendance to the business of the Office than the Lord President had been wont to do, consequently he, as Secretary, took far fewer decisions on his own and referred to the Vice-President many more matters than he had ever referred to the Lord President when there was only the one minister. Thus although the legal position of the Secretary had remained unchanged, the frequent attendance of the Vice-President had in fact lessened his responsibilities. Lingen stated that he transacted very little business with the Lord President under the new arrangements, nearly all the current business was despatched without it being brought to his attention. While the Vice-President transacted nearly all the business which might be described as ministerial on his own responsibility, yet Lingen believed there to be no doubt but that the Lord President was head of the Department. 'I have heard the Lord President state, in the clearest manner, when the subjects have been under discussion, that he considered his own authority supreme in the Office; and that when he made an order, there could be no question at all, if there was a difference of opinion between himself and the Vice-President, that his own opinion should prevail and not the opinion of the Vice-President. That I have heard said by Lord Granville.'[57] Lingen defended the existing arrangement of having two ministers rather than one minister of public instruction, probably responsible to the Commons, on the somewhat odd grounds that the task would be too 'humdrum' and would involve too much 'drudgery' to attract a man of cabinet rank, hence the present system was the only way of getting a spokesman for the Department into the Cabinet; moreover he felt that the head of the Department should be in the Lords because the bishops sat there.[58]

Perhaps the most extreme detractor from the importance of the office of Vice-President was one of its most memorable holders—Robert Lowe. He held that the responsibility for the conduct of the administrative work of the Department was 'single and undivided on the Lord President'. The Vice-President was simply a subordinate with no responsibility whatsoever. He told the Chairman of the Select Committee on being further questioned that he did not agree with Lord Granville's description of the office of Vice-President when proposing its creation in 1856. Granville had said that 'It would be desirable that some Minister should be appointed who should be responsible to the House of Commons for the proper distribution of the grants . . .', but Lowe maintained that the Vice-President was only there to have an expert knowledge of the Department for the purpose of explaining points in the estimates. He believed that the existing organization of the Department could not be improved, and that there was certainly insufficient work for a full Minister of Public Instruction—the duties of the Vice-President being 'very light'.[59]

A somewhat different view of the nature of his office was given by H. A. Bruce who was currently Vice-President at the time the Select Committee was making its inquiries. He told the Committee that the Vice-President was expected to decide all ordinary business himself. 'I conceive that although the Lord President may be primarily and chiefly responsible, the Vice-President is too largely implicated in the transaction of the business to do that which I think an Under-Secretary might fairly do, that is, discharge himself of all responsibility and place it upon his chief.' The Lord President and the Vice-President were fully responsible to their respective Houses of Parliament for the policy of the office.[60] Of other former office holders to give evidence at this time, both Lord Salisbury, who had been Lord President in Derby's ministry of 1858–59 and his Vice-President, Adderley, gave opinions which were a good deal closer to Lowe's than to Bruce's.

The evidence which the Select Committee of 1884 which was 'appointed to consider how the Ministerial Responsibility, under which the Votes for Education, Science and Art are administered, may be best secured' showed some increase in the degree of responsibility generally held to be attaching to the Vice-President. Again, the most important witness was certainly the Secretary to the Education Department, by now Sir Francis Sandford. He pointed out that things had changed a great deal since the Order in Council of 1856 had been issued. The Act of 1870 creating a form of local administration had produced a large number of issues which turned on such matters as the powers of local bodies and the relationship of these bodies with the central authority. These matters were naturally of much greater concern to members of the House of Commons than to members of the Lords, consequently the Department's spokesman in the Commons had gradually assumed a higher status than before. 'I should fancy that the Lord President is the Minister, I may say *de jure*, and the Vice-President very much the Minister *de facto*.' Unlike Lingen, Sandford saw disadvantages as well as advantages in the existing position. He felt the advantages were that the Department had representation in the House of Lords and in the Cabinet while it was also represented in the Commons by a Vice-President who ranked higher than an Under-Secretary or a Parliamentary Secretary, and was usually on the eve of promotion to cabinet rank. The disadvantages inherent in this arrangement Sandford felt to be a divided sense of responsibility—which arose from the dual control—and the outside public simply did not know who was the Minister of Education. He believed that many of the general public probably regarded the Vice-President as effectively the minister, though 'the Vice-President may perhaps feel that though he has the duties of the Minister of Education to perform, he does not hold the recognized position as such'.[61]

The Committee of 1884 also heard the views of Forster and Mundella. It is clear from their evidence that the position taken up by most of the witnesses before the 1865 Committee would hardly have been tenable by this time. Because of the very large vote involved and because of the interest of the localities in this matter, education was mainly a House of Commons business, and the formal head of the Department ought to sit in that House, this was the view of Forster. There was no longer any advantage in pretending that education was the business of the Privy Council, 'there is no meaning in the statement that the Privy Council are concerned in it, they are not'; moreover '. . . there is some disadvantage in these legal shams, for they are really that, because there are people in the country who believe that there is some meaning in them'. The real position, Forster asserted, was that the visible minister in the House of Commons now represented the invisible minister in the House of Lords, he added 'If you wanted another illustration, perhaps the illustration of the present Egyptian ministers at Cairo, under their English Under-Secretaries, might afford it'.[62] Mundella's views were similar in many respects. He emphasized how rapidly the work of the Department was growing, '. . . it is becoming increasingly heavy; I am told so in the office by the permanent officials; that every Vice-President has a much harder time of it, and that I have had a very much harder time of it than any previous Vice-President ever dreamt of; because as we get nearer filling up the supplies under the English Act, the questions of supply become more and more difficult and more and more keenly contested. Then there is such a largely increased interest in education; there are a vast number of bodies engaged now in it; and the school boards are composed of men who devote the better part of their lives to the work.'[63] His opinion was that a Ministry of Public Education should replace not only the Education Department, but also the various other government bodies concerned with different stages and aspects of education, and that such a Ministry should be something like the Ministry of Instruction Publique et Beaux Arts in France.[64]

While the legal position had not changed since 1856, the passage of events was having the practical effect of making the Vice-President into a Minister of Elementary Education, and by the 1880s there was really nothing that lay entirely outside of his field of activity for the functions that the Lord President still discharged were usually undertaken after consultation with the Vice-President or on the latter's initiative. Even the exercise of patronage in which the Vice-President had never engaged was only undertaken by the Lord President after consulting the former from 1883. The patronage consisted in appointing and promoting inspectors and examiners. At Mundella's request Gladstone, the Prime Minister, had ruled that in future patronage would only be exercised after consultation with the Vice-President.[65] The Lord President was, of course, consulted on major policy issues, and he continued to act as the spokesman for the Education Office in the Lords.

The relationship of the Committee of Council for Education to the actual work of the Department and the extent to which it exercised any influence over the decisions of the Lord President and Vice-President were naturally probed by the Parliamentary Committees inquiring into the administrative organization. It had clearly been intended in 1856 that this Committee should play an important part, its membership had been extended and the scope of its activities ostensibly widened to include workhouse, naval and military schools. By the end of the century probably the only relic of this Committee's authority was the form of correspondence used by the Education Office which contrived to express its decisions and opinions as those of 'My Lords'. Here, again, there appears to be a certain contrast between the opinions expressed about this institution's effectiveness in the 1860s and in the 1880s.

Lingen told the Select Committee in 1865 that the Committee of Council took no part in the regular administrative routine of the Office but that it deliberated upon Minutes or Draft Minutes or upon other questions of importance laid before it by the Lord President. The Committee met whenever some matter of importance arose, the Lord President issued the summons to attend, but the actual attendance varied greatly. No regular record was kept of its meetings, or of what it agreed except in so far as its decisions came to be embodied in official Minutes. The frequency with which meetings were held depended on the amount of business that might arise, there were, for instance, frequent meetings at the time that the Revised Code was being worked out. Normally the Secretary would draft any new minutes and the Committee would meet to amend and eventually approve the final draft before it was laid on the table of the Commons. Occasionally, there would be no actual meeting before a Minute was issued, but the draft would simply be circulated among members or the Lord President might take it to a Cabinet meeting instead. Lingen thought that the Committee was useful in that it could give a useful opinion on broad general questions.[66] Lowe believed that in his day Minutes were never issued without a meeting of the Committee. He considered that the 'quasi-legislative' function of the Department needed more than ministerial authority for its discharge, 'the business is too technical to be carried on in the House of Commons; and I think that it is quite right that the officials of the Department should be fortified by the calling in of a number of eminent persons, and that it should not be left to the single discretion of the Lord President, as would otherwise be the case'.[67] He claimed that the Committee had been of value in formulating the Revised Code although when pressed Lowe admitted that in fact it made no actual change in the proposals set before it.[68]

Lowe's predecessor, Adderley, Vice-President during the Derby ministry of 1858–59, held very different opinions. During his tenure of office a reference to the Committee occurred only once on a Minute 'and I recollect distinctly that what we had to do in consultation was to explain to the Committee upon what subject we wanted their advice, and the advice which they gave was very much to sanction the conclusion to which we had come already'. The other members of the Committee had apparently felt that they could hardly differ from the advice given by the Lord President and Vice-President since they knew nothing about the matter, and 'they rather complained of being called together for that purpose; . . . the unanimous feeling of everyone present was that it was perfectly unnecessary'.[69] Lord Salisbury's memory of these same years as Lord President supported Adderley's view, so far as the members of the Committee were concerned; he claimed that whenever he proposed a meeting '. . . it was generally ill-received'.[70]

The views of the Committee's importance expressed by Adderley and Salisbury proved to be a more accurate guide to the future than the opinions expressed by Lingen and Lowe. Sandford told the Select Committee of 1884 that the Committee of Council had 'perhaps' met once a year.[71] When the Select Committee asked Forster how frequently the Committee of Council had been summoned in his day, he could only reply 'I have a sort of dim recollection that there were one or two formal meetings, but they have not fastened themselves upon my memory at all'.[72] Mundella said that the Committee did not meet as often as once a year, when it did meet, it listened to what the responsible ministers had to say and followed their advice. The Committee consisted of 'cabinet ministers who do not come'.[73]

Few could be found who would defend the increasingly anachronistic arrangements which characterized the political leadership of the Education Department. Owing to a Parliamentary crisis, the Select Committee of 1865, which resumed its work in 1866, got no further than issuing the draft suggested for its final report by the chairman, Sir John Pakington. This draft proposed that in view of the evidence they had heard, they should recommend the abolition of the existing Committee of Council on Education and that in future there should be a Minister of Public Instruction with a seat in the Cabinet who should be entrusted with the superintendence of all matters relating to science and art and popular education.[74] In discussing these recommendations, the chairman argued that there was no real parallel to the Committee of Council for Education elsewhere in the machinery of the government and there appeared to be no advantage to be derived from this special arrangement for education. '. . . there can be no doubt that the position of the Vice-President does not at all fulfil the objects of those whose repeated suggestions that popular education should be promoted by the appointment of a Minister, were at last met by the Bill appointing a Vice-President in 1856.'

In 1867, the Vice-President produced a confidential memorandum on the future of the Education Department and of the Charity Commission. He suggested in this that the Committee of Council on Education should become the Committee of Council on Education and Charities and that a Council or Board of five members, including the Vice-President, should act as a sort of executive committee to transact all business.[75] The accession to power of the Liberal ministry under Gladstone in the following year led to the setting up of the Endowed Schools Commission and thus to a rather different solution to the endowed schools issue than that envisaged in the memorandum of 1867 which seems to have had no further influence.

The Select Committee of 1884 found the existing arrangement neither logical nor convenient. It recommended the establishment of a Board of Education under a President who should be a real and not merely a nominal minister, holding a position like that of the President of the Board of Trade. The office and duties to be discharged by this Minister ought to be generally recognized as no less important than those of some of the Secretaries of State.[76] This recommendation to create a Board of Education was not, in fact, implemented for some fifteen years during which time the administrative position had become even more confused and there had been a Commission inquiring at length into elementary education and another into secondary education.

The rapid growth in its expenditure combined with its anachronistic constitutional structure to lead the Education Department into difficulties with the Treasury from time to time during the years after 1870. The Minutes of the Committee of Council, which were the chosen instruments through which the Department at first offered grants and later virtually controlled the elementary school system, had financial consequences which could not always be accurately estimated by the Department.[77] The obvious reason for putting the Chancellor of the Exchequer on the Committee of Council on Education both before and after 1856 had been the financial implications of the Education

D

Department's work. The Treasury, alarmed from time to time at the increase in expenditure of the Education Department, was not slow to point out that the virtual decay of the Committee of Council as an effective body meant that it had to find the money to pay for offers concerning which it had not been consulted. A letter from the Treasury in 1871 put the point clearly:

'It appears to be the practice of the Committee of Council on Education to issue Minutes from time to time which, . . . involve prospectively most serious additions to the Annual Expenditure without affording to this Board the opportunity of previously expressing an opinion upon the financial part of the question: and it is only when the Estimates come before my Lords and when it is too late to discuss the question that they are informed of the obligations incurred by such Minutes.'

'My Lords are aware that the Chancellor of the Exchequer is a member of the Committee; but the Committee meets less frequently than it used to do, . . . in these circumstances, before Minutes pass beyond the stage of drafts they should be communicated formally to this Board, together with the best estimate that can be formed of the immediate and the prospective expenditure which they involve.'[78]

In 1881 the Treasury returned to the charge. In the nine years to the 31st March, 1880, Parliament had voted £20,000,000 for education. 'The magnitude and rapid increase of this expenditure have led the Chancellor of the Exchequer to consider what practical security exists that the holder of his office has had his own attention directly and effectually called to the preparation of Minutes or Bills by which such expenditure is promoted. . . .'

'The Chancellor of the Exchequer submits that his own rare presence at the meetings of the Committee (of Council), or even such conversations as he may be able to hold with the ministers at the head of the Education Department, on the subject of the measures which they have in contemplation cannot give him sufficiently exact knowledge and control of their vast expenditure.' The Education Department was obliged to accept an arrangement whereby before any proposal involving a serious increase in expenditure was adopted it was to be submitted to the Treasury showing just how much it would cost and 'what the objects are that are held to justify this increase in the public charge'.[79]

It is clear that whoever else might have attached significance to the constitutional arrangements for the governance of the Education

Department during the last thirty years of its existence, the Treasury did not do so, but took steps to secure its control over expenditure by means other than the Chancellor's membership of the Committee of Council.

In retrospect, the need to rationalize the central government's educational administration and to appoint a minister responsible to Parliament for all the work in this field seems self-evident and it is perhaps, difficult to feel much sympathy for successive governments which evaded or ignored the problem. Yet education had acquired a reputation among politicians in the nineteenth century that caused them only to contemplate any radical change with trepidation. It was so easy for even the best intentioned to stir the deepest feelings of some section of the community, religious or secular, and so to be very badly stung; in consequence any far-reaching reform was bound to be delayed until the last minute.

REFERENCES

[1] Newcastle Cssn., Report 1861, vol. 1, p. 21.
[2] Ibid., vol. VI, Q 68. Evidence of Lingen.
[3] Ibid., Q 229.
[4] Ibid., Q 369.
[5] Ibid., Q 377.
[6] Select Cttee., 1856, Q 3517. Evidence of Lingen.
[7] Select Cttee., 1865, Q 1040. Evidence of Adderley.
[8] Ibid., Q 711. Evidence of Lowe.
[9] Newcastle Cssn., Report 1861, Q 552. Evidence of Lingen.
[10] Ibid., vol. 1, p. 313.
[11] Ibid., p. 157.
[12] Copy of Minutes and Regulations of the Committee of the Privy Council on Education, reduced into the form of a Code, 7/2/1860.
[13] Select Cttee., 1865, Q 81. Evidence of Lingen.
[14] Cross Cssn., First Report, 1886, QQ 1015–1018.
[15] Ibid., QQ 672–9.
[16] Elementary Education Act, 1870, S 8, 9 and 10.
[17] Ibid., S 67.
[18] These notices constitute the first complete public survey of the elementary education of the districts to which they relate. They show the number, size and efficiency of the schools available as well as the size of any deficiency for which further provision needed to be made.—P.R.O. Ed. 1.
[19] Elementary Education Act, 1870, S 16.
[20] Cross Cssn., First Report, 1886, Q 453.
[21] In each case the Department sent one of its inspectors to hold a local inquiry and where there remained any doubts, his report was sent to the Vice-President or Lord President for them to take the final decision—Select Cttee. of 1884, Q 1306.
[22] Elementary Education Act, 1870, S. 18.
[23] H. Craik, The State in its Relation to Education, 1914 ed., p. 104.
[24] Select Cttee. of 1884, Q 1230. Evidence of Mundella.
[25] For further discussion of this question see E. Eaglesham, From School Board to Local Authority, 1956.

[26] Newcastle Cssn., 1861, vol. VI, Q 231. Evidence of Lingen.
[27] Ibid., vol. I, p. 231.
[28] Ibid., vol. I, p. 273.
[29] Report of the Committee of Council for Education for 1863–64, p. 187.
[30] Instructions for Inspectors, September, 1862.
[31] Select Cttee., 1884, QQ 2044–6. Evidence of Owen.
[32] Ibid., Q 158. Evidence of Sandford.
[33] Select Cttee., 1865, QQ 971–6. Evidence of Adderley.
[34] Ibid., Q 1204. Evidence of Tufnell.
[35] Ibid., Q 1160. Evidence of Tufnell.
[36] Ibid., Q 886. Evidence of Bruce.
[37] Select Cttee., 1884, Q 757. Evidence of Cumin.
[38] P.R.O. Ed. 23/71, 11/2/71–15/3/71.
[39] Ibid., 8/12/79–17/4/80.
[40] Cross Cssn., First Report, 1886, Q 1561. Evidence of Cumin.
[41] P.R.O. Ed. 24/63.
[42] Select Cttee. of 1884, QQ 1054–62. Evidence of Mundella.
[43] H. E. Boothroyd, A History of the Inspectorate, 1923, p. 33.
[44] Cross Cssn., First Report, 1886, Q 1589. Evidence of Cumin.
[45] Civil Estimate for 1857–58.
[46] P.R.O. Ed. 24/63.
[47] Select Cttee. of 1865, Q 330. Evidence of Lingen.
[48] Cross Cssn., First Report 1886, Q 1583. Evidence of Cumin.
[49] Ibid., p. 72.
[50] P.R.O., Ed. 23/71, 6/1/71–13/3/71.
[51] Ibid., 10/2/69.
[52] P.R.O. Ed. 24/63, 19/7/99.
[53] P.R.O. Ed. 23/71, 24/11/70.
[54] Ibid., 6/3/71.
[55] Ibid., 16/12/73–14/2/74.
[56] Supra, p. 8.
[57] Select Cttee., 1865, QQ 23–41. Evidence of Lingen.
[58] Ibid., QQ 107–12. Evidence of Lingen.
[59] Ibid., QQ 619–629. Evidence of Lowe.
[60] Ibid., QQ 828–834. Evidence of Bruce.
[61] Select Cttee., 1884, Q 46–52. Evidence of Sandford.
[62] Ibid., QQ 410–13 & 473. Evidence of Forster.
[63] Ibid., Q 1148. Evidence of Mundella.
[64] Ibid., Q 1116. Evidence of Mundella.
[65] Ibid., Q 1062. Evidence of Mundella.
[66] Select Cttee., 1865, Q 58–72. Evidence of Lingen.
[67] Ibid., Q 616. Evidence of Lowe.
[68] Ibid., QQ 674–6. Evidence of Lowe.
[69] Ibid., QQ 965–7. Evidence of Adderley.
[70] Ibid., Q 1343. Evidence of Salisbury.
[71] Select Cttee., 1866, Q 26. Evidence of Sandford.
[72] Ibid., Q 379. Evidence of Forster.
[73] Ibid., QQ 1154–5. Evidence of Mundella.
[74] Select Cttee. of 1866, para. 46. Chairman's Draft Report.
[75] Confidential Memorandum on the Constitution of the Office, October, 1867, by the Vice-President, p. 12.
[76] Select Cttee. of 1884, Report, para. 3.
[77] Supra, p. 10.
[78] P.R.O. Ed. 23/9, 27/1/71.
[79] P.R.O. Ed. 23/71, 2/3/81.

CHAPTER 3

THE DEPARTMENT OF SCIENCE AND ART

ON the proposal of William Ewart, a member for Liverpool, in 1835 the House of Commons set up a Select Committee 'to inquire into the best means of extending a knowledge of the Arts and of the Principles of Design among the people (especially the manufacturing population) of the country'. This Committee recommended the establishment of schools of Design. Consequently the Lords of the Privy Council for Trade recommended to the Treasury that the sum of £1,500 should be set aside in the estimates for a Normal School of Design and a Museum, the Treasury accepted the recommendation. Poulett Thompson, President of the Board of Trade, called a meeting of a number of Royal Academicians and others who were interested in this project, and in 1837 this group became the 'Council of the Government School of Design'. The school itself opened in Somerset House on 1st June of that year. In 1841 the government began to offer aid for the maintenance of provincial Schools of Design which it hoped to see established in manufacturing areas. The aid took the form of annual grants for the purchase of casts and for the payment and training of teachers and the preparation of models for use in these schools. The Board of Trade re-shaped the Council of the School of Design in 1842, increasing its membership and appointing an executive Director of the Normal School and Museum who was to be under the control of the new Council. By 1851 the Parliamentary grant for these schools under the Board of Trade had risen to £15,055, and there were seventeen provincial schools in such centres as Manchester, Birmingham, Leeds and Glasgow, which took about half of the annual vote. An inquiry by a Committee of the House of Commons in 1849 had shown certain weaknesses in the existing system so in 1852 the President of the Board of Trade abolished the Council of the School of Design, and set up within his ministry a Department of Practical Art in 1853.

The principal motive which led to the creation of the Science and Art Department was similar to that which had led the Committee of the Commons to recommend the establishment of Schools of Design in 1836—the desire to improve British manufactures. In an age when it was by no means universally accepted that the state should help education, state interference in promoting science and art might be justified 'in the influences which they exercise upon the material prosperity of the country'.[1] Those who entered this Department within the Board of Trade can hardly have imagined that they were setting up an organism that was to develop into the secondary education department of the Board of Education half a century later.

In the Speech from the Throne in 1852, the Derby-Disraeli ministry stated that 'The Advancement of the Fine Arts and Practical Science will be readily recognized by you as worthy of the attention of a great and enlightened nation. I have directed that a comprehensive scheme shall be laid before you, having in view the promotion of these objects, towards which I invite your aid and co-operation.' Before the ministry could carry out its intention, it fell from office and the establishment of the Science and Art Department was carried out by the new Liberal ministry with Cardwell as President of the Board of Trade. A letter from the Board of Trade to the Treasury in March, 1853, explained 'that the object in view is to extend a system of encouragement to local institutions for Practical Science, similar to that already commenced in the Department of Practical Art; that the systems should be combined on an enlarged scale; and that arrangements should be made for furnishing, through the instrumentality of one Department in connection with the Executive Government, having the support and being subject to the control of Parliament, the means for mutual co-operation and correspondence to every district of the Kingdom, where the local intelligence and energy of the inhabitants shall create schools of industrial science and art. . . . a recent and forcible expression of the public wants in reference to it will be found in the Surplus Report of the Royal Commissioners for the Great Exhibition of 1851.'[2] The opportunity was taken to reorganize the administration of other institutions for promoting Art and Science at the expense of the state; the Royal Dublin Society, the Mining Museum and School of Mines, the Industrial Museums of Scotland and Ireland and the Museum of Practical Geology were all in future to form part of the Board of Trade Department of Science and Art.

The increase in the amount of work with which the Committee of Council had to deal in connection with elementary schools led to the setting up of the Education Department in 1856. The Order in Council constituted the new Department to include '(a) The Educational Establishment of the Privy Council Office; (b) The Establishment for the encouragement of Science and Art, now under the direction of the Board of Trade and called the Department of Science and Art'. These two establishments were both placed under the Lord President of the Council who was to be assisted by a Vice-President of the Committee of Council on Education. This transfer of the Science and Art Department from the Board of Trade did not have any immediate effect, it was made in order to enable the President and Vice-President to render the working of any points of contact between primary education and the Science and Art Department's work more 'harmonious and consistent'.

The Science and Art Department met with little success in its early years in its task of encouraging the study of science. Various ideas were tried including that of paying the salaries of teachers of science in certain of the main centres of population such as Birmingham, Aberdeen, Stoke-on-Trent, Leeds and Bristol. It was in 1859 that the system of aid was established which led to a much wider study of the sciences and to the growth of the Department into something approaching a department of secondary education. Under the new Minute of 1859 there was to be an annual examination for a teacher's certificate along with local examinations throughout the country which were to be open to all. The Department offered payment to the teacher for holding a certificate and also payment in respect of his pupils who were successful in their examination, the payments being graduated in accordance with the grade in which the pupils passed. This system of payment by results was to be the hallmark of the Department's work for the next forty years. It was evolved by officials of the Department on the initiative of the Marquis of Salisbury, the political head. Cole, the Secretary, told the Select Committee on Scientific Instruction in 1868, 'I recollect an expression of the late Marquis of Salisbury: he said "You seem to have very little science, and unless we can get a scheme to make science common wherever the public want it, I shall abolish the name". The result of that was that, in obedience to his orders, we set about trying to invent a system which should be common to the whole country; and although it is a little modified every year, when the necessity for modification arises, the system in the main is very much what was established in 1859.'[3]

There can be no doubt but that the system of administering aid which the officials of the Science and Art Department hit upon was very successful in its day. Robert Lowe[4] told the Schools Enquiry Commission in 1868 that 'It is one of the most successful things that ever came under my notice, and I say so with the more freedom because the honour of it is due to Lord Salisbury and Mr. Adderley. . . . The result [of it] is that 4,666 thousand [sic] of young men are learning science throughout the country, and making great progress and proficiency, without any expense at all to the Government for finding buildings, schools, or libraries, or anything else. That result has been obtained by the efficiency of this plan, paying the master for the results obtained, and taking security by a previous examination that the master is competent to teach it. That is the most successful thing I have seen.'[5] The Royal Commission on Scientific Instruction and the Advancement of Science in 1872 found that the system had given a remarkable impulse to elementary scientific teaching, the number under instruction having risen from 500 in 1860 to 34,283 in 1870.[6] The Commission explained that much of the success of the scheme lay in its appeal to elementary schoolmasters who saw in it a way to increase their earnings. Pupils were recruited by the schoolmasters into their evening classes at the time when they left the senior classes of their elementary schools. 'The knowledge of the existence of such a class spread to others whose education had been neglected; and some who were desirous to fit themselves for positions in manufacturers or trade requiring some elementary scientific knowledge, resorted to these classes as a first step towards the attainment of that object.'[7] The number of students under instruction in the sciences continued to increase throughout the period of the Department's existence. The 34,283 students reported to the Royal Commission as being under instruction in 1870 had increased to 108,857 by 1890.

The increase in the number of science students was accompanied by an expansion in the variety of subjects for which payment would be made. Under the Minute of 1859 aid had been offered in six subjects; practical plane and solid geometry, mechanical physics, experimental physics, chemistry, geology and mineralogy, natural history including zoology and botany. By 1897 the number of subjects for which payment was offered had increased to twenty-five and included such subjects as building construction, naval architecture, steam and hygiene as well as the principal sciences. In each subject with the exception of mathematics, there were examinations at three levels, elementary, advanced and honours, in mathematics the examinations were divided into seven stages. The special examination for the science teachers' certificate was abolished in 1867 and anyone who had passed the Science and Art Department examination at the advanced or honours stage was recognized as qualified to hold a class and to receive payment for his pupils' successes.

The actual amount of the payments made on results were graded according to the standard of the papers which the pupil had passed. In 1893, for instance, the payment for a science subject at the elementary stage was £2 for a pass, at the advanced stage £2 10s. for a second and £5 for a first class pass, and £4 and £8 for a second or first class respectively in honours. A minimum number of attendances had to be made in the class of the teacher who claimed payment. These payments had been increased from time to time, first class honours pass had attracted a payment of £4 in 1870 while a second class at that time had gained a £2 grant. Payments by results could only be earned in respect of 'students of the industrial classes', this term was defined as

(a) Artisans or operatives in the receipt of weekly wages.

(b) Coastguards, policemen, and others who, though in receipt of weekly wages, do not support themselves by manual labour.

(c) Persons in receipt of salaries not large enough to render them liable to the income tax, as some descriptions of clerks, shopmen, etc.

(d) Small shopkeepers employing no one but members of their own family and not assessed to the income tax.

(e) Tradesmen and manufacturers on their own account, supporting themselves by their own manual labour, not employing apprentices, journeymen, etc., and not assessed to the income tax.

(f) The children (not gaining their own livelihood) of all such persons above mentioned.[8]

Apart from payments by results, the Science and Art Department offered prizes and Queen's medals to those students achieving a high enough standard in the annual examinations. A certain number of scholarships and exhibitions for full-time study were offered each year as well as aid to intending teachers who wished to attend the Normal School of Science and Royal School of Mines, South Kensington. Building grants were available to help in the construction of art schools from 1856 and for science schools from 1868; such grants were paid at the rate of 2s. 6d. per square foot of internal area up to a maximum of £500 for any one school. Further grants of up to 50 per cent of the cost were made for the purchase of apparatus for science classes, such grants being 'rigorously confined to articles of a non-destructible nature' and of 'a permanent and illustrative character which are required by the Teacher in giving instruction in Science'.[9]

In addition to these grants, a special grant in respect of attendance was available from 1872 to schools recognized by the Department as 'Organized Science Schools'. For recognition as a day organized science school, the principal conditions to be fulfilled were that instruction in science should be carried on methodically for at least three years in accordance with a course laid down by the Department and that at least fifteen hours a week should be devoted to subjects which were under the aegis of the Department. In schools so recognized the attendance grant amounted to 10s. a year until 1892, and after that to £1 a year for each student who made at least 250 attendances. The conditions to be met for recognition as an organized science school were liberalized in the Regulation of 1894 when the minimum amount of time which might be devoted to science teaching was cut from fifteen to thirteen hours a week. At the same time the grant system for such a school was changed so that in addition to the attendance grant, payment by results was to be confined to the advanced and higher courses while payment by results in the lower part of the school was replaced by a grant the size of which was dependent on the results of inspection, including the inspection of literary work. The heavy demands made by science subjects on the timetable in organized science schools meant that very few endowed grammar schools sought recognition as such, and of 264 endowed grammar schools receiving grant of some sort from the Department in 1894, only 16 were recognized as organized science schools.[10] The total number of organized science schools increased steadily, in April 1892 there were 64, in 1893 there were 82 and in 1894 there were 98. Many of these were established by school boards, one of the best known was the Central Higher Grade Board School in Leeds. The curriculum was further modified in 1895 when literary, manual and commercial subjects were made essential. The grants were again changed to a payment of £1 10s. for every 400 attendances and a variable grant of 35s., 30s., or 25s. for each pupil who had qualified for the attendance grant. The amount of the variable grant depended on the inspectors' reports on each school. Payments by results continued to be made in respect of the more advanced courses in these schools. After this liberalization of the conditions for recognition as an organized science school, more endowed schools sought this status and by 1897 there were 169 schools recognized by the Department for these grants including such better-known schools as Bradford Grammar and the Perse School at Cambridge.

Payments made for the study of art totalled considerably more than those for science, but the principle of payment by results remained the same. The actual number of students earning grant was much larger than in science because pupils in elementary schools were able to earn a Science and Art Department grant for their drawing. The number of persons taught in art classes in 1869 was 2,445,785, but of these 2,250,070 were pupils in elementary schools. In the same year the Department's grants for drawing in public elementary schools and training colleges amounted to £239,248 as against £169,923 in 'direct' payments for Art.[11] The growth in the work of the Art section of the Department may be seen by comparing these figures for 1896 with those for a quarter of a century earlier. In 1872 the total number of persons taught in art classes was 237,764 of whom 194,549 were scholars in elementary school drawing classes, the grant earned by these latter amounting to £9,964.

Some idea of the extent of the growth of the Science and Art Department can be gained from its total annual expenditure given in the following table. These figures include the grants made to the museums and other institutions which the Department took over in 1853. In the year 1851, before any consolidation took place, the annual Parliamentary votes on behalf of such institutions was in excess of £40,000; for the last year in the table, 1896, direct grants to institutions, South Kensington and Bethnal Green Museums and the cost of circulating objects from them in connection with the study of art amounted to £144,071.

The original Department of Practical Art had been accommodated at Somerset House, in 1852 it had moved to Marlborough House, and in 1857—as the Department of Science and Art—it moved again, this time to South Kensington where it was to remain until fused into the Board of Education. The Department came to be frequently referred to as 'South Kensington' during the later part of the nineteenth century, and as such was distinguished from 'Whitehall' as the Education Department dealing with elementary education was called. As the Science and Art Department met with a greater demand for its services, so did its staff grow. When the Department was formed in 1853, Lyon Playfair was appointed as Joint Secretary and Inspector General for Science while Henry Cole became Joint Secretary and

Inspector General for Art, having previously been General Superintendent of the Department of Practical Art. At the end of 1854 Cole became simply Inspector-General while Playfair became Secretary for the Science Department; on Playfair's resignation four years later, this latter title fell into abeyance.

The total expenditure of the Science and Art Department at three yearly intervals, 1854–96.[12]

Year	Total of expenditure
1854	£56,911
1857	£72,104
1860	£99,784
1863	£122,078
1866	£125,091
1869	£220,344
1872	£230,502
1875	£285,312
1878	£305,859
1881	£340,025
1884	£371,611
1887	£430,286
1890	£473,102
1893	£666,308
1896	£770,432

By 1860 the Department had a Secretary (Henry Cole), an Assistant Secretary, an Inspector for Science and an Inspector-General for Art as well as a clerical staff of eleven. It is of some interest to compare this with the position at the end of the century when the general administration was in the hands of a Secretary, aided by a Principal Assistant Secretary and an Assistant Secretary; the Science Division then had a Director, an Assistant Director, an Official Examiner (not to be confused with professional examiners), two Assistant Official Examiners and a Science Examinations Clerk; the Art Division was similarly organized except that it had only one Assistant Official Examiner. These functionaries had by this time come to be supported by 27 inspectors and a clerical staff of 108. The total number of staff employed in the Department had grown steadily rather than in a spectacular manner until the last decade of the century. Up to that time there had been four inspectors of schools, but the change in 1894 to variable grants paid partly on the results of inspection made necessary the creation of seventeen additional posts for inspectors.[13] The clerical staff also increased rapidly in the 1890s. In 1890 there was a chief clerk and 48 other clerks, by 1895 there were 107 clerks in addition to the Chief Clerk.

Apart from full-time staff, the Department employed a considerable number of acting inspectors and of local inspectors. Both of these grades were only called upon to act during the examination season each year. The local inspectors were only concerned with the conduct of examinations in Drawing in elementary schools. The country was divided into districts and for each district a local inspector, along with one or more assistants, adjudicated on part of the test paper worked by the pupils sending the rest to be marked to the Department at South Kensington. Forty-six of these local inspectors were employed in the examinations of 1890, seven in London and thirty-nine in the provinces. Acting inspectors were usually officers from the Royal Engineers, who were employed during the examination season to see that the Department's rules were being properly enforced. These officers were paid £1 per night, and their duties included seeing that at least three members of the local committee were present throughout the time while each paper was worked (usually from 7 p.m. to 10 p.m.), that the candidates were sitting far enough apart, and that the work was being done fairly.

For most of the half-century of its existence, the Science and Art Department came under the control of only two permanent heads. As we have already seen, Henry Cole had been at the head of the former Department of Practical Art and, after a brief period of joint rule with Lyon Playfair, he became Secretary of the Department of Science and Art until his retirement in 1873. Cole certainly did more than any other single man to build up the Department into the useful instrument of education that it became, during his period of office his political chiefs were changed no fewer than ten times. On his retirement Macleod—until then Assistant Secretary—was made Assistant Secretary of the Education Department (Whitehall) and Principal Officer at South Kensington. Sandford, Secretary at Whitehall became Secretary of South Kensington as well, and was given executive control of the Science and Art Department. Three separate Directors were appointed to take charge of the Science, Art and Museum Divisions. On Macleod's retirement in 1881, the Director of the Science Division, Donnelly, became Assistant Secretary and Permanent Head of the Science and Art Department, an office he was to hold for the remainder of the Department's independent life. Donnelly proved himself to be a doughty champion of the Department as it had evolved and a stern opponent of change. Before the Bryce Commission in 1895 he strongly defended payment by results and, as the Commission remarked in their Report, he 'stood quite alone' among their witnesses in defending the future independence of his Department from amalgamation with the Education Department at Whitehall.

Throughout its period of existence the Science and Art Department was supposed to be an agency for supporting local effort and enterprise, it was never intended that it should itself take the initiative in the localities. 'In the proposed United Department of Science and Art the motive power will thus be local and voluntary—the system, in the main, self-supporting', so wrote the Board of Trade in proposing the creation of the Department to the Treasury. In its Minute of 1853 accepting the Board of Trade's suggestion, the Treasury, in its turn, stressed the importance of local initiative so that local institutions might be rendered as self-supporting as possible 'because they [the Lords of the Treasury] entertain a belief that the utility of such institutions is great in proportion as they are self-supporting'.[14] The Directory of the Department reminded local people annually that 'The aid granted by the Department is intended to supplement and not to supersede local effort'.[15] The middle years of the nineteenth century in England constitute the golden age of the doctrine of self-help, of individualism and of the importance of limiting and reducing, if possible, the sphere of state activity. Therefore, even as the activities of the Department grew in importance and while it, in fact, took the initiative in the spreading of the study of the sciences and of art through offering payments for success in the examinations it organized, it continued to lay stress on local participation in its work and on individual self-reliance. In the Science Directory of 1870, the public was reminded that grants might be reduced or withdrawn at any time. 'The payment of fees by the students can be looked upon as the only solid and sufficient basis on which a self-supporting system can be established and supported. Though my Lords do not consider it necessary at present to lay down any rules making the payment of fees an absolute condition of the grants on account of Science instruction, yet as the payments from the State must be expected to diminish, and as aid on account of those persons who do nothing for themselves cannot be justified, Committees of schools and classes and teachers are strongly urged (should it at present not be the practice) at once to impose as high a scale of fees as they consider can be raised, not only on middle class students, but also on artisans.'[16]

From the beginning of the system of payment by results local committees had to be established before teachers could claim payments from the state for their pupils' successes. The requirements made by the Department of these local committees became more stringent as time went on. In the matter of their composition the Directory of 1860 merely required each committee to consist of five responsible persons. By 1890 the Directory specified that 'The Committee must consist of a Chairman, Secretary and at least three other members. The offices of Chairman and Secretary cannot both be held by the same person. All the members of the Committee must be well-known responsible persons of independent position, who have no personal interest in the teachers of the school. . . . It is very desirable that as many persons as possible in recognized positions of public responsibility in the district, such as mayors, provosts, town and county councillors, magistrates, members of school boards, trustees of grammar schools, clergymen of the Established Church in parochial employment, and ministers of religion in charge of legally recognized places of public worship, should be on the Committee. It is absolutely necessary that at least two such responsible persons should agree to act. The Chairman, who will be required to certify that the constitution of the Committee is in accordance with the above requirements, must be in a position of public responsibility as defined above.'[17]

The duties of local Science and Art Committees also became more closely defined with the passage of time. In 1860 the Directory stated that where there was an energetic local teacher, the chief duty of the local committee would be simply to give the teacher the necessary certificate for obtaining his payments. In 1868 as a former Vice-President of the Committee of Council for Education, Robert Lowe, could tell the Schools Inquiry Commission that science masters 'teach anywhere they can; in their own lodgings, in the street, or anywhere. We know nothing about their teaching.'[18] But in later years the Directory laid upon committees the task of providing and maintaining suitable rooms for class instruction with firing, lighting and apparatus. Outside of the examination period, the local committees came to be made responsible in every way for the conduct of classes. By the 1890s they almost invariably received any fees and any special grants for such purposes as providing apparatus and from this income met all the expenses, including any salary payment to be made to the teachers in addition to their payment by results.

Throughout the period of their existence, Science and Art committees were particularly concerned with the conduct of the annual examinations. From the point of view of the Science and Art Department, it was essential that the examination on which the main grants were dependent should be conducted in such a way as to eliminate any possibility of cheating on the part of the teacher, and the local committees and acting inspectors were the instruments chosen to see that the Department's interests were protected. The Regulations in 1860 required the members of the local committees to accept responsibility for giving out question papers, supervising the examination, collecting up the scripts, sealing them and posting them to the Department. Not fewer than three members of a local committee were to be present throughout each examination. In 1870 the Department stated 'It is through their [the local committees'] agency that more than 2,000 examinations were held in all parts of the country in 1869. Mistakes and irregularities have in some cases occurred, as might be expected, from the novel nature of the duties to some gentlemen.'[19] From 1870 the amount of work involved in conducting the examinations in the larger towns led the Department to authorize the election of a special Local Secretary by the local committees of a town. If there were more than three schools in a town, the Department could require the local committees to make such an appointment. He was allowed a fee of 10 guineas with an additional half guinea for each evening on which an examination paper was actually worked. The procedure for the election of a Special Local Secretary was for a special committee to be formed consisting of the chairmen of all the local committees and this meeting was to be convened by the chairman of that local committee in the town which had been longest in touch with the Department. This was often not as difficult a matter as the regulations might suggest for in the large towns the local school board—or a committee of it—might constitute itself as the local committee for a number of science schools and classes, even where the local committees varied from school to school they would in such cases have the secretary to the school board as their secretary, thus simplifying the administration. In Bradford in 1891 there were fourteen schools taking the Department's examinations, but eight of these belonged to Bradford School Board and the secretary to the School's Committee was in these eight cases the School Board Secretary.[20]

Apart from school boards, other local bodies could also be granted recognition as local committees for Science and Art Department purposes including governing bodies of endowed grammar schools and committees set up under the Technical Instruction Act.

During the Department's last years, the Bryce Commission pointed out that it was really among other things the central authority for technical education. Under the Technical Instruction Act it decided on the qualifications of schools suitable to receive aid from County or County Borough Councils; it also had the duty of sanctioning local expenditure on subjects of instruction not specifically authorized in the Act. This latter duty it interpreted in a liberal sense and authorized as 'technical' such subjects of study as musical notation, book-keeping and political economy. The new legislation on technical instruction also had some effect on the Department's payments by results. The aid given to schools and classes by the new county councils led the Department to withdraw the payment that was formerly made for passing the elementary stage examination in the second class and the money thus saved was used to increase the payments for results on the higher examinations.

The achievements of the Science and Art Department were considerable, but by the end of the nineteenth century secondary and technical education needed something different in the way of an administrative agency. The Bryce Commission recognized this and recommended that it should cease to exist as a separate department and that its functions should be absorbed in an enlarged and reorganized Education Department. In spite of the importance which it claimed to attach to local initiative, the Science and Art Department in fact left little or no room for its local committees to exercise judgment on any issue of weight or significance, they remained administrative devices in the service of a highly centralized grant-distributing machine. The Royal Commission found the Department's defects were inherent in its constitution, 'It is too centralized and too specialized, too little able to adapt itself to the changes it has been a major factor in effecting'.[21] The restricted list of school subjects for which payment was offered and the use of the examination results for assessing the amount of payment led to both unbalanced curricula and a style of instruction in Science not suited to children.[22] It was obviously much simpler for a more local authority to make grants on a capitation or attendance basis than for a central department to do so because it would be in a better position to see that such payments were really

E

meeting a genuine need in the district. Moreover, the Science and Art Department's relationship to such bodies as school boards was un-defined—unlike that of the Education Department at Whitehall—even although it came into contact with many local bodies in the normal course of its work. It had also built up for itself a tradition of independent action at the centre in that co-operation with the Charity Commission and the Education Department was lacking. The Bryce Commission noticed these defects in its Report when it suggested that the Department needed to be more liberal and to judge schools as wholes, not just by subjects and added, 'In dealing with schools, the Science and Art Department is much more independent of legislative control than the Education Department, and so tends to harass them by a too frequent change of rules'.[23]

REFERENCES

[1] Henry Cole, 'The Functions of the Science and Art Department' among *Introductory Addresses on the Science and Art Department*, London, 1858, p. 10.
[2] Letter dated 16.3.53 from Sir Emerson Tennant of the Board of Trade to the Treasury among Correspondence between Lords of the Committee of the Privy Council for Trade and Lords Commissioners of H.M. Treasury on the Constitution of the Department of Science and Art.
[3] Evidence of Henry Cole before the Select Committee on Scientific Instruction, 1868, Q 44.
[4] From 1862 Lowe abolished payments to teachers with science certificates following his proposal to abolish such payments to teachers with elementary certificates, considering it sound public policy to make the government's actions as uniform as possible—Sel. Cttee. on Scientific Instruction, QQ 51–2.
[5] S.I.C., 1868, Q 6650. Evidence of Lowe.
[6] Royal Commission on Scientific Instruction and the Advancement of Science, vol. I, 2nd Report, 1872, para. 41.
[7] Ibid., para. 44.
[8] Directory of the S. and A. Dept. for Science Schools and Classes, 1870. Section XXXVI.
[9] Ibid., LXIII.
[10] Bryce Cssn., 1895, p. 29.
[11] Annual Report of the Department of Science and Art for 1896, 1897.
[12] Figures from Annual Reports of Science and Art Department.
[13] Bryce Cssn., 1895, Q 1122. Evidence of Donnelly.
[14] Correspondence between Lords of the Committee of the Privy Council for Trade and Lords Commissioners of H.M. Treasury on the Constitution of the Department of Science and Art, 1853.
[15] From Science and Art Directory, 1890, para. XIII.
[16] Science Directory, 1870, para. V.
[17] Science and Art Directory, 1890, para. IX.
[18] S.I.C., 1868, Q. 6651. Evidence of Lowe.
[19] Seventeenth Annual Report of Science and Art Dept., 1870, p. X.
[20] Calendar of the Science and Art Department, 1891.
[21] Bryce Cssn., 1895, Report, p. 101.
[22] Ibid., vol. VII, p. 162, Mr. Laurie's Report on Leeds Higher Grade School.
[23] Ibid., Report, p. 100.

CHAPTER 4

THE ENDOWED SCHOOLS AND CHARITY COMMISSIONS

BOTH of these Commissions were government agencies charged with
the task of assisting the provision of secondary education. They were
to achieve their purpose by seeing that the best use was made of all
available endowments. The existing condition of the grammar schools
and the need which an increasingly industrialized and urbanized
society felt for secondary education forms one of the main themes of
the history of English education in the nineteenth century. Lord
Kenyon in the King v. Archbishop of York in 1795 said, 'Whoever
will examine the state of the grammar schools in different parts of this
kingdom will see to what a lamentable condition most of them have
been reduced'. He went on to speak of the 'empty walls without
scholars, and everything neglected but the receipt of salaries and
emoluments. In some instances that have lately come within my own
knowledge, there was not a single scholar in the schools though there
were very large endowments to them.'

Various attempts to undertake the reform of endowments for educational purposes in the first half of the nineteenth century failed. In
1820 Lord Brougham put forward a bill designed to exercise a measure
of control over endowed schools, but this was so widely amended in
the Committee stage that it was abandoned. According to Lord
Eldon's judgment in the Leeds Grammar School Case, there was no
precedent for the Court of Chancery to permit the conversion of
the school for teaching anything else except Latin and Greek. The
general effect of this case was to discourage further attempts by the
governors of school endowments from trying to broaden curricula
by appealing to Chancery.[1] The Grammar School Act of 1840
attempted to deal with this problem and to permit grammar schools
to widen the area of their recruitment where this was limited by their
foundation deeds, but the attempt to permit a broadening of the
curriculum was so hedged about with restrictions that it led to little
improvement. The Act confirmed the principle that the main purpose
of a grammar school was to teach Greek and Latin, but it permitted
the addition of other subjects provided that their addition did not in
any way encroach upon the principal aim of the foundation. The

57

effect of the restrictions favouring Greek and Latin was the more serious because of the very wide definition of the term 'grammar school' given in the Act.

The ineffectiveness of earlier attempts at reform was shown by the Report of the Schools Inquiry Commission in 1868. The Commissioners wrote that 'Of all the endowed schools in the country there is hardly one which is both entirely subject to the public voice and devoted without restriction to the public good . . . it is clear from the information which we have ourselves received that there are few endowments applicable to secondary education which are put to the best use, and very many which are working to little or bad use'.[2] Of the state they wrote, 'It might give test, stimulus, advice, dignity; it withholds them all, and leaves the endowed schools to the cramping assistance of judicial decisions, which may be quite right as regards the interpretation of the founders' words, and quite wrong as regards the wise administration of the schools they founded. Where the powers of the Court of Chancery have been applied with some success in the reformation of a school, the object has frequently been obtained only after much delay, after much expense, and sometimes by straining the law. The threat of opposition before the Court has wrecked many good schemes of reformation.'[3]

The situation which the Commission found in the London area was typical of the national condition. Here there were thirty-three endowed grammar school foundations; of these three no longer existed as schools at all, another had a master but no scholars, in another the masterships were suspended during the preparation of a new scheme, eight or nine were giving purely elementary education and were said to be inferior to a good national school, and none educated girls with the exception of Christ's Hospital with seventeen girls out of over one thousand pupils. Four metropolitan schools were selected for special commendation, one of these, City of London, had become a day school for 930 boys, and the other three had been created in the last thirty years out of funds left for eleemosynary, not educational, purposes; these were the Stationers', Whitechapel Foundation and St. Clement Dane's schools. 'In other words, . . . the most useful schools are those which have been most changed.'[4]

Apart from the condition of the individual schools, the Commission stressed the seriousness of the isolation of each grammar school and the lack of any organization to view the needs of an area as a whole.

'. . . the grammar schools stand side by side, affecting in many important ways the well-being of education and the growth and direction
of the English intellect; but each shut up, as it were, in itself, with no
authorized source of guidance to which they can resort, and no public
tribunal to call them to account for their stewardship of the high
interests which the State has permitted their founders permanently
to entrust to them.'[5] The Court of Chancery was quite manifestly not
suited to assume the role of an administrative agency for secondary
education, nor did the Charity Commission as then constituted, seem
suited. Charity Commissions in some form or other had been a
familiar feature of the government scene since 1818 when the first
Commission was set up under an 'Act for appointing Commissioners
to inquire concerning Charities in England for the Education of the
Poor'. The inquiry proved to be a much greater undertaking than
anyone had originally conceived it to be. By 1835 a Select Committee
found that the charities of six counties were 'entirely uninvestigated'
while those of six others had only been partially inquired into.[6] In
1855 a Charity Commission was established with power to do more
than merely to inquire, but its power to amend the rules of a charity
remained severely limited. It could do no more than inquire into a
charity unless a definite complaint were laid before it and to find
residents prepared to take the responsibility of coming forward to
invoke the Charity Commission was often difficult. Moreover, if
the charity had an annual value of more than £50 the Commission
could only act with the consent of a majority of the trustees and a
persistent minority could ruin a new scheme by an appeal to Chancery
'where costs only are certain'. The Commissioners hardly had the
necessary educational knowledge to examine the state of a school as
distinct from its endowment. Under the Charitable Trusts Act of
1855 the trustees of every charity had the duty of sending the Commission a copy of their accounts each year, but this provision was not
enforced and the Commissioners admitted in their Report in 1866
that the examination of so many sets of accounts was quite beyond their
resources. For these reasons, the Schools Inquiry Commission found
that the Charity Commission had also been unable to act as an administrative agent for secondary education.

To meet the needs of the existing situation, the Schools Inquiry
Commission under the chairmanship of Lord Taunton recommended
that the management of secondary schools should be shared between
the headmaster, the governors, a provincial authority and a central

authority. The headmaster should be responsible for the internal management of the school, that is to say for such matters as the appointment of assistant staff, discipline, text books, methods and school organization. The external management should be shared; the governors ought to undertake responsibility for the provision of buildings, fixing of fees, payment of all salaries and establishment of scholarships—subject in each case to the terms of the scheme sanctioned by the higher authority; it should also fall within their competence to appoint and to dismiss the headmaster and to fix the dates for school terms and holidays. A provincial authority would have such duties to perform as deciding the grades of different schools in relation to each other, deciding which schools should take boarders and which day boys, consolidating small endowments or suppressing them as schools and converting them to exhibitions, preparing schemes for submission to the central authority for the regulation of existing charitable trusts in their province in such a way as to improve the efficiency of the endowed schools and bringing to the notice of the Charity Commission all endowments for purposes other than education 'which appear to be useless, mischievous or obsolete and to propose schemes for their conversion to educational purposes'. It would be the duty of the central authority to receive the schemes submitted to it from the provinces and, if it agreed with them, to put them forward for parliamentary approval, it would also appoint inspectors who would report annually on each school in the country and audit the accounts of every endowed school each year.[7]

The Schools Inquiry Commissioners felt that a modified Charity Commission with its powers enlarged might serve as the central authority although they added that 'There is something to be said for appointing an entirely new Commission'. The principal advantage in using the Charity Commission was said to be that its experience would prove valuable and that disputes as to the proper limits of their jurisdictions between a new body and the existing Commission would be avoided. The suggestion was made that if a Minister of Education were appointed he should act as President of the Commission when it was dealing with educational business. The advantage claimed for this arrangement was that it would give the Commission a spokesman in Parliament and the support of the whole strength of the government at any particular time. Apart from the chairman, at least one other Commissioner should be appointed for his special knowledge of educational matters and it would also be desirable to appoint a member

of Parliament who would be able to answer any question that might
be asked in the House in the absence of the Minister. Before schemes
for the re-organization of endowments were finally given the force of
law, it was suggested that they should be laid before both Houses
for forty days and if there was no objection lodged during that time,
the ordinances should receive the assent of the Crown. The power of
the Charity Commission to modify educational endowments was not
to apply to those less than thirty years old.[8]

The constitution of provincial authorities provided Lord Taunton
and his colleagues with a well-nigh insoluble problem. In the absence
of county and county borough councils they proposed to take the
Registrar-General's divisions as 'provinces'. To each of these a permanent official would be appointed who would be the inspector for the
secondary schools of the area, with him would be associated six or
eight unpaid district commissioners chosen by the Crown from among
the more influential residents of the district. It would be their joint
duty, acting together, to draw up schemes for the management of all
endowed schools in their area and to submit them to the Charity
Commission. The Official District Commissioner being a civil
servant, would hold office on a permanent basis, but the unpaid District
Commissioners should hold office for periods of five years. The
Taunton Commission looked forward to popularly chosen county
boards and realized fully the value of popular participation in this
work, but it felt that the time was not ripe for the direct election of
boards. On the other hand it did suggest that towns with more than
100,000 inhabitants should be given the right to contract out of the
provincial authority and establish boards of their own consisting in
equal numbers of members named by the trustees of the larger endowed schools and by the town council with the Official District
Commissioner as a member *ex officio*.[9]

The third element in the external management of schools, the
governing bodies or Boards of Trustees, needed to be reconstituted.
The evidence gathered by the Commission had shown that the usual
method of filling vacancies was by co-optation and that too often
it was not so much the good of the school as the value of the patronage
acquired which was sought after. In order to overcome the stultifying
effects of these foundation governors, it was proposed that in future
schemes the existing foundation trustees should constitute about one-
third of the governing body, another third being appointed by the
municipality and the final third by the Provincial Board. No members

should be appointed for more than five years at a time, and those who absented themselves from all meetings for a year should lose their seats.[10]

The recommendations of the Commissioners led to the Endowed Schools Act of 1869.[11] The aim of this measure was set out clearly in the preamble as being to carry out the recommendations of the Commissioners who 'have made their Report and thereby recommended various changes in the government management and studies of endowed schools and in the application of educational endowments with the objects of promoting their greater efficiency and of carrying into effect the main designs of the founders thereof by putting a liberal education within the reach of children of all classes'. The Act was not to apply to the seven schools dealt with in the Public Schools Act of 1868,[12] to endowments less than fifty years old and to choir schools or seminaries, yet it gave very wide powers to a new central authority of three Commissioners who 'by schemes made during the period, and in the manner and subject to the provisions in this Act mentioned, shall have power in such manner as may render any educational endowment most conducive to the advancement of the education of boys and girls or either of them, to alter and add to any existing and to make new trusts, directions and provisions which affect such endowment, and the education promoted thereby, including the consolidation of two or more such endowments or the division of one endowment into two or more endowments'.[13] In exercising these wide powers, the three Endowed Schools Commissioners did not have to pay regard to the doctrine of cy-pres which had always guided the courts in their handling of charities. On the contrary, the Act of 1869 put forward the idea that existing educational trusts could be abrogated and new trusts substituted. The Commissioners might prepare schemes removing or appointing governing bodies and modify their powers as seemed necessary, moreover the religious belief of a person was not to affect his qualification for being a member of a governing body. Holy orders were not to be required of masters in endowed schools, the jurisdiction of the ordinary to license masters was abolished and the masters themselves were to be made liable to dismissal in all new schemes. By section 12 the Commissioners were instructed that 'provision shall be made so far as conveniently may be for extending [the benefits of endowments] to girls'. In order to increase the funds available for secondary education, the Endowed Schools Commission was given power to make schemes for the application of certain non-educational charities to the needs of schools. These included charities for marriage portions, for the redemption of prisoners and captives, for the relief of poor prisoners for debt, for doles in money or in kind and for any other purposes which appeared to have failed altogether provided that they were set up before 1800.

In these provisions the Act established a stronger central authority than the Schools Inquiry Commissioners had proposed in their Report but the Act did not establish any intermediate body between the Endowed Schools Commission at the centre and the governing bodies of individual endowments. For this reason it fell to the lot of the central authority not simply to receive schemes drawn up by a provincial authority, but to initiate schemes itself. The failure to establish provincial authorities by the government of the day seems to have been due to the lack of any suitable local bodies from which their membership could have been drawn. To compensate for their absence more work than was intended had to be given to the central authority, and to expedite matters in those circumstances a special Commission was set up at the centre instead of using the Charity Commission as suggested by the Report of 1868. So far as the grammar schools were concerned, this middle tier of the administration was not to come into existence until the twentieth century. The government of the day imagined that the task of reorganizing the schools could be accomplished in a few years and the Endowed Schools Commission was due to be dissolved on 31st December, 1872 or, by Order in Council, its powers could be extended for one more year. Even if provincial authorities had been established, it is very doubtful whether the greater part of the task of reorganization could have been accomplished in three or four years; without them it proved to be quite impossible. The comments of Lord Lyttleton, Chairman of the Endowed Schools Commission, when giving evidence before the Select Committee of 1873 which inquired into the working of the Act of 1869, make clear the difficulties which arose from the absence of provincial authorities. 'Without [provincial or district authorities] in some form, I conceive it is idle to look for more than an imperfect realization of the objects of the Report and of the Act, at least for a long time to come. . . . The Schools Inquiry Commissioners never intended that the immense, often invidious, always difficult functions in the reconstitution of endowments should be placed in the hands of a single central authority with the aid of Assistant Commissioners. They intended to rest the whole fabric on two great equal pillars—a central and a local authority, and to show, in perhaps the most striking manner, the wide difference between what was intended and what actually exists, it is enough to refer to the above named summary, in which it will be seen that it was the provincial, not the central, authority which was in the first instance to fix the grade of schools, to consolidate foundations and to propose entire schemes for their regulation. The absence of this integral part of the system—in other words, the lack of recognized, organized legal co-adjutors in our work throughout the country— has been felt by us during the whole of our existence. Such large measures—measures on the frequent expediency of which we believe all the best judges are agreed, and which, beyond question, are explicitly pointed out in the Act—on the consolidation, sometimes the partial or total transfer of endowments, and the consolidation of governing bodies, have rarely been even attempted by us, and much more rarely effected, from the invidiousness, often leading to complete impossibility, of forcing such changes on reluctant and prejudiced persons through the instrumentality of paper schemes promulgated by a newly constituted Board sitting in London, with the aid, on the spot, only of emissaries of its own, who are there regarded, and almost in proportion to their zeal and ability with nearly as much suspicion as the Board itself. The chasm is immense between this system and the same, supplemented by a powerful local organization of elements commanding, through the immemorial usages and traditions of the country, the respect and confidence of the whole population, such as the Schools Inquiry Commissioners had in view.'

Another major difference between the recommendations of the Taunton Commission and the provisions of the Act of 1869 was the omission from the Act of any machinery for establishing a central council for the examination and inspection of secondary schools. The Commission had proposed the creation of a council of twelve, half of the members being appointed by the universities and the other half by the Crown. This Council would have undertaken three main duties, firstly, to appoint examiners and to frame rules for the conduct of annual examinations to be taken by the schools; secondly, to make the necessary rules for the examination of candidates for the office of schoolmaster, to appoint the examiners and to grant the certificates; thirdly, to make an annual report on the schools giving as complete a picture as possible of what had been done and of what remained to be done. The lack of any administrative agency for dealing with the more purely educational aspect of the position in the endowed schools was a further weakness of the Act.

The procedure to be followed by the Endowed Schools Commission in carrying out their task was laid down in detail in the Act.[14] When the Commissioners were about to consider a charity, they had to give the existing trustees of the endowment an opportunity to produce their own scheme of reform in the first instance. If they failed to produce a satisfactory scheme, the Commissioners then set about preparing a draft scheme which was printed and circulated to all interested parties. Three months were allowed for objections to the proposals at this stage and, if the objections seemed to warrant it, a public inquiry would then be held before the draft with any amendments that seemed advisable was submitted to the Education Department. The Education Department had power to approve or reject any scheme; if it was approved, the scheme in its final form would be printed and circulated for information. At this stage objectors could appeal on any point of law to a Special Committee of five privy councillors of whom at least two were required to be members of the judicial committee. If there were no appeal or if the appeal were dismissed, the scheme was laid before both Houses of Parliament for forty days to give either House the opportunity of carrying an address against it. After surviving all of these checks successfully, the scheme was then made legally binding by Order in Council.

In the absence of provincial authorities, the Commission decided that if it were to create a system of secondary schools in each district, it would have to take the whole country area by area considering schemes for all the relevant charities at the same time and not work piecemeal, dealing with the most scandalous first. This led to delays for those who wanted a new scheme quickly and to the neglect of schools in which there was a crying need for reform; at the same time there was much resentment on the part of those who had hoped that their turn would not come for a long time, indeed, schools without notorious abuses found themselves under attack. Because of these difficulties and the opposition which was stirred by what seemed to be its injustice, the district approach had to be abandoned by the Commissioners.

From the start, therefore, the Endowed Schools Commission had to work through a somewhat clumsy procedure and against a great deal of opposition. At the same time it had to contend with the urgent demands of Mr. Forster at the Education Department that it should produce schemes more rapidly. D. C. Richmond, who later became a Charity Commissioner under the Endowed Schools Act and who served as Secretary to the Endowed Schools Commission itself, told the Select Committee of 1894 'I remember that Mr. Forster several times when he met me pressed me, "Cannot you send us more schemes?" and he was impatient at the slowness, as he thought, of the action of the machine which he had set going; he perhaps did not know how many legal difficulties, and how much opposition we should encounter; and so we were very much pressed then to make schemes, as he said, in the rough; and to some extent that was the case'.[15]

Further difficulties arose with the passing of the Elementary Education Act in 1870. Under this measure many small endowed elementary schools sought to be recognized as efficient, but in order to attain that status they frequently needed to apply for a building grant under the pre-1870 regulations before the period of grace for such applications ran out. However, the trustees of these schools could not lodge a valid claim for a building grant until they had ascertained whether the school's endowment and its site would be permitted to continue in use for purposes of elementary education by the Endowed Schools Commission. In dealing with these cases, the Commissioners decided as a matter of policy that the income from endowments might no longer be used to meet the normal maintenance and running expenses of elementary schools since under the Act there were other ways of raising money for this purpose; the endowment might only be applied to new buildings, sites and equipment. Income from endowments should be devoted to giving people advantages they would not enjoy under the Act and if the endowment did not exist. This led to great discontent for some places where the ratepayers had thought that they would use the endowments to avoid the establishment of a school board and the imposition of an education rate, or at least to diminish the rate they would otherwise have to pay, and found their proposed course of action barred.

The amount of work arising over these schemes for elementary schools and the objections to them of necessity diverted much of the energy of the Commissioners from the task of reorganizing the grammar schools. Consequently, in the Endowed Schools Amendment Act of 1873,[16] elementary schools with endowments of less than £100 per annum were exempted from the jurisdiction of the Commission and were empowered to negotiate new schemes directly with the Education Department. Certain other minor changes were introduced into the procedure laid down by the Act of 1869. The Education Department had hitherto only had power to approve or disapprove a scheme in its entirety, it was now given power to remit a scheme to the Commissioners with suggested amendments. Not every scheme need any longer be laid before Parliament, but only schemes objected to in certain ways by certain bodies and appeals on points of law were in future to be made to the Judicial Committee of the Privy Council instead of to a special committee thereof. Finally the opportunity was taken to deal with a difficulty which had arisen over the interpretation by the Courts of Section 17 of the Act of 1869. This Section directed that religious opinions should not affect the qualification of any person for being a member of the governing body of an endowed school. The intention had been to ensure that dissenters should not be excluded from such bodies, but the courts had interpreted it as meaning that clerics could not be appointed as governors *ex officio* of endowed schools. This had led to the Commission having difficulty with some of its schemes in the House of Lords; the new act therefore permitted clerics to remain as *ex officio* members of governing bodies where this was provided for in the original trust.

The measure of 1873 proved its value in smoothing out a number of the administrative difficulties which had arisen in the path of the Endowed Schools Commission, but it did not serve to make that body more popular generally or more acceptable to those who felt it threatened their interests in some way. Opponents of the Commission put forward three principal grievances; firstly, that money intended for elementary education was being applied to secondary schools; secondly, that money was being taken from the poor to be used to subsidize the education of the middle class; and thirdly, that at least two of the three Commissioners permitted their own pre-conceived notions to over-ride the wishes of benefactors.[17]

The first point has already been discussed, and it undoubtedly had enough substance in it to make it useful politically. The second accusation also appeared to many to be justified, and certainly proved to be a useful political weapon. The Commissioners were concerned above all else with improving the efficiency of the schools, this could often only be done by increasing their income through charging fees; in this way people who lived in certain places where there had been a right to a place in a free school—even if it were of poor quality— now found they were expected to pay something for a better education and that the only pupils to receive free education were now those who managed to win an exhibition awarded for success in a competitive examination. Thus there was substance in the charge that the Commission took from the poor to give to the better-off, and it is always possible to work up a frenzy of agitation around such an action however justified it may be in the circumstances of the time. Disraeli and his party were not slow to seize their opportunity.

The two Commissioners who attracted the wrath of the opposition were the Chairman, Lord Lyttleton, and Mr. Hobhouse. Lord Lyttleton, as brother-in-law of the Prime Minister, Gladstone, was an obvious target for political controversialists. Both men had, perhaps, spoken incautiously on occasion and they were not allowed to forget remarks that they had originally made within the precincts of the Social Science Association in 1869. According to the booklet, 'The Endowed Schools Commission: shall it be continued', Hobhouse had revealed his unfitness for the part of Commissioner in a paper to the Social Science Association when he said, 'To talk of the piety or benevolence of people who give property to public uses, is a misuse of language springing from confusion of ideas. As a matter of fact, I believe, as I have elsewhere said at more length, that donors to public uses are less under the guidance of reason and conscience, and more under the sway of baser passions, than other people.' In dealing with foundations there were two simple principles, 'The first is that the public should not be compelled to take whatever is offered to it; . . . the second principle is that the grasp of the dead hand should be shaken off absolutely and finally'. In the discussion following Hobhouse's paper, Lord Lyttleton had added 'that if he himself and Mr. Hobhouse were allowed to do what they certainly would feel it their duty to attempt, the pious founders would go to the wall'.[18] It was clear to their opponents that men who had given expression to such ideas could not possibly approach their work as Commissioners with that impartiality which the nature of the work required, and that they could not possibly inspire the governors of trusts with confidence. In these circumstances the Endowed Schools Commission should not be tampered with but abolished, and the whole business which it now transacted should be left once more to the Charity Commission as it was before 1869.

The general election of 1874 sealed the fate of the Endowed Schools Commission. The victorious Conservatives had undertaken to abolish it, and even if this election had gone the other way, its existence had become so much a party matter that its ability to undertake useful work and to suggest acceptable schemes would have been imperilled.

The Endowed Schools Amendment Act of 1874[19] abolished the Commission but it did not go as far as it had seemed that the Conservatives would go during the election, the Commission might be abolished but all its powers were transferred to the Charity Commission as from the end of the year. The Act also provided for the appointment to the Charity Commission of an additional Secretary and two additional paid Commissioners in order to deal with the business transferred. Neither Lyttleton nor Robey, Hobhouse's successor, were appointed as Charity Commissioners for endowed schools, but the third Endowed Schools Commissioner, Canon Robinson, who had stirred less antagonism, was so appointed.

The effect of this new arrangement in general terms was that there was a great deal less vigour in pursuit of the aim of creating a system of secondary education in the country—indeed, this aim virtually vanished and the provision of secondary schools came to be dealt with in a much more piece-meal manner more akin to the period before 1869. The Bryce Commission was to state twenty years later that 'more driving power was needed' than the Charity Commission could supply,[20] this was certainly the main defect of the arrangements from 1874 until the end of the century. The administration became more legalistic and formal and less enthusiastic. Sir George Young, who served on the Charity Commission, told the Select Committee on the Endowed Schools Act in 1886 that since 1873 there had been 'No marked change (in policy), but there has been a change I believe' in that there was now a closer concern for points of law and the treatment of endowments was less sweeping than the Endowed Schools Commissioners had desired.[21] D. R. Fearon, Secretary to the Charity Commission, told the Select Committee that the Act of 1874 had proved advantageous since under the earlier system the Endowed Schools Commission had been responsible for drawing up schemes while the Charity Commission was responsible for the continued operation of such schemes in the legal sense as endowed schools were not only educational institutions but also charitable trusts and subject to the provisions of the Charitable Trusts Acts. It has been very difficult for the trustees of schools to have to deal with two quite different bodies and the position was now much simplified. Moreover, Fearon added, when he was an Assistant Commissioner in the Endowed Schools Commission he was always needing papers at the Charity Commission. 'When I consider how, during the last few years, for example, in which I have been Acting Secretary of the Endowed Schools Department [of the

Charity Commission], the work that has gone on daily in my room has been constantly done in co-operation of the closest kind with the various officers of the Charitable Trusts Department, and their work has been constantly in close co-operation with ours, it is difficult for me to understand how we got on as well as we did.'[22] Thus from a legalistic and bureaucratic point of view the arrangements after 1874 were an improvement, but the over-riding aim of creating a system was lost from the administrative department responsible for endowed secondary schools during the last quarter of the nineteenth century.

As Fearon implied, the Charity Commission after 1874 derived its power and authority from two sets of enactments, the Endowed Schools Acts, 1869–74, and the Charitable Trusts Acts, the first of which was passed in 1853. The nature of the powers conferred by the Endowed Schools Acts has already been described. The Charitable Trusts Acts conferred additional powers in two main directions. In the first place many of the endowments which had been exempted from the Endowed Schools Acts did not enjoy exemption from the Charitable Trusts Acts. Under the latter the Commissioners still had to deal with the endowments of such exempted schools as Harrow, Rugby, Charterhouse, Shrewsbury and Westminster from time to time as well as with endowments of less than £100 per annum for elementary education. Under the Charitable Trusts Acts the powers to make schemes and to appoint trustees could only be exercised after application—usually by local people, and where the annual income exceeded £50, such applications had to come from the trustees or a majority of them. The second direction in which these Acts conferred powers additional to the Endowed Schools Acts lay in the continuing authority they conferred on the Commissioners to require the production of accounts and information at all times and not merely at the time of reconsideration of the trust scheme. It was this provision which rendered legal the work of inspection of schools which the Commission undertook in the last decade of the century. The Bryce Commission said of jurisdiction under these Acts that it was 'less extensive in power than that of the Endowed Schools Acts, but it includes a large number of educational endowments not affected by the latter, and when the area of jurisdiction is common to the two, it exercises a more permanent and pervading influence. It controls the trustees or governing bodies of educational endowments at almost every stage of their work. Thus, recourse to the Charity Commissioners is necessary before trustees or a governing body can dispose of an old, or acquire a new, school site, or erect thereupon buildings for scholastic purposes, or borrow money for these or other purposes of exceptional or capital expenditure or pension a master or mistress. . . .

'If the Endowed Schools Acts were repealed, and nothing was substituted for them, the only consequence would be that a particular mode of reorganizing certain endowments would thenceforth cease to exist. But if the Charitable Trusts Acts were repealed, and nothing was substituted for them, the consequence would be a revival of the lengthy and expensive process of the jurisdiction of the Chancery Division of the High Court, in all the above-mentioned respects, over these educational endowments.'[23]

From 1874 there were five paid Charity Commissioners, the Chief and the other Commissioners appointed under the Charitable Trusts Acts and two Commissioners appointed under the Endowed Schools Amendment Act of 1874 which was continued annually under the Expiring Powers Continuation Acts. By 1894 the Commission had a staff of more than seventy including a Secretary, two Assistant Secretaries, eight Assistant Commissioners and six temporary Assistant Commissioners, four principal clerks, two accountants, fifty other clerks, and a number of messengers. There was no head of the department in the usual sense of that term since the Chief Commissioner was only *primus inter pares*, this arrangement was intended to avoid the bottleneck that would be created if all decisions were referred upwards to one man, the looser arrangement enabled any Commissioner to speak with full authority for the department.[24] The actual cost to public funds of running the department climbed steadily. In the fiscal year 1894–95 it amounted to £40,380, ten years earlier it had been £30,521. The two Commissioners of the Endowed Schools Department divided their work on a geographical basis, Sir George Young was responsible for England north of the Humber, for Wales and the counties bordering on it, and for the South West; the remainder of England was the responsibility of the other Commissioner, D. C. Richmond.

The procedure adopted by the Commissioners of the Endowed Schools Department in drawing up a scheme did not vary greatly from that of the former Endowed Schools Commission, but was marked by a more cautious approach and a greater effort to avoid stirring too much opposition, consequently schemes took a very long time to go through. Fearon told the Select Committee of 1894 that however non-contentious a scheme might be, it was hardly ever passed

F

in less than a year, and sometimes took several years to get through.[25] The procedure opened with a general inquiry into the main facts of a particular endowment by one of the Assistant Commissioners, he would usually travel to the district, meet the trustees informally and any other persons concerned and then report his conclusions to the Commissioner to whose area the case belonged. The Commissioner considered report and might take one of three courses: drop the matter, ask his Assistant to make some further inquiry, or produce 'Heads of a Proposed Scheme' which would be circulated to all of the Commissioners. The document was discussed by the whole Commission and, possibly after amendment, approved as the basis for a scheme. The draft scheme was prepared and sent to the trustees for their confidential consideration and remarks. In the light of these remarks, the draft scheme was sometimes brought before the Board for amendment before the next stage—publication. Publication took the form of sending drafts to the governing body of the endowment, to the principal teachers, and to any local bodies that might be interested such as school boards, the draft was also advertised in two local papers of opposing political views and deposited in the locality for inspection, copies were usually put on sale at a low price. Two months were allowed from publication for objections or suggestions. After the two months the Commissioner responsible considered any representations and brought the case before the Board again. In a contentious case, an Assistant Commissioner then held a public inquiry and reported the result of it to his superiors who, if they decided to continue with the case, then formally framed the scheme and submitted it to the Education Department. That Department could accept, reject, or suggest amendments to the Charity Commission. If the Department accepted the scheme, it was again published and a further interval allowed for objections. The Charity Commissioners might again become involved at this stage for, if objections were made on a point of law to the Judicial Committee of the Privy Council, it was the Commissioners and not the Education Department which appeared as respondents to defend the scheme. If the scheme survived any attack at this stage, it was laid before both Houses of Parliament, and if no address was presented by either of them during a period of two months, the royal assent was given and the scheme came into operation.[26]

Amid this formidable array of checks and balances, the only really constructive role fell to the Commissioner who drew up the scheme in the first place, and it is of interest to hear from one of the Commissioners how he and his colleague set about this task. 'We enter very carefully indeed into the educational side of every scheme. The investigation is a complete one, first, into the history and property of the endowment dealt with, next into the work that the endowment is now doing, and the needs of the locality in which it works. . . . Having informed ourselves as fully as we can about the endowment, we then approach the question, what educational work shall we design for it in the future; and in that matter we have the assistance of skilled Assistant Commissioners; and, I think I may say, that the educational part of the scheme is as carefully considered as the financial or any other part of it.'[27] The changes suggested from time to time by the Education Department originated outside of it in the objections or suggestions made by third parties. According to Sir George Kekewich, Permanent Secretary of the Education Department, for a scheme to be 'approved' by the Department was merely a formality required by law and such approval really meant that no one had objected or that they had not objected sufficiently.[28] He felt that if the Department were to approve schemes in fact as well as technically, it would need to guide the policy of the Commissioners and to do much of their work of inquiry all over again. In practice, the Department always sought to avoid schemes falling through when there was a difference between it and the Commissioners on a matter of policy by giving technical approval. Even after the Act of 1873 neither the Department—nor indeed Parliament—could actually insert amendments into schemes, it could only remit them to the Charity Commission with suggestions for certain amendments and refuse to approve schemes until they were amended. If, as sometimes happened, the Charity Commission preferred simply to drop a scheme to which some amendment had been proposed then that was the end of the matter.

In the circumstances under which the Commission worked, it was a considerable achievement to have dealt within twenty-five years with endowments whose annual income amounted to about five-sevenths of the total thought to be subject to the Endowed Schools Acts. The schemes for individual schools usually dealt with two broad issues, they regulated the general scope of the school's work and organization and regulated the constitution of the governing body. The position of the headmaster was defined; he was, of course, subordinate to the governors but was usually empowered to appoint and control his own assistants; he was assigned a fixed minimum salary, in most cases with an 'incentive' payment in the form of a percentage of the fee paid by each pupil. The scheme laid down fairly wide limits within which the fees charged must fall, e.g. £8 to £12 in senior departments, along with a minimum age for the admission of pupils and a maximum age to which they might remain. The curriculum was usually defined in general terms by listing the subjects in which a school was to offer instruction. The aim of most of these provisions was to ensure that there was no overlapping between schools of different grades—if a third grade school had to dismiss its pupils at fourteen, then obviously it could not compete with a first grade school keeping its pupils until they were ready to proceed to the university.

The constitution of the governing body was frequently a more controversial matter. There was no set pattern to be followed in all circumstances, the Commissioners tried to vary the constitutions of these bodies to suit the needs of different localities. The governors would generally include some representatives of the old governing body, some people who might be presumed to have a specialist knowledge of education and representatives of the district. The size of these different elements varied greatly; there would, for instance, be little point in putting many local representatives on the governing body of a school which served mostly boarders. There was a marked tendency to increase the size of the representation given to local rate-payers and the like throughout these years. The Select Committee on the Endowed Schools Act of 1886 stated among its recommendations that 'It is essential to the welfare of endowed schools that the sympathies of the locality be enlisted by giving to the people a large share in the management by representation, direct or indirect, through elected bodies'.[29] In his evidence before the Select Committee on the Charity Commission in 1894 D. C. Richmond, one of the Commissioners, said, 'It may be regarded as a fundamental principle in these schemes, if we have a free hand, that the representative element should preponderate'.[30] Before 1888, school boards and municipal councils were offered the right to nominate some members of governing bodies of endowed schools; the Local Government Act of that year created County Councils and it became increasingly usual to reserve places for the County's nominees in new schemes drawn up after that date. Indeed, Richmond in his evidence spoke of this as 'the most important Act in relation to the work under the Endowed Schools Acts since the original Act of 1869. Although Parliament has not given county councils any special *locus standi* as regards our work under the Endowed Schools Acts, yet it has given us bodies to which we can apply, and who we can interest in our work, and with whom we can co-operate, and co-operation is, I am happy to say, going on increasingly.'[31] The Local Taxation (Customs and Excise) Act of 1890 made such co-operation more important and more fruitful for the schools.[32] The Endowed Schools Department of the Charity Commission took the initiative in getting in touch with the counties and inviting their secretaries—who were appointed under the Technical Instruction Act of 1889—to discuss the opportunities which the unexpected windfall opened up. The representation of county councils on the governing bodies of endowed schools was the natural concomitant of this co-operation. The first county to accept a scheme for close co-operation was Surrey, where the county council was given representation on all governing bodies and in exchange gave all the endowed schools annual grants to develop their scientific and technical education. The Commissioners saw in the new councils and the money which they received under the Local Taxation Act a way of making up deficiencies in the provision of endowments.

The creation of county councils meant that many schemes for the government of schools which had been made before 1888 ought to be re-caste if the greatest advantage was to be taken of the change in circumstances. Moreover, there were other changes which often made it advisable to revise earlier schemes, in some cases the annual value of town property held as part of endowments had doubled or trebled since the original scheme was made, while agricultural values fell disastrously in the last quarter of the nineteenth century with the depression in English farming. The Endowed Schools Commission had originally been regarded as having a temporary task to undertake, and even after its powers had been transferred to the Charity Commission, the dependence of the two Endowed Schools Commissioners on the Expiring Acts Continuance Bill each year meant that this section of the Charity Commission seemed to have a somewhat insecure and temporary existence. The question of when it could finally be wound up arose from time to time although its work was clearly of a continuing nature.

The enforcement of schemes once they had been drawn up was rather more efficient after 1887 than before that year. The regular inspection of schools which had been made the subject of schemes only began after the Report of the Select Committee on the Endowed Schools

Acts had drawn attention to the absence of any systematic attempt to supervise the working of schemes and recommended the appointment of additional Assistant Commissioners for this purpose. The Secretary to the Education Department, Sandford, had told the Select Committee on Education, Science and Art (Administration) in 1884 that there should be regular inspection of endowed schools and that such inspection should be under its own control; the only exception he was willing to allow was that the task of inspecting first grade schools might be 'farmed out' to the Universities. This Committee had recommended the future Minister of Education—whose early appointment they looked for—should be given power 'to direct any inquiries or inspection to be made which he may deem necessary'.[33] Nothing had come of these recommendations and Richmond had to admit that little had been done in the course of his examination before the Select Committee of 1886–87. He was asked 'Practically as regards both the organization of the schools and the qualifications of the teachers, and as regards the financial regularity with which the accounts are kept, you have no permanent and continuing control?' He replied 'In respect of accounts . . . all trustees of charitable endowments are, by law, bound to send their accounts to us, and we prescribe a form in which the accounts of endowed schools shall be sent, in considerable detail, to us; but we have not a staff to analyse and act to any great extent upon the results that we might obtain from those accounts'.[34] The other Endowed Schools Commissioner, Sir George Young, explained that inspectors of charities might be sent down at any time to require information about a charity, but he declared himself opposed to regular educational inspection of schools. In spite of Sir George's opposition, the next Report of the Charity Commissioners indicated that the Select Committee's opinion had prevailed for it showed that in 1887 'a systematic inspection, within certain geographical limits, of all the schools and educational endowments appropriated by schemes under the Endowed Schools Acts, to Secondary and Higher Education' had been instituted.[35] No additional staff was appointed and it was not possible to cover more than five counties a year. In theory the inspection was administrative in its nature, but since the general working of the scheme was the subject of inquiry, including such matters as the number of pupils, the tuition fee, subjects of instruction, adequacy of buildings and equipment, the educational quality of the establishment could not but be revealed. 'Taken together with the report of the [schools'] examination, a copy of which is required to be sent to the Charity Commission, the inspection is found by the Commissioners to "afford material on which a fairly confident estimate of efficiency can be based".'[36]

It was the lot of the Bryce Commission to make a thorough contemporary assessment of the work of the Endowed Schools and Charity Commissions in the field of secondary education. In terms of statistics, during the quarter century ending on 31st December, 1894, the Commission has established 851 original schemes and 127 amending schemes. The condition of the endowed grammar schools was far better than it had been in 1868 and this improvement could be seen in the larger proportion of such schools giving education which could properly be called secondary, in the higher standard of work in many of them and in the increased number of pupils in attendance. The West Riding of Yorkshire was taken as an example of these improvements. Here, the number of endowed grammar schools offering secondary education was found to have increased from 28 to 36, the number of first grade schools had increased from 3 to 8 and in general, the grammar schools had largely regained the ground which they had lost to the private secondary day schools. The improvement which the Endowed Schools and Charity Commissions had been instrumental in causing was particularly noticeable in the greater energy and much stronger sense of public responsibility in the governing bodies of grammar schools.[37] There can be little doubt but that the central government's machinery for secondary education achieved a great measure of success in its task of reviving the endowed schools.

On the other hand it had certainly failed to create that system of secondary education which the Taunton Report had recommended, nor had it achieved the avowed aim of the government in 1869 when it wrote into the preamble of the Endowed Schools Act that its object was 'to put a liberal education within reach of the children of all classes'. From the time of the abolition of the Endowed Schools Commission, the principal object of concern had been the needs of the individual school rather than the needs of the area, and even before 1874 the Commissioners had been compelled by the pressure of circumstances to abandon their attempt to review all the educational charities of an area together. The failure of the government to set up any sort of district authority for secondary education had really made it difficult to consider the needs of localities as distinct from those of individual schools. In some areas the necessary raw materials— educational charities—from which to build up a system were sadly deficient. Sir George Young pointed out in 1886 that one of the worst areas was Cornwall; if this county were represented by the deficiency figure of 80, then the next worst ranged thus—Lancashire 50, Durham 50, Cheshire 39, Wales 37, Sussex 35, Cumberland 32, Staffordshire 31 and Hampshire 28.[38] The Act of 1869 provided two ways of overcoming this difficulty, firstly, the removal of educational endowments from one place to another and secondly the diversion of other charities to educational purposes. Neither of these amounted to much in practice, partly because there were too few endowments of a suitable nature and partly because any class or group likely to suffer loss through such removal or diversion put up so much resistance that the Endowed Schools Commissioners soon learned not to attempt either operation except in the most extreme circumstances.

Administratively, the procedure through which the Commissioners were obliged to operate was slow and cumbrous. The relationship of the Charity Commission to the rest of the government and the nature of its communication with Parliament led to increasing difficulty with the passage of time. The source of the trouble lay in its essentially political function as central authority for much of secondary education which the Commission was trying to discharge in a semi-judicial manner. This problem stemmed in its turn from the absence of local authorities for secondary education for, in default of such provincial councils to aid the central body, the government of the day intended to take the main responsibility for supporting each scheme. Mr. Forster, as Vice-President of the Committee of Council for Education was in charge of the Endowed Schools Bill in the Commons in 1869 and he explained that the government must itself be responsible for each scheme, the Commissioners 'are merely officers assisting the government . . . the scheme finally proposed by them is to be submitted to the Educational Department of the Privy Council. . . . The responsibility will rest on the government whether they approve the scheme. If they do approve it, they will lay it before Parliament and it will become law, if not objected to within forty days by either House. Everything the Commissioners do will be a waste of paper until it has passed the ordeal of Parliamentary assent.'[39] The Lord President of the Council told the House of Lords, when they were debating this measure, that 'We felt, however, that Parliament would justly require for work of that description distinct Parliamentary responsibility'.[40]

The abolition of the Endowed Schools Commission meant that its work passed to the Charity Commission, a body which had never had, nor was to seek, any particularly close contact with the Education Department. Legally it remained true that the Charity Commission merely prepared schemes under the Endowed Schools Acts for the approval of the government, but the same Commission's relationships with the same endowed schools when there was not actually a new scheme in preparation were governed by the Charitable Trusts Acts which did not require the Commissioners to seek anyone's approval for their actions. Thus the Charity Commission adopted an independent position and the Education Department regarded its consent to the schemes that the Commission drew up as merely 'formal'—to use Sir George Kekewich's term to the Select Committee of 1894, he added 'I have always thought that the control [of the Department] is very shadowy and illusory'.[41]

The consequences of this situation were that the Commissioners had increasing difficulty in getting their endowed schools work completed because they lacked the necessary support, both in dealing with recalcitrant local people and in trying to persuade the Treasury of the need for more staff at different times. The Chairman of the Select Committee of 1894 wrote in his draft report that the Estimates for the Commission did not appear to have any minister really responsible for defending them, that urgently needed bills were not brought forward, and that when schemes were attacked in the House they were perfunctorily defended. He thought the trouble was partly due to Parliamentary jealousy of any department not entirely under its control, and that the position was comparable to that to the Poor Law Board at the time of its abolition in 1847 when Disraeli said 'When we look at the nature of our Parliamentary Constitution, we shall find that any attempts to carry on the business of the country without the interference by Parliament, the palpable interference of Parliament, have always proved a failure'.[42]

Remedies for this situation had been suggested by three Parliamentary Select Committees by the time the Bryce Commission reported. In 1884 the Select Committee which inquired into the administration of Education, Science and Art suggested that a Minister of Education be appointed and that one of his duties should be the general supervision of endowed schools. The Select Committee of 1886–87 on the Endowed Schools Acts supported the same recommendation. The Select Committee of 1894 reported that 'to the position and function of the new Minister of Education recommended by previous Committees of your House there should be added the control of endowments. Such a Minister would be really, as well as technically, responsible for the schemes which he presented to Parliament. He would be in a position to defend the Estimates of his Department on their merits, and he would be able to bring pressure on the Treasury, in order to secure needful provision for his work.'[43]

The case against subjecting the endowed schools work to more direct Parliamentary control was put by a Departmental Committee appointed by the Treasury in 1893 to inquire into the Charity Commission. The first question this Committee had to decide was whether the Commission should remain as it was or whether it should assume the more usual form of a ministry. The Committee decided against any change in the existing form of organization and if a Minister of Education came to be appointed it felt that he should not take over the administration of endowed schemes, but that he should work closely with the Commissioners. The reasons for these recommendations were two. A board was advantageous because the work was deliberative and consultative to a greater degree than in other departments and the action of a board carried more weight with the public than would that of a single individual. The other reason why direct control by a minister was unsuitable was because of the 'quasi-judicial' character of the work of the Commissioners 'whose operations do not, therefore, lend themselves to the direction and control of a Parliamentary head to the same degree as those of an ordinary administrative department of state'.[44]

This particular constitutional tangle was only one of the factors which the Bryce Commission had to take into consideration when making its recommendations, and the solution it proposed for resolving this problem was part of its broader answer to the whole question of the future organization of secondary education. Such an answer had to be based on an assessment of the overall value of the work of the Charity Commission as a Department of Secondary Education. It criticized the existing Charity Commission on the grounds that it was divorced from political responsibility, that it was provisional and temporary in its jurisdiction, partial in that it looked only to endowments and not to secondary education as a whole, and isolated in that it looked at schools one by one rather than at the needs of an area taken together. 'While it is this in fact it was meant by the Schools Inquiry Commission to be exactly the reverse—permanent, national, co-ordinative and organizing.' The Charity Commission was to be an executive department with the task not only of scheme-making, but of organization and administration in the broadest sense. The endowments were considered to be merely the financial basis to be used for the organization of a national system, 'a public fund appropriated to education'. The actual functions of the Commission are thus much narrower than our predecessors proposed that they should be, and this has resulted in a corresponding restriction in the field and effects of its operation. Its action has necessarily been too piecemeal and too divorced from the educational policy of the period to accomplish all that was expected and desired.'[45]

REFERENCES

[1] B. Simon, *Studies in the History of Education*, 1780–1870, pp. 105–7, where there is a full discussion of the significance of this judgment.

[2] S.I.C., 1868, vol. 1, p. 106.

[3] Ibid., pp. 107–8.

[4] Ibid., p. 222.

[5] Ibid., p. 223.

[6] Select Cttee. on Charity Cssrs. Reports, 1835.

[7] S.I.C., 1868, pp. 627–9.

[8] Ibid., pp. 632–3.

[9] Ibid., pp. 637–44.

[10] Ibid., p. 645.

[11] 32 & 33 Vict., c. 56.

[12] 31 & 32 Vict., c. 118.

[13] 32 & 33 Vict., c. 56, S 9. In some directions the Act was not as far reaching as Forster's first draft of the bill had been. This would have also required—*inter alia*—that pupils in all schools other than the seven public schools of the Act of 1868 should be examined centrally by an Educational Council, and that no endowed school could employ a teacher who did not possess a teaching diploma. Proposals such as these were abandoned after provoking very strong opposition among those public schools not included in the Public Schools Act of 1868. David Newsome in his *History of Wellington College* describes the part played by Benson, the school's headmaster, in opposing the bill. He quotes him as writing to Temple, a supporter of the measure, 'You think our connection will not be weakened by severance from the Category of Public Schools and union with decayed grammar schools, consolidated doles of parish bread and hitherto scholarless school houses. Half our boys are brothers of Eton, Harrow, Winchester, Rugby boys—and they will mind it—and their parents will . . .' (p. 140).

[14] 32 & Vict. c. 56, S 31–41.

[15] Select Cttee. on the Charity Cssn., 1894, Q 962. Evidence of Richmond.

[16] 36 & 37 Vict., c. 87.

[17] An antagonistic literature grew up around the work of the Commission; a typical attack on its existence was *The Endowed Schools Commission: shall it be continued?*, pp. 60, London, 1873, where the grievances are fully developed.

[18] Ibid., quotations from the *Journal of the Social Sciences Association*, 1869, pp. 595 and 609.

[19] 37 & 38 Vict., c. 87.

[20] Bryce Cssn., 1895, vol. 1, p. 89.

[21] Select Cttee. on the Endowed Schools Act, 1886, Q 910. Evidence of Young.

[22] Ibid., Q 5886. Evidence of Fearon.

[23] Bryce Cssn., 1895, vol. 1, p. 20.

[24] Select Cttee. on the Charity Cssn., 1894, Q 972. Evidence of Richmond.
[25] Select Cttee. on the Charity Cssn., 1894, Q 2121. Evidence of Fearon.
[26] Ibid., QQ 2037–46.
[27] Select Cttee. on Education, Science and Art (Administration), 1884, QQ 1551–2. Evidence of Richmond.
[28] Select Cttee., 1894, Q 3514. Evidence of Kekewich.
[29] Select Cttee., 1886, recommendation No. 12.
[30] Select Cttee., 1894, Q 855. Evidence of Richmond.
[31] Ibid., Q 906.
[32] The effect of this Act was to make available to local technical instruction authorities the funds originally intended as compensation for displaced publicans.
[33] Select Cttee., 1884, Report, para. 4.
[34] Select Cttee., 1886, Q 132. Evidence of Richmond.
[35] 36th Report of the Charity Cssrs., p. 27.
[36] Bryce Cssn., 1895, vol. 1, p. 59.
[37] Ibid., pp. 42–5.
[38] Select Cttee., 1886, Q 631. Evidence of Young.
[39] Hansard, vol. CXCIV, col. 1370.
[40] Hansard, vol. CXCVII, col. 609.
[41] Select Cttee., 1894, Q 3519. Evidence of Kekewich.
[42] Ibid., Draft Report of Chmn., para. XVI.
[43] Ibid., para. XII.
[44] Report of a Departmental Cttee. appointed by the Treasury to inquire into the Charity Commission, 1893, p. 3.
[45] Bryce Cssn., 1895, vol. 1, pp. 94–5.

Chapter 5

THE CREATION OF THE BOARD OF EDUCATION

THE need for some central authority charged with the oversight of elementary, secondary and technical education had become very pressing by the end of the nineteenth century. Although the Education Department, the Science and Art Department and the Charity Commissions between them offered the aid or guidance of the state to schools of most varieties, their efforts were unco-ordinated with the consequence that in some fields there was overlapping while in others neglect. The want of a more rational system of educational administration became particularly obvious when the situation in this country was compared with that which obtained in continental states.

Not only was the need for a unified central authority pressing by the 1890s, but it was also coming to be increasingly widely recognized; this may be seen in the evidence of witnesses who appeared before the Royal Commission on Secondary Education and in the Report of the Bryce Commission itself. 'It has been seen that each of the three central authorities now connected with Secondary Education has a strictly limited province. The Charity Commission under the Endowed Schools Acts, can deal only with certain endowed schools, and with these only for certain purposes; while the processes involved are complex and tedious. The Department of Science and Art can take cognizance only of certain subjects out of the number of those which are comprehended in Secondary Education. The Education Department touches Secondary Education only through the higher work of certain elementary schools, and (less directly) through the training of teachers and the relation in which it stands to the university colleges and the day training colleges; and, while the sphere of each authority is thus narrowly circumscribed, those authorities have no organic connection with each other. One Department may consult another on specific affairs common to both, and they may make joint arrangements for a particular purpose; but that does not affect their ultimate independence of policy and action. That independence may be illustrated by taking any part of the educational field in which the separate agencies happen to meet. A grammar school may be worked

83

under a scheme framed and administered by the Charity Commissioners; it may be earning grants, or may also include an organized science school, subject to the regulations laid down by the Department of Science and Art; and it may be receiving scholars from elementary schools, whose earlier training has followed lines prescribed by the Education Department.'[1]

Apart from the limitations and overlapping of the jurisdictions of existing departments, it was impossible for the State to meet the growing need to have a policy and an aim and thus to give a lead to local authorities and to the governing bodies of schools. The creation of local authorities for technical instruction in 1889 and the augmentation of their resources in the following year by the local Taxation Act[2] led to the steady development of local publicly-financed support for many secondary schools during the last decade of the nineteenth century. Some guidance from the centre was essential if the greatest value was to be obtained from these new resources. The central agency which was given the oversight of these arrangements was the Department of Science and Art. When defining the subjects that might be included within the definition of 'technical instruction' and thus qualify for a local subsidy, the Department took a very broad view and permitted almost every subject normally studied in secondary schools with the exception of classics. The consequence of this liberal interpretation was to increase further the administrative confusion in the field of secondary education.

As we have noted above, in 1868 the Taunton Commission had foreseen the need for a central guiding authority and had proposed the creation of an agency much more vigorous and positive than the Charity Commission proved to be. It had recommended that the Minister of Education should preside over the central commission when it was dealing with educational matters, that he should represent it in Parliament, and that it should exercise continuous administrative powers. The actual drawing up of schemes for individual schools—of which the educational work of the Charity Commission came almost entirely to consist—had been regarded as a task suited to local authorities, knowledgeable concerning local needs.[3] As the Bryce Commission pointed out, the Charity Commission in its existing form under the Endowed Schools Acts was in many ways the reverse of what the Taunton Commission had intended.[4]

It was against this background that the Royal Commission made its recommendations for a central authority to deal with secondary education. The Commission was anxious to preserve both local initiative as against the future central authority and the independence of individual schools to govern themselves without interference from the future local authority. 'We conceive, in short, that some central authority is required, not in order to control, but rather to supervise the secondary education of the country, not to over-ride or supersede local action, but to endeavour to bring about among the various agencies which provide that education a harmony and co-operation that are now wanting.'[5] The central authority should consist of a department under a minister answerable to Parliament; the same minister and permanent secretary should also be responsible for elementary education so as to avoid duplication and to ensure a reasonable harmony between the different branches. The Commission thought that the new work would be in some ways sufficiently different from the elementary work with which the existing Education Department was familiar to require a different approach, consequently there would need to be at least some officials appointed especially to deal with secondary work. The educational work of the Charity Commission and the Science and Art Department should both be absorbed by the enlarged Education Office. Alongside the Minister, the Bryce Commission proposed the establishment of an Educational Council which was to consist of persons with special knowledge of educational problems who could advise the Minister on 'judicial' and 'professional' matters, and itself undertake to manage a register of teachers. The Council might consist of a dozen members of whom one-third could be nominated by the Crown, one-third by the Universities of Oxford, Cambridge, London and Victoria, and one-third might be chosen from among the teaching profession.

The Commission had no desire to extend to secondary education any administration so detailed in its scope as that which the Education Department already exercised in the elementary field. The imposition of a national code with examination and inspection to ensure its enforcement was said to be quite out of keeping with the true functions of a central authority for secondary education. These functions were stated to be the maintenance of a general oversight of the actions of local authorities, the provision of information and advice to local authorities and to schools, the consideration and approval of schemes for re-organizing endowments, the hearing of objections and appeals from local authorities and other bodies and the administration of grants from the central government which, it was recommended, should replace the existing system of science and art grants. It would be the duty of the central office to draw up rules under which local authorities might disburse the proceeds of government grants, the office having power to withhold the grant from recalcitrant and unsatisfactory authorities; it would also have power to appoint inspectors. Certain questions should only be dealt with by the minister after he had heard the opinion of the Educational Council, these included regulations for the inspection of schools by local authorities and ministerial nominations for membership of local authorities for secondary education.

In 1895, the year of the publication of the Bryce Report, the Conservative Party was returned to power. The new Lord President of the Council was the Duke of Devonshire, and Sir John Gorst became Vice-President; with these two men lay the primary responsibility for deciding what action should be taken to implement the recommendations of the Committee. Devonshire's interest in and acquaintance with the educational problems of the day was limited. Gorst became member of Parliament for Cambridge University in 1892 after a varied career during which he had held a fellowship at St. John's College, helped in the pacification of the Maoris in New Zealand and had served as an organizer for the Conservative Party. He had a genuine interest in education, but while serving as Vice-President this did not always show itself to the best advantage since he was liable to let his political venom cloud his vision. Educational politics in the 1890s were dominated by the sense of impending crisis which overhung the voluntary elementary schools. These schools had increasing difficulty after 1890 in making ends meet faced as they were with the competition of the rate-financed board schools which were raising their standards. Soon after the return of the Conservative government to office, the church addressed a memorial to the Prime Minister demanding, among other things, larger grants for voluntary schools and the provision of denominational instruction in board schools where parents sought this. Lord Salisbury, the Prime Minister, and the Conservative party generally favoured the voluntary schools. Thus in 1896 Gorst introduced his ill-fated Education Bill with the twin aims of dealing with the problem of educational administration and relieving the financial plight of the Church schools.

The Bill marked an important development in government thinking in that it proposed to make county councils the local authority for all types of school—elementary, secondary and technical—and in this way to co-ordinate developments within each locality. The Bill also offered a larger grant to voluntary schools, along with exemption from rating and easy terms for loans for capital expenditure, while it placed a limit on the rating power of school boards and would have obliged them to provide denominational instruction at the request of parents. Not only did this Bill arouse the opposition of the non-conformists and of the school boards, but it also stirred many municipal boroughs and urban districts to vigorous action against what they conceived to be an attempt to increase the powers of the county councils within their boundaries. The Bill encountered so much hostility on this latter point that it was withdrawn by the government and a simple measure giving an additional grant to voluntary schools was passed during the next year.

The question of reorganizing the administrative structure could hardly be entirely abandoned, however, and at the beginning of 1898 the Lord President submitted a memorandum on this subject to the Cabinet.[6] In this document, Devonshire explained that he believed it was the plans for the local administration of elementary education which had led to difficulty in 1896, and that even if that measure had been enacted, the new authorities would have had difficulty in re-organizing secondary school provision in the absence of guidance from the centre—guidance which the centre itself was ill-equipped to give. The new local authorities would have been in contact with the Education Department, the Science and Art Department and the Charity Commissioners. 'These have never, so far as I know, been accustomed to look at educational problems as a whole, or to work together for the co-ordination of educational agencies . . . it has certainly never been the duty of any minister to form an opinion and to influence his colleagues and Parliament, in favour of any definite direction or aim to be given to Secondary Education even in State-aided schools.' The memorandum went on to complain that this was 'an indefensible condition of things' when the Science and Art Department was disbursing £276,000 per annum in grants, local authorities were spending £800,000 on technical and secondary schools and the school boards were spending a great deal of public money on what were really secondary schools. A central authority was really an essential preliminary to the establishment of satisfactory local authorities for secondary education. 'What I should propose, therefore, would be simply to take power to create a central authority to which might be transferred by Order in Council all the duties and powers of the

G

Education Department, the Science and Art Department and such of the powers of the Charity Commissioners as relate to education.' Devonshire recommended that there should be a minister with a parliamentary secretary drawn from the other house, there should also be a permanent secretary and two under secretaries, one for elementary and one for secondary education. An Educational Council on the lines recommended by the Royal Commission ought also to be provided for in the same Bill.

This memorandum from the Lord President marked the beginning of work on a new Education Bill which eventually became the Board of Education Act, 1899[7] and which, therefore, created for the first time a central authority responsible for the various fields of education. Sir Courtenay Ilbert, Assistant Parliamentary Counsel, who was in charge of preparing the new bill, drew up a memorandum[8] two days after that sent to the Cabinet by the Lord President in which he set out five points to be covered by the new legislation, viz.:

> To separate the Education and Science and Art Departments from the Privy Council and to rearrange ministerial responsibility;
> To permit the new central office to take over by Order in Council the Charity Commissioners' power from time to time;
> To authorize the central office to inspect secondary schools;
> To extend the Technical Instruction Act of 1889 and the Local Taxation Act of 1890 so as to permit local authorities to contribute to the cost of inspecting non-technical secondary schools;
> To authorize the establishment of a Consultative Committee.

The preparation of a draft bill that was acceptable within the government itself took some while and no fewer than fourteen drafts were produced before a form was found which appeared to satisfy all the interests concerned.

The principal source of difficulty was the Charity Commissioners, who put up a stiff resistance to the drafts of bills which would have cut their powers. The outcome of following their advice would have been that the only endowed secondary schools with which the new authority would have been concerned were those cases which were still without schemes of any sort because of great local difficulty or hostility. All endowed schools which had no scheme and where none was intended, would have remained under the Charity Commission, while those schools under schemes already would still have been under the supervision of the Charity Commission acting for the new Board of Education. Thus the new Board would have begun its career with only the worst cases and would have incurred odium and unpopularity for reviving old controversies. These points were developed in notes prepared in the Education Department in May, 1898, by way of comment on a letter dated 13th May from the Charity Commissioners.[9] Sir George Kekewich, Secretary to the Education Department, felt that sufficient powers needed to be transferred to the Board from the Commissioners to enable it to see that educational endowments were fitted into local arrangements for secondary education, and to see that endowed schools were being properly run in accordance with the scheme under which they were governed. Ilbert pointed out that there was no need to incorporate any precise division of powers between the Commission and the Board in the bill since an accommodation could be obtained through the wording of the Orders in Council to be issued subsequently. In this way the issue with the Charity Commission was postponed rather than overcome. The only important change introduced into this section of the bill was to add that 'any question as to whether an endowment or any part of an endowment is held or ought to be applied to educational purposes shall be determined by the Commissioners'.[10] The aim behind this addition was simply to avoid criticism of the minister's decisions which might have been presumed to be biased in favour of education.[11]

A point that has aroused a good deal of curiosity both at the time the bill was published and since is the reason why a Board of Education was established instead of a Ministry, for this Board of eminent politicians never met as such and the President in fact acted as a Minister. The first draft of the bill did propose the appointment of a Secretary for Education without any mention of a board, but when the second draft appeared this had been changed to a President with a Board. The change appears to have been the work of Ilbert who had written three days before issuing the second draft, 'the disadvantage of a single Secretary, as compared with a Board, is that there is no one to act for him in case of illness'.[12] There certainly appears to have been no more important reason for, as the Duke of Devonshire said in replying to the debate on the second reading in the House of Lords, 'As far as I remember the point was mooted when the Bill was first prepared, but I quite admit that I am unable, at the present moment, to recollect the reasons which weighed in favour of a board rather than a secretariat. It has the advantage, at all events, of numerous precedents, and it is perfectly well understood that there will be no board at all.'[13]

The amalgamation of the Science and Art Department and the Education Department and the creation of an Educational Council did not cause any difficulties at the drafting stage.

When the bill was finally published there was not a great deal of criticism of what it attempted to do, most public criticism was directed to what it appeared to omit. Many would have agreed with James Bryce, who said that 'it was a slender and meagre measure as regards the central authority, a very imperfect and inadequate instalment, an evasion of the most important question'. There was a good deal of criticism from those who felt that local authorities were a necessary preliminary to a thorough reorganization of secondary education.[14] Criticism of actual proposals contained in the bill centred around three points, the transfer of powers from the Charity Commission, inspection of secondary schools and the internal organization of the new office.

One of the principal critics of the proposal to transfer powers from the Charity Commission to the new office was Lord Cranborne. His criticisms really seem to have sprung from a feeling that the new ministry would in the nature of things show a less judicial disposition in handling matters concerned with endowments than did the Charity Commission which he considered to be 'quasi judicial'. Ilbert prepared a memorandum in reply to Cranborne's criticisms for Devonshire to show to the Prime Minister. In this, Ilbert pointed out that the functions of the Charity Commissioners were not really judicial but administrative, and that the real difference was that the Board of Education would be—whereas the Charity Commissioners were not— directly represented in Parliament by a minister; thus the Charity Commissioners were perhaps less amenable to immediate political influence but, on the other hand, they were also less exposed to public criticism. He felt that any misuse of power by an administrative department was subject to much readier correction if that department was directly represented in Parliament by a responsible minister who could be questioned as to the acts of himself and his subordinates.[15]

There was some criticism of Section 3 of the Bill which provided for the inspection of such secondary schools as desired to be inspected 'on such terms as may be fixed by the Board of Education with the consent of the Treasury'. Critics said that the schools most needing inspection were likely to be those which least desired it and were least able to pay for it; moreover it also created an unfortunate distinction between the richer schools and the poorer. But the point which stirred up most agitation among educationists was the future organization of the new ministry, whether the new ministry was to have three branches, one each for elementary, technical and secondary education, or whether only two with technical and secondary being combined in one. There was a clash of opinion here between headmasters of the better-known schools and the secretaries of county council technical instruction committees, the former favouring three branches and the latter two.

The main motive behind the opposition of the headmasters and of the universities to the combination of technical and secondary branches was the fear that such a unified branch would merely be the old Science and Art Department under a new name. That Department had long been regarded by those responsible for the running of the older endowed schools as an enemy of the interests of a true education, its one concern had always seemed to be to use the funds at its command to force more science on the schools regardless of the need for a balanced curriculum. Moreover, the Science and Art Department had been largely concerned with grants to municipal schools of science, evening classes and classes in higher grade schools, all of which were regarded as socially inferior to the better-known endowed schools; these latter were hardly likely to welcome the apparent social demotion which could have been implied in their becoming clients of a re-named Science and Art Department.

The headmasters were anxious to have an assurance written into the Bill on this point or else a public pledge from the Lord President or Vice-President that there would be a secondary branch quite distinct from the technical. In July, 1899, while the measure was before Parliament, the headmasters subjected the government to considerable pressure. Typical of the sentiments expressed in the letters and telegrams received at the Education Department was that from Edmund Warre, headmaster of Eton addressed to Kekewich in which he wrote, 'I saw the Duke and had a conversation with him and assured him that we should feel much aggrieved and indeed feel bound to oppose the bill altogether, if secondary education were, in the Departmental organization for Education allotted to any other place than one on a footing of equality with Primary Education and Scientific and Technical Education as clearly indicated in the Queen's Speech. Any attempt to subordinate it and degrade it to a sub-assistant secretary's care would be felt as a distinct breach of faith, and as exploding all kind expressions of desire for its welfare. . . .'[16] The Duke of Devonshire also wrote to Kekewich on the same day, and commented that 'I saw Dr. Warre to-day. . . . If I am not able to reassure him, I am afraid we shall have trouble in the House of Commons as soon as the Bill comes back from the Standing Committee.'[17] The Committee of the Headmasters' Conference resolved on 11th July '. . . that an arrangement by which the three main factors of National Education are thus placed on a separate, equal and independent footing is the best method of safe-guarding the interests of all three, and of securing their satisfactory development in the future'.

Faced with these circumstances, the Lord President had already asked M. E. Sadler, then head of the Department of Special Inquiries and Reports, to prepare for him a memorandum on the future organiza-tion of the Board. In this memorandum Sadler argued strongly on the side of the headmasters 'There is every sign', he wrote, 'of growing indignation at the very idea of an organization of the Board of Educa-tion which would degrade and weaken the position of the great public schools and of Oxford and Cambridge'.[18] This memorandum produced a certain amount of friction with the Science and Art Department whose head, Abney, saw it as an attack and accused Sadler of being strongly partisan in a bitter note to Kekewich. However, the headmasters carried the day at this stage against the Science and Art Department and the County Technical Education Officers. Although no change was made in the Bill, on 17th July Gorst stated in the Commons that '. . . it is not intended to entrust this work to either of the existing departments, but to a third official whose responsibility to the Principal Secretary will be distinct from, and equal to, that of the two existing assistant secretaries. Instructions to that effect will be given to the Departmental Committee which will consider the organization of the Department.'[19] In August, 1899, the Bill establish-ing the Board of Education was enacted.

The Act gave very wide powers to the government and it could be made to mean much or little. It came into force at the beginning of 1900 and for two years or so had little practical effect, the oppor-tunities it presented for reorganizing the central administration and thus giving a definite lead towards building a better school system for the country were not taken until Morant became Permanent Secretary at the Board. The principal reasons for the delay seem to have been a lack of determination on the part of the Lord President and, more important, a good deal of obstruction on the part of senior officials who could see no good reason for radical changes in the organization. The new Board was not, in fact, organized on a tripartite basis until after the passing of the Education Act of 1902, while the transfer of powers from the Charity Commissioners proved to be a very long drawn out affair.

The Board of Education Act came into force on 1st April, 1900. In January of that year, Devonshire corresponded with Kekewich on the problem of finding a suitable person to head the new secondary branch. He wondered whether Sadler might not be suitable, but 'I confess I should not have great confidence in Mr. Sadler whose educational goals would probably lead him into extreme counsels, but he would at least have the advantage of starting with the confidence of the schoolmasters, though not perhaps of the county councils. But whoever it is, I think we must decide upon it without more delay. . . .'[20]

While the Lord President hesitated over this new appointment, Abney, who was Principal Assistant Secretary of the Science and Art Department, carried on a campaign to prevent the work of that Department from being split up between the two separate secondary and technical branches. In a memorandum written at the end of February he claimed that the Science and Art Department alone had educational experience of secondary schools. The headmasters wanted a man with a 'literary or classical' bias to head the new secondary branch and to put the science which the Department had fostered in the schools under his control. 'In other words, modern secondary education is to be made subordinate to literary and classical education with the natural result that it would wither and become practically extinct.' The only way of saving the situation was to have only two branches, one for elementary and one for higher education. 'It is a question whether the fruits of the victories of the war waged during the last twenty-five years between modern and literary education shall be disallowed to the former.'[21] Abney followed up this memorandum with one to the Lord President in which he suggested that if there were to be three branches, that for secondary education should have two Principal Assistant Secretaries, one for Arts and one for Science. He suggested a public announcement might be on the following lines, 'The name of the Science and Art Department is abolished. A branch of secondary education is set up with two subdivisions, viz. the Arts branch and the Science branch. . . .'[22] Such a solution to the problem

would have been no answer at all to the criticism of current administrative arrangements which the Bryce Commission had expressed
when it pointed out that the subsidization and encouragement of certain
subjects by the Science and Art Department had led to a lack of balance
in the curricula of many schools, and that no one at the centre had the
duty of looking to the welfare of a school considered as a whole.

With the Act due to come into force on 1st April, a decision could
not be delayed much longer. On 8th March Gorst reported to the
Lord President that the City and Guilds leaders hoped to see a separate
technical or technological branch quite distinct from the existing
Science and Art Department.[23] A week later he submitted a scheme
of tri-partite division to Devonshire at the latter's request. In this
Gorst had organized the new central authority round three Principal
Assistant Secretaries, one for each of Elementary, Secondary and
Technological education, and he suggested a pattern for the distribution
of work between the three. This was the scheme eventually adopted
in 1903, but at this stage Devonshire was not prepared to make such a
radical change—in spite of his pledge. He claimed that such a scheme
would cut Abney off from some of the functions from which he ought
not to be spared in a note to Kekewich on 15th March. At the same
time Abney's scheme was not 'at all satisfactory. While nominally
abandoning the title of Science and Art, he leaves that Branch of the
Department practically where it is, but under two co-ordinate heads
instead of one.'[24] Devonshire's final solution was contained in a note
he sent to Gorst on 26th March. In this he said he felt that Gorst's
plan might well answer as a permanent arrangement for the future,
but the removal of Abney from some of his functions and the difficulty
of finding anyone to head the technical branch ruled out such a scheme
for the present. 'I am inclined to think that . . . there would not be
much difficulty in retracting our pledges, and in reverting for the
present at least to a Bi-partite Division, and in putting Abney at the
head of a Secondary Education Division in which the museums
would be included. He might have Assistant Secretaries for Literary,
Scientific, Art and Technological divisions and divide the old and the
new work between them. I do not quite know what the latter division
would include, but probably from what we have heard both from the
schoolmasters and from the technical education people, the recognition
of such a division would go far to satisfy their remaining scruples.'[25]

The Treasury duly gave its consent to the new appointments in
June and the opportunity given by the Act to bring about a fundamental

reorganization of the central offices was, for the moment, lost. The old Science and Art Department had acquired two more Assistant Secretaries and had been renamed. In other respects there was little change in its organization. At this stage it still continued to be accommodated in South Kensington away from the Elementary Department at Whitehall. In July, 1902, Gorst proposed that the posts of the two Principal Assistant Secretaries for elementary and secondary education should be abolished; he wrote to Devonshire 'they perpetuate the division between the two branches of the office. This, notwithstanding the Board of Education Act, is as great now as when we took office seven years ago.'[26]

Resistance to proposed change similar to that put up by Abney on behalf of the Science and Art Department was shown by the Secretary to the Charity Commissioners, D. R. Fearon. Fearon fought his action within the Walpole Committee. This Departmental Committee was appointed in July 1899 to consider what changes in the staff and organization of the Education and Science and Art Departments were necessary 'to bring those departments into closer relation to each other'.[27] Its appointment was caused partly by the retirement of Sir John Donnelly from the Secretaryship of the Science and Art Department and the abolition of his post and partly by the probable passage of the Board of Education Bill. Fearon was not a member of the Committee as originally constituted; it consisted of the Chairman, Walpole, from the India Office, Spring-Rice from the Treasury, Abney from the Science and Art Department and Kekewich and Tucker from the Education Department. Fearon was added in November when the Committee's terms of reference were widened to consider the future organization of a secondary branch. The choice of Fearon to represent secondary education rather than someone like Bruce, an Assistant Commissioner with a lively interest in the schools, appears to have been proposed by Spring-Rice. A letter remains which he sent to Kekewich at the end of July when the addition of someone concerned with secondary education was first mooted. 'If someone', he wrote, 'has to be added to our Committee to "represent" [save the mark!] Secondary Education, would not Fearon be a good choice? He is thoro'ly sensible and practical; and the contemplated transfer of educational work from him to you would be a good pretext.'

'It would never do to have on a business committee some educational theorist or advocate of a doctrinaire idea.'[28]

The Committee issued a Report on the establishment of a secondary education branch for the new office in March, 1900. The Report listed the various powers of the Charity Commission which might be transferred to the Board, viz.:

(1) Powers which enabled the Charity Commissioners to enforce administrative inspection of secondary schools:

(2) Powers of the Commissioners in the matter of the Treasury Grant to schools established under the Welsh Intermediate Education Act:

(3) Powers exercised by the Commissioners, under the provisions of the Charitable Trust Acts, for the general administration of endowments in Wales and Monmouthshire regulated by schemes under the Endowed Schools Acts:

(4) Administration of the Endowed Schools Acts:

(5) Powers of the Commissioners for making schemes for educational endowments, under the Charitable Trusts Acts.

The Committee stated that it understood Devonshire was only prepared to consider transferring the first three of these groups of powers at that time, and that the two latter should remain with the Charity Commission. This meant that the new Board would have a very limited function in secondary education outside of Wales and Monmouthshire. Not surprisingly, the Committee had difficulty in finding work for the proposed new branch, and recommended a staff of only four including an inspector and two clerks. The main work would clearly still be with the Charity Commission. What had led Devonshire to limit so narrowly the functions to be transferred? Apparently he based his decision on a recommendation made by the Walpole Committee itself two months earlier and that recommendation was in its turn based on a memorandum drawn up for his colleagues by Fearon.

Fearon's memorandum was a remarkable document for it seemed to suggest that the legislation recently passed by Parliament to bring together the various central educational agencies should be largely left in abeyance so far as the Charity Commission was concerned for an indefinite period. He argued that 'the great power of altering charitable trusts given by the Endowed Schools Acts in the case of a limited but important class of endowments, without regard to the doctrines of chancery, was originally allowed by Parliament and has hitherto been tolerated by the nation, only because it was felt that the alterations would first be considered and promulgated by a body which had a minister at its head, and to which appeals would be made on other than legal grounds. The Charity Commission, in short, as has been said more than once in Parliament was intended to be a buffer between trustees and the governments. The removal of this buffer will certainly expose the new Board of Education to some severe pressure, which will come from reformers on the one hand and obstructives on the other. And it should be carefully considered by the Committee whether it is desirable to expose a newly created Department, with so large and unknown a field of educational enterprise before it, to this pressure....'[29]

A Draft Order laid before Parliament on 17th May, 1900, transferred to the Board of Education powers relating to educational endowments in Wales and Monmouthshire and conferred power on the Board to exercise concurrently with the Charity Commission authority which would permit it to carry out administrative inspections of schools already under schemes in England. The actual business of making schemes for endowed schools in England remained with the Charity Commission.[30] Thus the senior officials of both the Science and Art Department and of the Charity Commission met with a considerable measure of success in their efforts to preserve their particular 'empires' from that drastic upheaval with which they had seemed to be threatened by the Board of Education Act. The attitude of these officers was certainly not one of deliberate sabotage; it was simply that a new act had been passed which left a great deal to the discretion of the government, it could have heralded wide reforms or it could have been made to mean little. Those intimately concerned with working a system frequently find it difficult to appreciate the need for radical change, this seems to have been the position of Abney, Fearon and their colleagues. In these circumstances the senior officials on whom the government relied for advice went no further than they could help in developing a unified central office.

The sense of independence which the re-named Science and Art Department maintained may have been due in part to its physical isolation at South Kensington while the Elementary Branch continued to inhabit inadequate accommodation in the Whitehall area. The former Education Department—and the new Elementary Branch—was housed in five separate buildings at the time of the passing of the Board of Education Act and there was no central building in which a Secondary Branch could be accommodated. Even before the Act it had been intended to build new accommodation for the Education Department, the shortcomings of the existing arrangements were illustrated by the Report of a Departmental Committee which looked into the problem in 1896. The main centre consisted of 87 rooms scattered over portions of four floors in the Treasury Buildings in Whitehall. Here the corridors had had to be used for storing documents and 'the passages, instead of being reservoirs of fresh air, are a standing source of unwholesomeness, affecting each room in a greater or less degree'. Fifty-six officials worked in a temporary structure in King Street; thirty-four worked at Trafalgar Buildings, Charing Cross where 'The lavatory is now turned into a library and rows of folio returns confront the washing basins'. The remaining two office buildings in use were a corrugated iron building in Charles Street and 43 Parliament Street. The Committee complained that this 'chance-medley' of buildings defied the due organization of work and that sections dealing with each other could not be put into proximity. The financial administration 'is at present in two divisions, half a mile apart. Fee grants are calculated and paid at Charing Cross, the annual grants at the Census Buildings, while the Assistant Secretary, who acts as Financial Secretary, necessarily sits at Whitehall. . . .'[31] A new building offering the opportunity of bringing the central office together in one place was eventually completed in 1908. Thus in the years immediately following the passing of the Act it was not possible to encourage any sense of unity of purpose by bringing the various elements that were supposed to merge to form the new office into physical proximity with each other.

REFERENCES

[1] Bryce Cssn., 1895, vol. I, p. 64.

[2] Local councils were permitted to aid schools other than elementary from the rate fund by the Technical Instruction Act of 1889 (52 & 53 Vic., c 41). The sum likely to be available was greatly increased by the Local Taxation (Customs and Excise) Act of 1890 (53 & 54 Vict., c 60) which diverted to local authorities moneys originally intended as compensation for publicans—popularly known as 'whiskey money'.

[3] S.I.C., 1868, vol. I, pp. 633–7.

[4] Bryce Cssn., 1895, vol. I, p. 93.

[5] Ibid., p. 257.

[6] P.R.O., Ed. 24/8, 26/2/98.

[7] 62 & 63 Vict., c 33.

[8] P.R.O., Ed. 24/8, 28/2/98.

[9] P.R.O., Ed. 24/8, 21/5/98. Notes by H. M. Lindsell, Advising Counsel to the Education Department.

[10] 62 & 63, Vict., c 33, S 2.

[11] P.R.O., Ed. 24/8, 9/6/98.

[12] Ibid., 28/2/98.
[13] Parliamentary Debates, 24/4/99, col. 353.
[14] P.R.O., Ed. 24/8, A Precis of opinions on the Board of Education Bill, 1899.
[15] P.R.O., Ed. 24/8, 22/7/99.
[16] P.R.O., Ed. 24/64, 7/7/99, Warre to Kekewich.
[17] Ibid., Devonshire to Kekewich.
[18] Ibid., Memorandum on the future organization of the internal departments of the Board of Education by M. E. Sadler.
[19] The Times, 18/7/99.
[20] P.R.O., Ed. 24/64, 20/1/00, Devonshire to Kekewich.
[21] Ibid., 26/2/00, Abney to Kekewich.
[22] Ibid., March, 1900, Abney to Devonshire.
[22] Ibid., 8/3/00, Gorst to Devonshire.
[24] Ibid., 15/3/00, Devonshire to Kekewich.
[25] Ibid., 26/3/00, Devonshire to Gorst.
[26] P.R.O., Ed. 24/67A, 11/7/02, Gorst to Devonshire.
[27] Minute of 4/7/99.
[28] P.R.O., Ed. 24/62, 25/7/99, Spring-Rice to Kekewich.
[29] P.R.O., Ed. 24/63, Memorandum on the Question of the Transfer of the Administration of the Endowed Schools Acts from the Charity Commission to the Board of Education by D. R. F[earon].
[30] The transfer of business from the Commission to the Board was completed by 1/4/03 (Cd. 1763).
[31] P.R.O., Ed. 24/60.

CHAPTER 6

THE BOARD AND MINISTRY OF EDUCATION FROM 1903

I

THE transformation of the administrative agencies which had only been nominally unified after 1899 into an effective office of the central government, became urgent with the passing of the Education Act of 1902,* 'The period following the Act of 1902 was a great period of constructive administration, the fruitfulness of which is mainly attributable to Sir Robert Morant, the Permanent Secretary from 1903 to 1911'.[1] In 1899, while a member of the staff of the Office of Special Enquiries, Morant had prepared a precis of opinions on the Board of Education Bill in which he pointed out that the Bill gave very wide powers to the new Board of Education to make or to ruin the educational system and that the interpretation put upon the Bill would be of great importance. It now fell to the lot of Morant as Permanent Secretary not only to put the great Act of 1902 into force, but also to make the most of the opportunities conferred by the Act of 1899. It was really he who built the Board into an effective central office, capable of providing the new local authorities with guidance in the various fields of education. His remodelling of the central administrative machinery in the years after 1902 was certainly not one of his least important achievements.

The original proposal to organize the Board's work in three branches was carried out and each of the branches was placed in the charge of a Permanent Assistant Secretary. The Elementary Branch dealt not only with the provision, administration and inspection of elementary education, but also with the training and examination of teachers and pupil teachers for elementary schools. The Secondary Branch took over all matters concerning the inspection of secondary schools and educational endowments while the Technological Branch undertook the administration and inspection of technical institutions and evening classes in receipt of government grant and all business concerning the Victoria and Albert Museum, the Royal Colleges of Science and of Art and the Geological Survey.

In December, 1903, Morant reorganized the Elementary Branch so as to enable it to work more closely with the new local authorities.

* The administrative consequences of this measure are discussed more fully in chapter 9.

The administrative work of the Branch was split into three divisions; these were, Group A to cover the Northern, North-Eastern and North-Western inspection divisions (the seven Northern counties), Group B covering the West Central, East Central and Eastern divisions (the twenty Midland counties), and Group C covering the South-Eastern, South-Western and Metropolitan divisions. Each of these groups was roughly equal in the size of its population and the number of its elementary schools. The administration of each group was put in the hands of an Assistant Secretary aided by a Senior Examiner and a number of Junior Examiners. The effect of this form of organization was to identify the work of the office more closely with that of the Inspectorate and to enable Assistant Secretaries to become familiar with the problems of particular localities while, viewed from the standpoint of the local authorities, their officers could get to know the Board's officers for their areas. The legal work could not be broken down in this manner, therefore all of this was transferred to a Legal Division within the Branch which was established at the time under Selby-Bigge—later to become Permanent Secretary to the Board.[2]

A principal duty of the Board came to be to see that local authorities fulfilled their statutory obligation of providing sufficient satisfactory elementary school places. By the Act of 1899, the Board was charged 'with the superintendence of matters relating to education in England and Wales' and in fulfilment of this duty it attempted to stimulate lax authorities by the threat of a reduction in grant. This weapon came to be used much less frequently and it was never very effective outside of elementary education because there was no legal obligation on authorities to provide higher education. The total amount of work which fell upon the Secondary was much less than that falling on the Elementary Branch. In 1907 Morant pointed out in a memorandum on the organization of the Board that the Secondary Branch had a considerable amount of legal work because of its Charity Commission background. The files were badly in need of reorganization for they had grown immense and contained a mixture of legal, educational and administrative material. The answer to this problem was, he believed, to be found in forming a distinct Legal Division within the Secondary as had been done in the Elementary Branch. 'It is possible . . . that the legal and quasi-legal work arising within each of the three branches of the Board's work may eventually be grouped together into one legal branch', but the absence of suitable premises made such a solution impossible at the present time. The Secondary Branch was to have three territorial divisions on the same lines as those already existing in the Elementary; it was also to take over from the latter Branch all pupil-teacher work. Morant explained that the new arrangements would make more necessary than ever the frequent interchange of knowledge and opinions among officers; 'I am particularly to emphasize that this interchange should be as much as possible by means of oral communication and discussion—men going to one another's rooms freely for this purpose. Matters should not be delayed by writing minutes for these purposes, except in so far as a record of reasons for arriving at particular decisions render it necessary.' With this end in view 'it has been arranged to place all the Secretaries and Examiners of the Secondary Branch in contiguous rooms on one floor'.[3]

In the same memorandum, Morant recorded that the government had decided to establish a separate department to deal with the work of the Board in Wales. At the time of writing Morant contemplated that an Assistant Secretary would be in charge and he expressed the hope that eventually it would be possible to appoint Welshmen to staff the new department. This department was created as a result of political pressure. Morant personally and the Board generally had incurred the wrath of Welsh Nonconformity in applying the provisions of the Act of 1902 which obliged local authorities to give rate aid to Church schools. After the Liberals were returned to power in the election of 1906, attempts to amend the provisions of the 1902 Act were frustrated by the Conservative majority in the House of Lords, but the new ministry could ensure that the influence of Morant was removed from the Welsh scene and that the administration and enforcement of the hated Act was carried out by those sympathetic to the views of Welsh Nonconformists. Consequently when the department was set up in 1907 it had a Permanent Secretary at its head reporting directly to the President of the Board and independent of Morant. Alfred Davies was appointed to take charge of the new department. He was a solicitor in private practice in Liverpool where he had been playing an active part as a Liberal and Nonconformist in local affairs. He wrote to Morant after the news of his appointment had been made known apparently expressing some surprise that 'The earliest to tender their congratulations were two of the staunchest Conservatives and Churchmen in this city'.[4] Morant appears to have swallowed his feelings as best he could, but there is some sign of how he felt about this diminution of his authority by the Lloyd George faction in the Liberal Government in some of his correspondence with his new colleague. Davies wrote to Morant asking for a supply of Board of Education notepaper and envelopes for replying to letters concerned with his new office during March, 1907; Morant refused to send any replying that 'you will not be an official of this Board until 1st April; it would be impossible that you should write any letters on the official paper before taking up your duties'. Before sending this, Morant passed it to McKenna, the President, with a note asking him 'Will the enclosed suffice and not be too rude?'[5]

The new department took over elementary and secondary work for Wales from the beginning, but it was not immediately able to take over all of the work which it eventually handled because some technical education work was still accommodated at South Kensington and the transfer of this had to await the completion of the new buildings. A Welsh Inspectorate was set up at the same time under O. M. Edwards, a lecturer in modern history and author of various works on Welsh history and literature. According to the biographical note prepared for distribution to the press, Edwards had been 'closely connected with Welsh educational and literary movements—being indeed one of the main sources of inspiration of recent developments in these directions'.

Also in 1907 the Medical Branch was set up following the passing of the Education (Administrative Provisions) Act which, among other things, imposed upon local authorities the duty of providing medical inspection at least three times during the school life of each child. The duties of the new Branch were set out as follows: (1) to advise and supervise local authorities on medical inspection matters; (2) to consider and sanction such arrangements as may be proposed by local authorities concerning the health and physical condition of children; (3) to collect and collate information from local authorities and to issue an annual report.

The establishment of the new Branch led to a sharp encounter between the protagonists of a personal health service for school children run by the educational authorities on an *ad hoc* basis, and those who saw the school medical service as part of the general sanitary and health service run by local authorities and the state. Morant adhered firmly to this latter view and appointed Dr. G. Newman, Medical Officer of Health for Finsbury and Lecturer in Public Health and Sanitary Administration as the first Chief Medical Officer at the

H

Board. The appointment was attacked by both the *British Medical Journal* and *The Lancet* which gave their support to the other group led by a Dr. Kerr who was employed by the London County Council as Assistant Medical Officer (Education). Morant set out his views in a letter towards the end of 1907, ' . . . the important point in my view is that we should as far as possible make this new Medical Inspection of Schoolchildren the means of extending public action generally in regard to the medical and sanitary condition of the families whose children attend the elementary schools—and that word condition must gradually include the home, and not be restricted to the school.

'On the other hand there is a certain comparatively small clique of so-called "School Doctors", who consider that the predominant, indeed almost the exclusive, point to make for is the medical man's work on the school premises; and they are on that account keenly fighting against any association of this new work with the Medical Officer of Health and with the public machinery for public health in the large towns.

'We have definitely taken the line against them, as shown by our appointing as Head of our small staff here a man who is not a school doctor . . . but who is an especially capable Medical Officer of Health.'6

By the outbreak of the First World War this Branch had come to deal with the administration of the Provision of Meals Acts, the Mental Deficiency Act of 1913 in so far as it concerned local education authorities, grants for and the inspection of physical education, grants for play centres and for day nurseries. When the new Ministry of Health was established in 1919 the association of the school medical service with the general provision for public health was marked by the appointment of the Board's Chief Medical Officer as Chief Medical Officer at the new ministry while continuing to discharge his responsibilities for the medical work of the Board.

In addition to the Medical, two other general branches evolved which operated across the whole span of the Board's activity at this time, the Finance and Legal Branches. The head of the Finance Branch, the Accountant-General, was responsible as 'Accounting Officer' for the accuracy of the Board's accounts. The Legal Branch was formed when better accommodation became available and it brought together the work of the legal divisions within the main existing Branches. The work was divided into two sections, one for endowments and another for other matters. In the case of endowments it was held that educational considerations were always to be regarded as paramount, thus this business was dealt with by the appropriate administrative branch advised by the Legal Branch. So far as other matters were concerned, such as the compulsory acquisition of land or instruments of government, the rule was that no matter involving a legal issue should be dealt with except after reference to the Legal Branch.

In April, 1910, Morant established a Universities Branch at the Board for 'Experience has shown that the technological and professional instruction (including the training of teachers for elementary and secondary schools) given by the Universities and aided by grants from the Board could not be properly dealt with as part of the ordinary administration of the Board as applied to institutes which have less autonomy, responsibility and prestige than the Universities'.[7] Morant was determined to win for the Board control of the general grant for Universities that was administered by the Treasury on the advice of a grants committee and thus to make his newly-constituted Universities Branch the sole medium of state aid to institutions of university standing. The main difficulty he encountered was the opposition of some of the Universities and, above all, the opposition of the Chancellor of the Exchequer, Lloyd George. It was not until 1911 that the general grant was taken over by the Board, and even then the Treasury proved extremely difficult.[8] M. F. Heath, who had succeeded Michael Sadler as Director of the Department of Special Inquiries and Reports, became Principal Assistant Secretary for the new Branch, and one of his first duties was to travel round the Universities re-assuring ruffled Vice-Chancellors.

Thus in the decade or so following the Education Act of 1902 the central administrative agency for education was built up. Since that time its name has been changed from Board to Ministry, its legal powers have been modified, and its various fields of activity have expanded greatly, yet in all the essentials the present administrative organ had been brought into existence by the time of the First World War, and largely under the direction of Robert Morant.

II

The organization of the staffing of the Board of Education remained peculiar to itself until the early 1920s, when the system was assimilated to the general grades which prevailed in the civil service as a whole.

The administrative work of the Board fell on the shoulders of the Assistant Secretaries and Examiners, the latter being divided into senior and junior grades: the career pattern was that a man entered the office as a Junior Examiner and might hope eventually to rise to the level of Assistant Secretary—although many went no further than the grade of Senior Examiner. This pattern of staffing had developed in the old Education Department and a similar system had been in use in the Science and Art Department. Recruitment of staff was undertaken directly by the Board without the agency of the examinations of the Civil Service Commission. Until 1901 all who wrote in for posts had their names entered in what was called the 'Candidates' Book' with a summary of their education and a note of the names of those who supported the application. The Candidates' Book had reached three volumes by the time it was abandoned in favour of forms of application.

An analysis of the educational backgrounds of the 92 higher staff in 1910 showed that no fewer than 58 were from Oxford, 23 were from Cambridge, 1 from London, 2 from Trinity College, Dublin, 1 from the Royal University of Ireland and 2 from the University of Wales, while 5 held no degree; 26 of the men from Oxford and 16 of those from Cambridge held first class degrees, while an analysis by subjects showed that 36 of the Oxford men had taken Greats and 14 Cambridge men had read Classics. The schools attended by these same men are given in the following table.

In 1907 Morant set down his views of what the Board of Education should expect of its senior staff. He emphasized 'the increasing need of attaining and maintaining a high standard of knowledge of educational problems in the widest sense. It is a truism to say that the successful treatment of educational problems involves the consideration of constantly changing conditions, domestic, social, economic and political, and if the best use is to be made of the influence exercised by this office, through its ordinary administration it is essential that the administration should be guided and informed by intelligence well versed in the study of both the special and the general problems of education.' Opportunities were constantly being missed and 'it requires both knowledge and imagination to see the bearing of administrative details on educational progress'.

'It is not sufficient in an office like ours that an officer of the higher staff should merely "get through the papers on his table" with regularity and despatch, or apply to each case as it comes to him the

The Schools that Higher Officials at the Board of Education in 1910 had attended.[9]

School	Junior examiners	Senior examiners	Assistant Secretaries and higher posts
Eton	6	3	2
Harrow	1	2	2
Winchester . . .	4	1	6
Rugby	1	–	–
Charterhouse . . .	2	1	–
Westminster . . .	2	–	1
Shrewsbury . . .	3	1	–
Bedford . . .	2	–	–
King Edward's, B'ham .	1	–	–
Clifton	1	–	–
Dulwich . . .	1	–	–
King's College School .	2	–	–
Marlborough . . .	7	–	2
Merchant Taylors . .	1	–	1
Repton	2	1	–
Rossall	–	–	1
St. Paul's . . .	4	–	–
University College School	1	–	–
Wellington . . .	2	–	–
Other H.M.C. Schools .	4	2	–
Other Secondary Schools .	6	9	4
Totals . . .	53	20	19

general rules and precedents which may happen to have been collected or to have grown into a sort of formula from somewhat similar incidents on previous occasions.'

The currents of public opinion were constantly changing, and 'it is therefore incumbent upon every Assistant Secretary and every Examiner, as well as on each responsible head of a Branch, to use every endeavour to keep himself abreast of the best that is written and said from day to day on the subject of education. The officers of the Board of Education ought to be and can be a body of experts in the general problem of education. . . .'[10]

The great advantage of this system whereby members of the higher staff spent the whole of their careers in the service of the Board was that it did permit them to became specialists in educational matters.

Yet the system had its drawbacks, not enough responsibility was given to Junior Examiners so that self-reliance and initiative were lost during the very long wait for promotion to the senior grade. One who was brought up under the system wrote that to go on year after year referring cases that were not in any way outside normal procedure and usually to see these cases not even settled by the Senior Examiner but going on and on up the office tended to kill a man's sense of responsibility. '... I may be exaggerating this point somewhat, but it is not wholly untrue to say that a man becomes ripe for promotion from a junior examiner grade just when he has lost his powers of initiative, decision and self-reliance.'[11] The writer of these critical remarks considered that assimilation with the rest of the civil service and recruitment through the Administrative Class Civil Service Examination could not possibly provide an answer to the problem 'if we are really to know something about education'. In fact, quite soon after the First World War the old system was ended and the Board's higher staff came to be recruited through the general arrangements for the civil service and were no longer required to have any particular knowledge of the educational system.

Apart from the higher grades, the Board of Education employed about 1,800 men, women and boys in clerical and miscellaneous classes. Responsibility for the deployment of this large body and the general efficiency of their organization lay with the Chief Clerk. It was his duty to see that the whole of the office worked smoothly; the Chief Clerk in 1908 described himself in these terms, 'as well as being a sort of General Manager and Metropolitan magistrate combined, the Chief Clerk finds himself something like the Vicar of a considerable parish. Into his ear are poured the ambitions and disappointments of men, women and boys.' In the course of his duties he apparently formed strong opinions of departments with disruptive tendencies; after the formation of the new department for Wales in 1907, the Chief Clerk commented in 1908 that 'The new Welsh Department alone is responsible for additions to [my] work so unnecessary and so troublesome that I cannot trust myself to write of them'.[12]

III

The period between the two World Wars did not bring any fundamental change in the central government's machinery for administering education. In 1918 the Machinery of Government Committee issued its Report on the manner in which the exercise and distribution by the government of its functions might be improved. One member of this small committee was Morant, so it was not entirely surprising that governmental arrangements for the administration of education were found to be good.[13] The committee decided that the distribution of duties among government departments should be guided by a general principle, the principle being distribution in accordance with the nature of the service to be rendered to the community since this would lead to a minimum of confusion and overlapping. In the case of education the principle of concentrating the main functions of central government in relation to a specific service in a single department was already recognized. 'It is not, therefore, necessary for us to do more than to draw attention to some of the characteristics in the present organization which bear most closely upon our enquiry.'[14]

One change which was made the next year no doubt contravened the main principle enunciated by this committee for the Board ceased from acting as the agency which distributed grants to institutions of University standing. In 1919 these grants were increased to £1,000,000 and extended to Scottish Universities. The government decided to revert to paying these grants through the Treasury, advised by a grants committee.

The most important change in the internal administrative organization of the Board between the wars was its further 'territorialization' in the 1920s. At the end of the First World War the Board had four main branches, Elementary, Secondary, Technological and Universities; two special branches, Legal and Medical; two general branches, the Accountant-General's and the Establishments Section; there was also the Welsh Department and the Office of Special Enquiries and Reports which included the library. In 1918 Sir Edmund Phipps, a senior officer of the Board, sent a paper to the Permanent Secretary (Selby-Bigge) urging the abolition of the main branch organization and its replacement by a territorial form of organization.[15] Although this reform was rejected at the time the eventual acceptance of the main idea behind the scheme lends considerable interest to the arguments that Phipps put forward.

The principal disadvantage of the existing branch system, even with each main branch broken down into three areas was that this arrangement did not lend itself to the handling of matters in which the whole of an authority's activities or policy should come under review; it was, for example, very difficult for the Board to decide whether expenditure was more urgently needed on a new elementary or secondary school. The existing separation of the Elementary, Secondary and Technological Branches made close consultation necessary for this purpose, and this was only done slowly through the exchange of minutes. Frequent conferences between officers was probably desirable, but in practice this was very difficult for 'it seems not to suit men's ways of working'. The stress which the new Education Act of 1918 lay on the 'progressive development and comprehensive organization in respect of an area' and the need to bring about co-operation between Part II and Part III (Elementary only) authorities in an area made it necessary to arrange that only one man in each rank should be responsible for all duties proper to his rank in respect of any local authority. This change could be achieved by fusing the three main branches and dividing the amalgamated body into nine territorial divisions. Such a scheme would have only one real disadvantage for under the present system when the officer of a local authority came to see someone at the Board, the Board man could claim to have superior experience of a particular branch's work to that possessed by the local man, under the proposed reform this would no longer be the case. On the other hand local authorities would no longer be able to play off one branch of the Board against another as they had done in the past. Phipps suggested that no change need be made in the position of the Inspectorate who would still be divided into elementary, secondary and technological, it would be the function of the office man to co-ordinate for each area the advice of the inspectors.

These suggestions met with a cool reception from the Permanent Secretary, nearly eight months later he forwarded a paper on the proposed amalgamation of the branches on a geographical basis to the President of the Board, H. A. L. Fisher.[16] Selby-Bigge made the most of the difficulties likely to arise; efficient organization depended upon specialization, and the amalgamation of branches would place a much greater strain on men; it was inconceivable that men could be trained to grapple simultaneously with the great variety of problems presented by elementary, technological and secondary education; the quality of men available made such a scheme impracticable for for most of the Senior Examiners were quite incapable of adjusting themselves to a wider field of work; the local authorities were not well served by their officials who were badly chosen, it was vital that the Board's officers should speak to them with the 'authority of knowledge and experience'; finally the present system had precision and lucidity of method, 'The credit for all this is not due to myself but to Sir Robert Morant; and my instinct at present is to proceed with great caution in departing from the main lines of the system which he established'. Selby-Bigge added a remarkably frank post-scriptum saying that he would probably not remain as Secretary for more than four more years and might be retired after eighteen months. 'It would not be right for me to devolve responsibility for the office reorganization on anyone else, and I am too conscious of my own limitations to believe that I could take responsibility for a fundamental change of office machinery together with the other work which would fall upon me [under the new Act]. This, of course, may be due to timidity on my part, but, on the merits of the proposal, I do not see my way clear to adopt it, and if it is to be adopted it had much better be done by my successor.'

The immediate outcome of these proposals was that the President decided against undertaking any reform. Fisher wrote: 'The Secretary's Minute convinces me that it would be impossible at the present juncture, if only for reasons of personnel, to embark upon the large scheme of reorganization outlined by Sir E. Phipps'. He proposed instead to rely on divisional inspectors to view the schemes of local authorities as a whole. The need to reorganize the main branches of the office became increasingly clear as actual problems arose in working the new educational legislation. Consequently a modified form of the scheme contained in the Phipps paper came to be adopted. The country was divided for purposes of elementary, secondary and techno-logical education into nine divisions and a territorial system for adminis-trative officers up to the rank of principal was introduced. Thus one officer of the Board became responsible for all grades of education within a particular area, and he would be acquainted with the whole of an authority's problems and organization. The branch organization was maintained above the principal level and the territorial officer was obliged to refer to the appropriate Assistant Secretary any impor-tant problems that might arise to ensure that such matters should be dealt with in a manner consistent with national policy.

The inspecting staffs of the Education Department, the Science and Art Department and the Charity Commission had been absorbed into the service of the Board of Education, but as the Elementary, Technological and Secondary Inspectorates they remained largely separate entities. In 1926 the higher branches of the Inspectorates were brought together; there were three Chief Inspectors, one each for

Elementary, Secondary, and Technological, one of these was designated Senior Chief Inspector to co-ordinate the work of the Inspectorate generally. The country had been divided into nine territorial divisions for the purposes of elementary school inspection for some years and Divisional Inspectors were now given the task of co-ordinating the work of their colleagues and were to report directly to the Senior Chief Inspector. During the 1930s the process of 'aggregation' took place in the Inspectorate, that is to say the Women's Inspectorate ceased to be maintained as a separate body, the title of Chief Woman Inspector being dropped on the retirement of its holder in 1938. The principle of unification was taken further in 1944 when a Departmental Committee recommended a unified Inspectorate; its other recommendations included an increase in the numbers of inspectors, the abolition of the grade of Assistant Inspector, and the replacement of the three Chief Inspectors by a Senior Chief Inspector and six Chief Inspectors. All of these recommendations were implemented in the years following the Second World War.

IV

When the Second World War began the Board of Education staff remained at work in their London headquarters initially, but in view of the general effects of the aerial bombardment of London during the summer and autumn of 1940, the government decided to evacuate the greater part of the staff to Bournemouth. During the following winter the educational policies of the nation were reviewed at the official level and the act which was eventually passed in 1944 converted the Board into the Ministry of Education and increased its powers and responsibilities. The very change in title from President of a Board to a Minister was intended as a symbol of change in the status of the head of the office, many believed that it would give greater prestige to education generally in the eyes of the nation. The duty of the Board had been limited by the Act of 1899 to the superintendence of educational affairs and this general definition survived until 1944 when the Minister was given the rather more positive duty 'to promote the education of the people of England and Wales and the progressive development of institutions devoted to that purpose, and to secure the effective execution by local authorities, under his control and direction, of the national policy for providing a varied and comprehensive educational service in every area'.[17]

The Education Act of 1902 had given the Board numerous specific duties; among the most important of these were approving schemes and making provisional orders for education committees, making orders for the appointment of managers of non-provided schools, sanctioning loans and settling disputes between managers of non-provided schools and the local authorities. The duty of administering government grants and setting out the conditions on which they would be paid continued to give the Board—as it had its predecessors—the opportunity to enforce minimum standards of efficiency, and this position continued until the passing of the Local Government Act in 1958.*

Within two years of the enactment of the legislation of 1902 the weakness of the position of the Board when confronted with defiance by local authorities became apparent for it found itself unable to enforce the provisions of the Act of 1902 in parts of Wales without the aid of special legislation. Strong opposition to giving rate aid to Church schools led a number of Welsh authorities to refuse to operate the provisions of the 1902 settlement for non-provided schools. Carmarthen, Merioneth, Rhondda, Mountain Ash and Pontypridd disclaimed all responsibility for non-provided schools and simply passed on to their managers any Parliamentary grants due in respect of their schools as soon as the money arrived from Whitehall—they would assume none of their liabilities towards these schools and give no aid from the rates. In Caernarvon a different policy was adopted, here the authority undertook all administrative functions, it appointed the teachers and the cleaners, prescribed textbooks, fixed salaries and so forth and corresponded directly with the teachers, thus depriving the voluntary managers not only of control but also of knowledge of what was happening in their own schools. The Caernarvon lead was followed in Brecon, Merthyr Tydfil, Radnor, Glamorgan and Denbigh.[18] Faced with such widespread illegality, the Board of Education was obliged to attempt to take some action. The only action open to it was that contained in Section 16 of the 1902 Act. This Section provided that if an authority failed to fulfil any of its duties, 'the Board of Education may, after holding a public inquiry, make such order as they think necessary or proper for the purpose of compelling the

* After 1902 when both local and central authorities had been reorganized, there were some grounds of hoping that the grant system itself might be simplified. These hopes were largely unrealized until after the First World War, when more than 50 separate grants were reduced to two main grants, one for elementary and one for higher education. Even after this, special grants continued to be offered from time to time to encourage particular projects, e.g. for teacher training in 1923.

authority to fulfil their duty, and any such order may be enforced by mandamus'.

The Board felt that in the circumstances then prevailing in Wales the imprisonment of the members of Welsh authorities for failing to comply with a mandamus would merely create martyrs and strengthen the opposition to the 1902 measure, but it did proceed to hold a public inquiry in the case of Carmarthen so that:

(1) the facts of the situation might be clearly demonstrated to Parliament and the public,

(2) the length and futility of the remedies in the Act might be demonstrated and the need for further powers proved, and

(3) to gain time until Parliament was in a position to provide increased powers.[19]

The immediate consequence of the situation in Wales was the passage of the Education (Local Authority Default) Act in 1904.[20] This strengthened the position of the Board considerably, for it empowered it in case of default by a local authority to pay money direct to the managers of schools and to deduct this amount from the grant normally payable to the local authority. The effect of this measure, when enforced, would be to make refusal of rate aid to non-provided schools pointless since an authority would have to raise an extra sum for its own schools from the rate to make good the amount deducted from its Parliamentary grant and paid directly to the managers of non-provided schools.

Since 1904 powers on these lines have been reserved firstly to the Board and later to the Ministry of Education. The Minister's powers in dealing with defaulting local authorities or governors or managers in the Education Act of 1944 took three forms; in the first place he was given wide powers to declare an authority in default, and to give such directions as he might think expedient, such directions being enforceable by mandamus; secondly he was given power to ensure the appointment of suitable bodies of governors or managers in case of default by a local authority; and thirdly the Act enabled him to deduct from the grant of any authority which had failed to fulfil its duty of maintaining voluntary schools such sum as might seem suitable and to pay it directly to the managers or governors.[21] Apart from these powers of enforcement, the Act of 1944 secured for the Minister the right to take the initiative in a much more effective manner than could his predecessor, the President of the Board; he could now direct any recalcitrant authority to make such improvements in their provision as he might decide, if he felt that an authority were acting unreasonably 'he may . . . give such directions as to the exercise of the power or the performance of the duty as appear to him to be expedient' even where the Act made the exercise of the power or performance of the duty contingent on the opinion of the authority itself.[22] In these circumstances, the power of the Minister to make deductions from the grant of an authority on the grounds that it had failed to maintain a satisfactory minimum standard of service became less important. Nevertheless when the system of specific grants for particular services came to be replaced by the general or 'block' grant system in 1958, the new Local Government Act gave power to reduce the general grant if the 'appropriate' minister[23] should consider that an authority had failed to maintain a reasonable standard in a service covered by the grant.[24]

The considerable increase in the power and authority which the central administrative agency has exercised since 1944 was described in the Explanatory Memorandum of 1943 as 'a recognition of the principle that the public system of education, though administered locally, is the nation's concern, the full benefits of which should be equally available to all alike, wherever their homes may be'.[25] However great the variations in educational opportunity may still be between one area and another, there can be little doubt but that they are much less important than they were before 1944.

V

The situation in Wales after 1902 and the delicacy with which the government felt bound to tread even after the enactment of the Defaulting Authorities Bill in 1904 illustrates that in this country no amount of legal power can ensure a smooth passage for an educational policy which runs strongly counter to the wishes of most people in any particular area. Thus it can be argued that education is a field in which advisory committees should be given a prominent part in helping the government to evolve policy. The central Education Department could hardly hope to secure and retain public confidence if it did not avail itself of the advice and aid of advisory committees constituted so as to make available the knowledge and experience of those sections of the community closely concerned with the Department's work.

The Act which created the Board of Education did, in fact, provide for the establishment of a Consultative Committee 'consisting as to not less than two-thirds of persons qualified to represent the views of universities and other bodies interested in education'. The Consultative Committee was set up by order-in-council in 1900 and had three functions: to frame regulations for a register of teachers, to advise the Board on the inspection of secondary schools and to advise the Board on any matter which the Department referred to it. The Committee only ever fulfilled the last of these functions. The men controlling the Board were determined to ensure that the Committee was kept occupied with inquiries into topics in the field of education which were not directly concerned with the Board's immediate policies. Many headmasters of secondary schools and other educationists had seen in the device of a committee some sort of safeguard against departmental bureaucracy, and had hoped that it would enable those concerned with education and the schools to play an active part in the Board's administrative work. The question of preserving ministerial responsibility fully and not permitting it to be in any way undermined had been aired in the debate on the Board of Education Bill in 1899. The Committee on the Machinery of Government in 1918 commended the sort of arrangements that had been followed with the Consultative Committee of the Board of Education and felt that such advisory bodies might play an increasingly useful and important rôle; ' . . . the preservation of the full responsibility of ministers for executive action will not, in our opinion, ensure that the course of administration which they adopt will secure and retain public confidence unless it is recognized as an obligation upon departments to avail themselves of the advice and assistance of advisory bodies so constituted as to make available the knowledge and experience of all sections of the community affected by the activities of the Department'.[26]

The Consultative Committee was suspended during the First World War, but it was reconstituted by order-in-council in 1920. Between the two wars the Committee published seven reports; possibly the three most important were 'The Education of the Adolescent' (the Hadow Report) in 1926, 'The Primary School' in 1930, and 'Secondary Education' (the Spens report) in 1938. These three reports served to draw together ideas which were circulating on the reorganization of primary and secondary education, to focus attention on the problems which such a recasting of the educational system would involve and to suggest possible solutions. Apart from their immediate impact, these reports had an obvious effect on the terms of the Education Act of 1944, and on the period of reconstruction which followed it. The value of the Committee's work and the general respect which this aroused led to legislative provision for a similar body in the Act of 1944. The Act provided that there should be two Central Advisory Councils, one for England and the other for Wales, and that these Councils should advise the Minister 'upon such matters connected with educational theory and practice as they think fit, and upon any questions referred to them by him'.[27] The members of each Council were to be appointed by the Minister, and were to include persons who had had experience of the statutory system of public education as well as persons with experience of institutions not forming part of that system; thus while members are chosen from a wide variety of educational fields, they are not chosen after consultation with interested organizations. The Central Council for England has continued to work in much the same way as the former Consultative Committee in that it has taken one topic at a time, spent two or three years studying it and then published a report. Legally since 1944 the Central Council may take the initiative and choose its own topic, but in fact it has been occupied for most of the time working on topics set it by the Minister. In 1947 it issued its first report, 'School and Life', and then began on its own initiative a study of the educational needs of young workers, but it had to set this aside when the Minister asked it to carry out an inquiry into the leisure time interests of school children, this report appeared in 1948 under the title 'Out of School'. Other reports which the Council has published include 'Early Leaving' in 1954, '15 to 18' (the Crowther Report) in 1959, and 'Half Our Future' (the Newsom Report) in 1963. The Central Advisory Council for Wales has confined itself to matters of special interest to education in that country, and its publications include 'The Place of Welsh and English in Schools in Wales' and 'Education in Rural Wales'. In its volume on Advisory Committees in British Government, P.E.P. has suggested in connection with the Central Advisory Council for England that while statutory provision gave permanence and some independence to a committee, it could lead to too rigid an approach. The existence of several other advisory committees and the fact that schools are run by local authorities and not by the Ministry were said to result in difficulty in finding suitable problems for the Council to tackle 'in order that its interludes of inactivity may not be unduly prolonged'.[28] On the other hand some might feel that there are so many questions connected with the educational system that might with advantage be investigated that the 'interludes of inactivity' referred to are certainly not due to a lack of suitable problems.

Apart from the Consultative Committee, various other standing advisory committees were appointed by the Board of Education. In 1913 the Victoria and Albert Museum Advisory Council and the Science Museum Advisory Council were set up: the Juvenile Organizations Committee was appointed by the Home Secretary in 1916 and transferred to the Board in 1919; the Adult Education Committee began its life in 1917 as a committee of the Ministry of Reconstruction and became a standing committee of the Board of Education in 1921; two of the most important committees to be set up were the Secondary Schools Examinations Council in 1917 and the Standing Joint Committees on Scales of Salaries for Teachers in 1919 and 1920, the latter became known as the Burnham Committees in memory of their first chairman, Lord Burnham. All of these committees proved to be of considerable value and four of them—the two Museums' Advisory Councils, the Examinations Council and the Burnham Committees—have continued to operate since the Second World War, though in some cases after re-organization. Two new advisory committees which have been established since the war and which have had a considerable impact are the National Advisory Council for Industry and Commerce and the National Advisory Council on the Training and Supply of Teachers.

The National Advisory Council on the Training and Supply of Teachers was set up in 1949. In a sense it may be regarded as a substitute for the Central Training Council recommended in the McNair Report on the training of teachers. This Report spoke of the Council having 'an independent existence just as the University Grants Committee, though within the framework of the Treasury, has an independent existence'[29] and suggested that it should have from three to five members. The National Advisory Council has never enjoyed anything approaching the independent existence of the University Grants Committee and its membership is probably too large for it to develop much in the way of an effective initiative in opposition to the current Departmental line. The Council is simply advisory and meets under the chairmanship of a nominee of the Secretary of State although it is permitted to elect its own vice-chairman. Its functions are two-fold, to keep under review the supply and distribution of teachers in ways most suited to meet the needs of the schools and to advise on the training and qualifications of teachers. All other matters, such as salaries, fall outside of its province, thus even if it feels that inadequate salaries are causing a shortage of teachers with particular qualifications, it cannot report on this as such and recommend a suitable increase. The Council has three standing committees, one on training and qualifications, another for supply and distribution and, since 1957, a third for teachers in further education.

The members of the Council are nominated by certain organizations and the Secretary of State cannot refuse a nomination; the nominees do not commit their organizations by what they agree to in the Council. The nominating bodies include the local authority organizations— the County Councils Association nominates four, the Association of Education Committees four, the Association of Municipal Corporations four, London County Council two, the Welsh Joint Education Committee two—the teachers' associations—the National Union of Teachers six, the Association of Teachers in Technical Institutions two, the Joint Four Secondary Organizations two, the Association of Teachers in Colleges and Departments of Education five, the Association of Technical Institutions and the Association of Principals two jointly—the area training organizations nominate six members and the Committee of Vice-Chancellors two. The Minister may nominate four members and four representatives of industry and commerce are appointed after consulting the National Advisory Council on Education for Industry and Commerce. It is, perhaps, worth noticing that among the bodies which nominate to this Council, neither the Association of University Teachers nor the National Association of Schoolmasters is represented.

The Council is obliged by its constitution to meet at least twice each year and in fact it has often met more than twice. The secretary to the Council is a civil servant, and any statistics or additional information which may be needed are supplied by the ministry. The three standing committees of the Council make their own arrangements for meeting and secretarial duties are undertaken by civil servants. The fruits of their deliberations come before the Council through their minutes. The Council issues reports from time to time some of which are influential, for instance, the Report on 'Graduate Teachers of Mathematics and Science' of 1953 made seven suggestions for increasing the supply of teachers and some attempt was made to follow up each of these.[30]

I

The Secondary Schools Examinations Council was in one way rather more than an advisory committee for it acquired certain semi-administrative functions. When it was set up in 1917 various examining bodies were conducting examinations for secondary schools according to their own ideas and without co-ordination. The Board of Education aimed at bringing these to conform to a single pattern to be known as the School Certificate, but it could only proceed by persuasion, it had no power to compel the university examining bodies to conform. Thus there was an informal agreement that if the universities would co-operate, the Board would approve their examinations for normal school leaving purposes. In order to achieve these ends, to maintain adequate standards, to decide the form of certificates to be granted and to deal with any other matters arising out of these examinations the Board established the S.S.E.C. 'All matters falling within the functions of the Co-ordinating Authority stand referred to the Council, which conducts on the Board's behalf all ordinary business, correspondence and conferences connected with the co-ordination of examinations; but the Council are directed to consult the Board before committing themselves on questions of principle or policy which are controversial or specially important. . . . [The Council] reports to the Board and the Board's officers may attend its meetings and speak, but not vote. It has proved itself a most useful instrument of delegated administration.'[31]

The Council had a membership of twenty-one, ten of whom represented the University Examining Boards, six the teachers, and five the local authorities. In 1936 when the Board sought a change of policy to which the Examining Board nominees were believed to be opposed, it reconstituted the Council so that the University Boards had only a third of the seats, a third being given to the local authorities and a third to representatives of the teachers.[32] During the first twenty-years or so of its existence the Council was successful in co-ordinating the activities of the examining bodies.

A committee of the Secondary Schools Examinations Council under Sir Cyril Norwood reported in 1943, it recommended the abolition of the School Certificate and that there should be no external examinations before the age of eighteen. This began a period of crisis which lasted for about a decade during which Ministry policy was, in general terms, anti-external examinations. During this period the former S.S.E.C. was broken up and representation changed so that those immediately concerned with running the examinations—the

University Examining Boards—were excluded. The consequence of this was that the Ministry attempted to push through fundamental changes in the examinations being administered by the eight examining bodies while it had no machinery for consulting with them. Hence regulations were made which proved to be unworkable and had gradually to be withdrawn, usually after complaints to the remodelled S.S.E.C. from the teachers' associations.

After its reconstitution in 1946 the Secondary Schools Examinations Council had thirty-one members, of these five were nominated by the Ministry, eight by the local authority associations, eleven by teachers' organizations and seven by the Universities directly—no longer through their examining boards.[33] There can be no doubt that the exclusion of the examining bodies from the consultative machinery rankled strongly with those bodies themselves. This was recognized by the Chairman of the S.S.E.C. when he said in 1957 that 'I believe that we are only now coming near to a restoration of friendly relations between the examining bodies as a whole and the newly constituted Council, towards which they understandably felt no strong affection from the start'.[34]

Since 1946 there has been an arrangement whereby the Chairman of the S.S.E.C. might summon the Secretaries of the examining bodies if he so wished to discuss points of administrative detail, but it was ruled from the beginning that they were not to be consulted on matters of policy. It does seem to have been a weakness in these arrangements that the users and organizers of the examinations were no longer brought together at the national level. The history of the S.S.E.C. suggests that advisory bodies are at their best when they are dealing with matters about which there is little or no political controversy for this body gave of its best in the 1920s and 1930s; after secondary schools and their examinations came to be of greater interest to politicians, the Council's usefulness declined.

The Secretary of State for Education and Science has now abolished the S.S.E.C. as such and has transferred its functions to a newly-constituted Schools Council. From 1st October, 1964, this Council was 'to assist the Secretary of State to carry out his responsibility for the direction of policy and the general arrangements for secondary school examinations and to discharge on his behalf the functions of a central, co-ordinating authority'. The committees of the S.S.E.C were to continue to operate 'until the Schools Council is ready to make arrangements for their functions to be carried out within the framework of the Council's own organizations'. The Council has a field of reference stretching beyond examinations; it has taken over from the former Ministry Curriculum Study Group the duty of keeping curricula under review, it also may survey teaching methods and aspects of school organization so far as they affect the curriculum. In the spring of 1965 it had various study projects going forward under its aegis such as 'Primary French', '5–13 Mathematics and Science' and 'Project English'. At the time of writing it is much too soon to attempt any evaluation of the worth of the new arrangements in this area.

The advisory committee of the Department of Education which has probably had more publicity than any other is the Burnham Committee on teachers' salaries. Although this committee has advisory status it is practically a negotiating committee. When H. A. L. Fisher was President of the Board of Education he was impressed by the need to improve teachers' salaries on a national basis, and in 1918 he set up a Standing Joint Committee on Teachers' Salaries on which both teachers and local authorities were represented and they met under the chairmanship of Lord Burnham. The Committee's object was said to be to 'secure the orderly and progressive solution of the salary problem in Public Elementary Schools, by agreement, on a national basis',[35] and in November, 1919, it issued a unanimous report. In 1920 a Joint Committee was set up to deal with salaries in secondary schools and later in the same year yet another was established to deal with salaries in technical schools; Lord Burnham was also chairman of both these committees. The scales adopted by these various committees were not mandatory, but they were in fact adopted in the areas of virtually all the local authorities, and there were only very occasional refusals to accept the negotiated agreements between 1920 and 1944. If the position regarding teachers' salaries during the twenty years preceding 1920 is compared with that of the following twenty years, the full measure of the success of the Burnham advisory bodies becomes apparent.

Before the Second World War the Board of Education held that the 'settlement of the basis and details of the remuneration of teachers is primarily within the province of the local authorities, and should in the first instance be the subject of agreement between them and the teachers for whose employment they are responsible'.[36] The Education Act of 1944 might be said to have made a dent in that doctrine when it made the Burnham Committees part of the statutory machinery. The Act required the Minister to appoint one or more committees consisting of representatives of the authorities and of the teachers, it became the duty of such committees to submit their recommendations to the Minister who could make an order requiring that the remuneration of teachers should be in accordance with the report he had received or he might reject the report entirely.[37] The Minister was restricted in that he could only accept or reject a report as it stood, he could not modify it in issuing his order.

The Burnham Main Committee, which deals with the salaries of teachers in both primary and secondary schools under the 1944 arrangements,[38] has a chairman nominated by the Secretary of State and two joint honorary secretaries, one from the authorities' panel and the other from the teachers' panel. Until 1965 the authorities' panel was composed of nine representatives of the County Councils' Association, six of the Association of Municipal Corporations, six of the Association of Education Committees, three of the London County Council and two of the Welsh Joint Education Committee. The teachers' panel has sixteen representatives of the National Union of Teachers, four of the Association of Teachers in Technical Institutions, two of the Incorporated Association of Assistant Masters, two of the Assistant Mistresses Association, two of the National Association of Schoolmasters and one each of the Incorporated Association of Headmasters, the Incorporated Association of Headmistresses and the National Association of Head Teachers. There are three other smaller committees, those for technical schools and institutions, for farm institutes and for training colleges.[39] The four committees have the same chairman.

The work of these committees is in its nature spasmodic, when new recommendations need to be made—usually at intervals of two or three years—the committees meet often but they seldom meet in the periods between such negotiations. A great deal of the work of the Main Committee is carried on in separate meetings of the panels for until a panel has arrived at some sort of agreement within itself it is hardly in a position to state its case to the opposing panel. The Chairman has no vote, and in the case of complete disagreement between the panels unofficial arbitration has been resorted to in the past with the agreement of the Chairman and of both panels. Legally there was no provision for arbitration, thus the findings of the unofficial arbitrators could not be binding.

In the past the government did not take any direct part in the working of the Burnham Committees and, until 1963 had accepted their recommendations. In 1963 the Minister asked the Main Committee to make certain changes in its recommendations, the Committee refused to do so and the Minister, lacking any power to modify the report himself, rejected it. As the law stood, nothing could be done in this situation to adjust teachers' salaries to allow for the continuing fall in the value of money without a special Act of Parliament. Thus a special Act was passed giving the Minister power to issue orders fixing the salaries of teachers until 1st April, 1965, and using this power the Minister imposed his own scale of salaries against the wishes of the representatives of both the local authorities and the teachers. It was clear that the situation of the Burnham Committees would never be the same again. Even if their constitution were to remain unaltered, the precedent created by the Minister in rejecting their recommendations and legislating to enforce scales of salaries acceptable to neither employers nor employees brought about a new state of affairs.

The Minister was especially anxious to play a more direct part in the negotiating procedure at an early stage. After protracted discussions with the various parties concerned with Burnham, the Remuneration of Teachers Bill was introduced late in 1964. This has been enacted and the main changes it has made in the arrangements are two: in the first place the Secretary of State is to be represented on the management panels of the committees; secondly, in case of disagreement between the panels, there is provision for arbitration. Section 3 of the Act provides that the Secretary of State shall arrange arbitration if this proves to be necessary, and that he may ask the Minister of Labour to appoint the arbitrators. Under these arrangements, the Secretary of State is no longer able to reject the findings produced by the new machinery, the only way of preventing the findings from taking effect is for each House of Parliament to resolve 'that national economic circumstances require that effect should not be given to the recommendations'. Under Section 7 of the Act any order may be made with retrospective effect.

The new machinery operated for the first time in 1965. The two panels of the Burnham Main Committee disagreed and the Minister of Labour appointed three arbitrators. Their findings differed little from the final offer made by the employers' panel which had been rejected by the teachers.

The Burnham Committees might be regarded more strictly as negotiating than simply advisory, this is certainly true of their current position under the Remuneration of Teachers Act. Yet the rejection of the Burnham Report in 1963 and the events which have followed have served to draw attention once more to the real standing of advisory committees and their recommendations. If a group of specially qualified or chosen persons conduct an extensive inquiry into a problem and arrive at broadly agreed conclusions, it can well be argued that there should be a predisposition on the part of a minister to accept those findings. Constitutionally a minister carries responsibility for policy, and therefore he must himself decide his course of action. But in education, where even now, much still depends upon the goodwill of local authorities and teachers, the Secretary of State would do well frequently to seek and to heed the advice of those who actually run the schools and teach in them.

REFERENCES

[1] L. A. Selby-Bigge, *The Board of Education*, 1927, p. 19.

[2] P.R.O., Ed. 23/216F, Memorandum on the Office Organization by Morant, January, 1907.

[3] Ibid.

[4] P.R.O. Ed. 24/581, Davies to Morant, 14/2/07.

[5] Ibid., Morant to Davis, 6/3/07.

[6] P.R.O. Ed. 24/280, Morant to Masterman, 4/11/07.

[7] Board of Education, Annual Report for 1909–10 [Cd 5616] 1911, p. 40.

[8] P.R.O. Ed. 24/519.

[9] P.R.O. Ed. 23/216D, 'A Patronage Office', a paper on the recruitment of the higher grades by the Chief Clerk, 1910.

[10] P.R.O. Ed. 23/216F, Memorandum on the Office Organization by Morant, January, 1907.

[11] Ibid., Notes on Reorganization, by R. Wood, 29/8/18.

[12] P.R.O. Ed. 23/216C, Statement by E. B. Phipps, Chief Clerk, 11/9/08.

[13] Morant himself had been transferred from the Board of Education in 1911 after the indiscretions of the so-called Holmes circular, and had since devoted himself to building up the National Health Insurance organization.

[14] Report of the Machinery of Government Committee [Cd 9230] 1918, p. 52.

[15] P.R.O. Ed. 23/216E, Sir Edmund Phipps to the Secretary, 26/2/18.

[16] Ibid., L. A. Selby-Bigge, to H. A. L. Fisher, 11/10/18.

[17] 7 & 8 Geo 6, c 31, S 1.

[18] P.R.O. Ed 24/577, Confidential Memorandum on the Defaulting Authorities Bill, 25/6/04.

[19] Ibid.

[20] 4 Ed. 7, c 18.

[21] 7 & 8 Geo 6, c 31, S 99.

[22] Ibid., S 68.

[23] This meant the Minister of Education in relation to educational services.

[24] 6 & 7 Eliz. 2, c 55, S 3.

[25] Cmd 6492.

[26] Report of the Machinery of Government Committee [Cd 9230] 1918, p. 11.

[27] 7 & 8 Geo 6, c 31, S 4

[28] P.E.P., Advisory Committees in British Government, 1960, p. 22.

[29] Teachers and Youth Leaders, 1944, para. 160.

[30] A discussion on the effect of this Report appears in P.E.P., op. cit., pp. 188–192.

[31] Selby-Bigge, op. cit., pp. 209–10.

[32] R. Vernon and N. Mansergh (editors), *Advisory Bodies*, 1940, pp. 203–4, 'The control of the Council thus passed out of the hands of the University representatives,

with the result that in 1938 a majority recommended that a Board should award a certificate without requiring a pass in both the language and science groups. To this the Board agreed. . . .'

[33] Cmd 7426, p. 22.

[34] Lecture given by Sir John Wolfenden, Chairman of the S.S.E.C., entitled 'The S.S.E.C. and the Evolution of Policy on External Examinations' reprinted in External Examinations in Secondary Schools edited by G. B. Jeffery, 1958.

[35] Cmd 443.

[36] Selby-Bigge, op. cit., p. 265.

[37] 7 & 8 Geo 6, c 31, S 89.

[38] The reclassification of the schools for all children over the age of eleven as secondary led to the unification of the Elementary and Secondary Committees as the Burnham Main Committee after the Act of 1944.

[39] The recommendations of the Training Colleges Committee are not mandatory.

Chapter 7

SCHOOL BOARDS AND
SCHOOL ATTENDANCE COMMITTEES

THE first public local authorities for education were the school boards established under the Act of 1870. The Liberal Party had been returned to power in the election of 1868 with a large majority, and the new Vice-President was W. E. Forster, a Radical who had made a name for himself as an advocate of popular education. In order to spur the government on, the Education League was founded by such Radicals as Dixon and Chamberlain in 1869; its avowed aim was to secure the establishment of a system of free, compulsory and lay education. Elementary education was entirely in the hands of the 'volunteers' and they were manifestly failing just where the social need was most urgent, in the poorer quarters of the big cities. This failure was underlined by the report of an inquiry ordered by the House of Commons in March, 1869, into the education of the poorer classes in the cities of Birmingham, Leeds, Liverpool and Manchester.[1]

The inquirers—J. G. Fitch for Birmingham and Leeds and D. K. Fearon for Manchester and Liverpool—had considerable difficulty in obtaining reliable figures. The overall picture in Birmingham and Leeds was as given in this table:

	Population	Population from 3 to 13	Number in average attendance in	
			(a) inspected schools	(b) other schools
Birmingham .	360,846	83,125	16,053	10,783
Leeds . .	253,110	58,307	12,422	7,070
	613,956	141,432	28,475	17,853

Fitch commented: 'Thus it will be seen that the existing system of state aid administered through the agency of the religious bodies, reaches 28,475 out of 141,432, or 20 per cent of the total population' of the two towns. Using a different basis for his calculations, Fearon concluded that in Manchester there were 20,841 children who were not on the roll of any school in the city; in Liverpool he estimated that the total number of children requiring elementary schooling was about 90,000, but only 42,096 of these were on the rolls of inspected schools, and only some 32,000 were in actual attendance.[2] The poor quality of the education given in these cities was stressed by both inspectors who found that very few children passed beyond standards III or IV. The main hindrance to the development of primary education was said to lie in the difficulty of achieving any sort of regular attendance. The uniformity of the building grants offered by the Committee of Council led to difficulties in building schools in cities where sites were very expensive and Fitch put his finger on the fundamental weakness in relying on the voluntary approach when he wrote 'The parishes in which the richer people live are necessarily those in which there is least need for a primary school; and the districts in which the poor most abound are not unfrequently the districts in which the Church is most slenderly endowed and in which voluntary subscriptions are raised with the greatest difficulty'.[3]

In England and Wales as a whole there was accommodation for 1,765,944 children in grant-aided elementary schools on 31st August, 1869, but the average attendance over the year amounted only to 1,062,999.[4] Moreover the length of school life of those who attended the elementary schools tended to be short and the number of pupils in the three lower standards tended to be much greater than the number in the three higher standards. During the year 1869–70, 573,921 were presented for examination in Standards I to III, while only 191,663 were presented in Standards IV to VI.[5] Thus there was both an overall shortage of places, and even the existing supply of places was not being fully used.

It was against this background that Forster drew up a 'Memorandum of Suggestions for Consideration in Framing the Education Bill'.[6] He set out the aims of any legislation as

'(1) To cover the country with good schools;

(2) To get the parents to send their children to school'.

The present system 'being a mere partnership with educational volunteers, leaves undone all the work which the volunteers do not care to undertake . . .'. In creating a system to achieve his aims, Forster suggested three principles should be borne in mind:

'1. The least possible encouragement to parents to neglect their duty:

2. The least possible expenditure of public money:

3. The least possible injury to existing schools'.

Thus, as he told the House of Commons when introducing his Bill in February, 1870, 'Our object is to complete the present voluntary system, to fill up the gaps, sparing the public money where it can be done without . . .'.[7]

Since the object was defined as to create a system which would fill up the gaps left by voluntary local agencies, it would have been possible for the State to attempt to provide the places needed and to meet the expenses entirely from the Treasury. The Government of the day advanced two reasons for not attempting this solution, that it would give enormous power to the central administration and that it would be an extremely difficult undertaking in an administrative sense for a central office.[8] Thus a system of local educational administration was created to fill up the gaps and since this was its purpose it was only a partial system in that it was only established in those areas suffering from a shortage of school places.

An outline of the main features of the local administrative system for the next thirty years is set out in Forster's confidential memorandum of October, 1869.[9] He found the basis in the plan suggested earlier by Lowe. The country must be divided into educational districts and every district would be responsible to the central government for the education of its inhabitants. 'I cannot but think that all hope of success depends on this formation and responsibility of local districts, without which it is hard to see how a national system is possible.' Officials of the districts would furnish returns showing the local position and the Government would then be able to assess the amount of educational destitution in a locality and, where it was proved, 'notice could be given that if, within a certain time, the bad schools be not improved, or the new schools not erected, the district must raise the sum needed to supply the deficiency. Opportunity would thus be given to those who prefer the present management to keep it, and to those who dislike rates to do without them, but their preference and dislike would not be allowed to keep a district in destitution.'

On the question of what unit of population to take as the educational district, Forster proposed that the municipal borough was the obvious solution so far as the towns were concerned. In country areas a choice had to be made between unions and parishes. He felt the balance lay in favour of the parish 'as more simple, more in accordance with educational tradition, and less tainted with the idea of pauperism'. So far as the financial burden was concerned Forster wrote that 'An educational assessment on income-tax payers has been proposed, and this would be fairer (than rates) were it not that wage receivers escape the income tax, and therefore a highly paid artisan would not be rated for a school to which he sent his children while the struggling shopkeeper would have to pay whether he sent them or not. . . . When we resort to a compulsory provision, it would seem necessary to levy a rate, remembering that if we keep, as we might, the present proportion, the taxes would pay as much as the rates. But at present the parent generally pays one-third of the cost. Should he escape this third? Surely school fees should be the rule. The duty lies primarily with the parent. If he pays towards the schooling of his child, he will be more likely to see that he goes to school. . . .'

In the matter of attendance, Forster believed that direct compulsion would be necessary eventually. He thought it should be the duty of the local agency to enforce this through specially appointed officials who should first of all warn neglectful parents and then, if necessary, take them before the magistrates to be fined.

The Education Bill which was based on these ideas was finally enacted on 9th August, 1870.[10] The administrative provisions of this Act are of especial interest not only because they created the first local education authorities in this country, but also because they brought into existence the only local authorities to be established solely for educational purposes ever to be directly elected by the ratepayers. The Act provided that each voter should have the number of votes equal to the total membership of the school board and he could give them all to one candidate or distribute them among the candidates in any manner (S.29). This system of cumulative voting led to a great deal of controversy during the next thirty years, and it was the subject of inquiry for a Select Committee of the Commons in 1885.[11] The original Bill had proposed that school boards should be chosen by town councils in the boroughs and by the vestries in parishes. When the matter was discussed in Committee, Sir Charles Dilke proposed that the boards should be elected by ratepayers and this suggestion was only defeated by a majority of five. The government felt that this showed the strength of feeling in the House in favour of direct election so that when Lord Fredrick Cavendish brought forward his proposal for direct election by the cumulative vote a little later, the government accepted it. It was adopted by the House of Commons without a discussion, and was welcomed by the nonconformists and minority groups in general as a guarantee that they would be able to obtain representation for their views on local boards.

The Education Department was given a good deal of power in deciding controversies arising out of school board elections (S.33); it also decided initially the size of a board within the limits of five and fifteen members set by the Act (S.31). Once a board had been formed, it might itself make resolutions concerning the future size of its membership and submit them for approval to the Education Department. The school boards themselves were given authority to appoint such officials as they might think fit and to determine their salaries.

The procedure laid down by the Act to determine whether a school board was needed followed fairly closely that suggested by Forster in his memorandum. The Education Department was to obtain returns from boroughs and parishes throughout the country giving particulars of the elementary schools and of children requiring elementary education. These were to be checked by inspectors of returns appointed for the purpose and the Department was then to publish a notice of its decision as to the school accommodation for each district. A month was then allowed for representations from local ratepayers or school managers and a local inquiry could be held if necessary; after any inquiry or at the end of the month the Department issued another order to districts where accommodation was insufficient directing that the additional school places should be supplied. Six months were then to be allowed and if at the expiration of the period the necessary places had not been supplied or were not likely to be supplied by voluntary means then the 'Education Department shall cause a school board to be formed for the district . . . and shall send a requisition to the school board so formed requiring them to take proceedings forthwith for supplying the public school accommodation mentioned in the requisition, and the school board shall supply the same accordingly' (S.10). When the Bill was before the Commons a new section (12) was inserted which permitted the Department to take steps to form a school board on application by the council of a borough or by the electors of a district without going through the preliminaries of inquiry and returns. If a shortage of school accommodation developed later in an area where there had been sufficient in 1870 and where no school board had been established, the Education Department could at any time begin the procedure to bring a school board into existence and overcome the shortage.

The size of London and its existing forms of local government seemed to indicate a need for a different approach. The shortage of places in the metropolis was apparent and the Act provided for the immediate formation of the London School Board (S.37). The Education Department was given the duty of dividing the capital into electoral divisions and allocating the number of members to be elected by cumulative voting from each division to the central Board. The first election was to be held as soon as possible after the passing of the Act and subsequent elections were to take place triennially in November. The Act contained a special clause authorizing the payment of a salary to its chairman if the School Board for London so wished, but in fact no salary was ever paid even although the post made such demands on the energies of its holder that he could hardly undertake his duties except on a full-time basis. The powers of the Board were similar to other boards in supplying and maintaining schools.

As well as possessing a general power to provide, equip and maintain elementary schools, school boards were provided with a form of procedure which enabled them to purchase sites compulsorily; a provision which was particularly necessary in the more congested areas of the larger cities (S.20). The Act permitted boards to delegate to a body of at least three managers any of their powers of control and management of a school or group of schools; the only power which they could not delegate was that of raising money (S.15). School boards were able to remit the fees of children whose parents were considered to be too poor to pay and they could also pay the fees of poor pupils who attended voluntary schools within their area (Ss. 19, 25). The Bill in its original form gave boards the option of aiding voluntary schools out of the rates to meet deficiencies as an alternative to building schools themselves. This proposal was heartily attacked from both sides, the Radicals attacked it because they objected to any form of rate aid for denominational schools, while Churchmen feared prejudice in some school boards. On account of these objections, Gladstone withdrew this proposal.

The financial provisions in the Act (Ss. 53–62) appeared to be straightforward, but in fact finance became a fruitful source of friction both within many localities and between the localities on the one hand and the Local Government Board on the other. All the expenses of a board were to be paid out of a fund to be known as the school fund. School fees, grants from the Central Government, loans and any other reserves were to be carried to this fund and any deficiency was to be met from the rates, for this purpose school boards were enabled to issue precepts on the normal rating authority. It was thought that capital expenditure would normally be met by raising loans and the Bill authorized the raising of loans provided that they were repaid over a thirty-year period; this was extended to fifty years when the Bill was before the Commons. The Public Works Loan Commissioners were authorized to advance loans to boards on the recommendation of the Education Department. Accounts were to be made up half-yearly and audited by the district auditor appointed by the Poor Law Board—soon to be replaced by the Local Government Board—who had the power to surcharge members of a school board with any expenditure which he considered improper.

In his memorandum, Forster had suggested that compulsory attendance was bound to come, and the first step towards it was contained in the Act for it permitted—but did not compel—school boards to make bye-laws requiring the attendance of children at elementary schools between the ages of five and thirteen. Many of the bigger boards were quick to make use of this authority, but it was to be more than a decade before compulsory attendance became universal.

The Education Department acted rapidly and within seven days of the new Bill becoming law sent out a circular to local authorities calling for the educational returns specified by the Act. Supplies of two forms were distributed, a general return to be completed by the local council and a return to be completed by each school and forwarded to the council which was to send the general and the school returns together to the Education Department. The forms for the greater part of the country had been returned by the beginning of 1871 so that early in the year the Department was able to begin the process of deciding which districts were lacking in accommodation. Many places did not wish to wait while these inquiries were undertaken, and the Department seems to have been surprised by the number of applications which it received under Section 12 of the Act from town councils for the immediate creation of school boards. Consequently regulations had to be drawn up at an early stage for the election of boards. Most of the bigger municipal boroughs requested that steps be taken to form a board and by 21st June, 1871, orders for the election of school boards had been issued for 96 boroughs with a population of 4,379,487 as well as 188 civic parishes with a population of 896,257.[12] Birmingham, Liverpool, Leeds and Manchester were among the boroughs to request boards under Section 12. Once boards were elected, they set about ascertaining as accurately as possible the need for school places in the different divisions of their districts. In Sheffield, for instance, the new board met for the first time on 15th December, 1870, and soon after it set up a Statistical Enquiry Committee to undertake this duty.

The Education Department laid down a scale by which the number of members to be elected for a board was governed by the size of the population,[13] viz.:

(a) boards of districts with a population of fewer than				5,000 had 5 members
(b)	„	„	„	„	15,000 „ 7	„
(c)	„	„	„	„	40,000 „ 9	„
(d)	„	„	„	„	70,000 „ 11	„
(e)	„	„	„	„	100,000 „ 13	„
(f)	„	„	„	over	100,000 „ 15	„

In the first set of General Regulations which the Department issued to govern school board elections, individual electors were required to sign their voting papers and to give the address of the property for which they were rated. The passing of the Ballot Act in 1872 led to a new set of Regulations for elections from the Department in order to apply the ballot to future school board elections throughout the country with the exception of elections for the London School Board where elections had been by ballot from the beginning.

Since the Education Act provided for the establishment of the London School Board without inquiry it was possible to make arrangements for the first election to be held as early as November, 1870. The election is of some interest as it was the first to be held in this country by ballot and the first in which the system of cumulative voting was employed. There were 135 candidates for 49 seats and, as in so many of the early school board elections, the vital issue appeared to be that of religious instruction in the schools. The candidates' addresses contained little in the way of definite policies apart from the religious issue. The first meeting of the new board was held on 15th December at the Guildhall at the invitation of the City Corporation. As in other great cities, the first task that confronted the London School Board was to try to obtain some fairly accurate assessment of the number of school places needed in the various divisions of its area. Early in January, 1871, the Board appointed a Committee on Returns to try to prepare the necessary statistics. The Committee was too ambitious, it attempted an actual enumeration of the children of school age instead of using the Education Departments' method of estimating that one-sixth of the total population would need school places; the consequence was that the figure obtained proved greatly to underestimate the need in the long run.[14]

Probably the most rapid progress in creating the new administrative machinery outside of London was in the bigger cities. Developments in Sheffield were fairly typical. Here the forthcoming creation of a board stirred great interest and no fewer than ninety-five candidates were nominated for the fifteen seats although there were a number of withdrawals, and only fifty-two candidates actually went to the poll. The board consisted of ten nonconformists, four members of the Church of England and a Roman Catholic. At its first meeting, the board appointed a local banker as its treasurer, formed a sub-committee to seek suitable premises for an office and decided to advertise for a suitable person to act as its Clerk. In January the board met to select a Clerk from a short list of three, a schoolmaster, a clergyman, and a local newspaper reporter. The reporter was appointed at a salary of £300 per annum and held office throughout the thirty-three years of the board's existence, and became the first Chief Education Officer under the Education Committee created by the Act of 1902. The greater part of the efforts of the board and its servants during the first months of its existence was directed towards ascertaining as accurately as possible the extent of school provision required in the various divisions of the city. In March four standing committees were appointed, each consisting of the Chairman and Vice-Chairman of the board along with five other members; the committees were

(a) General Purposes

(b) Finance

(c) Sites and Buildings

(d) Education and School Management.

Thus, by the spring of 1871 something recognizable as a local education authority had been created in Sheffield.[15]

The administrative machinery for actually managing schools among the larger school boards was of two kinds. Probably the majority of boards managed their schools directly from the central office and delegated no powers to local bodies of managers. There were no local managers in Birmingham, Manchester, Leeds, Bradford or Hull. On the other hand both London and Liverpool relied largely on local managers for the day-to-day management of their schools. In Liverpool, the entire duty of management was remitted to local bodies by the board; the members of these bodies were nominated by the school board in the first place, but as vacancies occurred these were filled up by managers co-opting local people. The system was said to be very

K

successful in attracting the support of influential citizens to the board schools and in 1885 the chairmen of local managing bodies included eight merchants, six ministers of religion, two clothiers, two medical men, a county court judge and a journalist. The board's inspector attended local managers' meetings as technical adviser and thus maintained the necessary liaison between managers and board.[16]

London School Board first had to decide its policy on this issue when schools began to be transferred to it which already had managers, it decided that each such school should have eight managers, four of whom were to be nominated by the outgoing body, one was to be a member of the school board and three were to be nominated by the divisional members of the board. In the case of new schools built by the board, all eight managers were to be recommended by divisional members. As the number of schools increased, so it became necessary later on to arrange for the grouping of schools under one body. An honorary correspondent was appointed by each committee of managers to keep in touch with the school board; here, also, the increase in the amount of work made it necessary eventually for the board to appoint a paid official in each division with an office and a staff to act as correspondent to all bodies of managers in the division. By the end of the century most schools were grouped for management purposes, where two schools were grouped together there were twelve managers and where three schools formed a group there was a committee of fifteen.

The duties of managers were very varied, according to Article 44 of the Board's regulations 'It is the duty of managers to foster the schools under their care by every means in their power, to see that the rules laid down for the guidance of teachers are adhered to, to smooth down the difficulties of teachers by constant encouragement and sympathy, to have at heart the mental, moral and physical welfare of the scholars, and to see that they are brought up in habits of punctuality, of good manners and language, of cleanliness and neatness, and also that the teachers impress upon the children the importance of cheerful obedience to duty, of consideration and respect for others, and of honour and truthfulness in word and act'.[17] This involved in fact making an annual report on the work of the school and being present when H.M.I.s were visiting; investigating complaints against teachers made by parents (complaints from some parents were often numerous); checking registers and log books from time to time; selecting and appointing assistant teachers. The appointment of head teachers was undertaken by the managers alone until 1889 when the system was changed because there seemed to be a tendency for managers to appoint heads from within the school, so then the Board took over the appointment of head teachers. In 1892 the system was again changed and a sub-committee of the school management committee selected three candidates for each post from among whom the managers made an appointment.[18]

The Royal Commission on Elementary Education strongly favoured the appointment of local managers for their schools by the larger boards. The Commission argued that if school is a place for the formation of character as well as intelligence then frequent visits by, and personal contact with the managers were essential. 'In our opinion it would be very advantageous if school boards, and especially the larger boards, were in the supervision of their schools, always to associate themselves with local managers.'[19]

One of the matters which engaged the attention of the new boards at an early stage was that of compulsory attendance. Liverpool was one of the first boards to adopt bye-laws requiring attendance under Section 74 of the Act, these received the approval of the Education Department on 26th June, 1871. These bye-laws compelled parents of children aged from five to thirteen to see that their children attended school regularly except that children over the age of ten who had reached standard five could be totally exempted from attendance, while those over the age of ten who had reached standard four were only obliged to attend for fifteen hours each week.[20] Similar bye-laws were adopted by most of the bigger school boards although many of the small rural boards showed a marked reluctance to take action. But even if all the school boards in the country had been enthusiastic and had exercised their powers fully this would not by any means have solved the problem of school attendance since in those districts where there was no shortage of voluntary school places there was no authority that could make bye-laws requiring attendance. By 1876 about 50 per cent of the population were living in areas with bye-laws. In that year an Elementary Education Act[21]—known as Lord Sandon's Act—was passed with the aim of spreading compulsory attendance. Employers were forbidden to employ children under ten, while those who were ten but were under fourteen could only be employed if they had attained a certain standard or could prove a certain number of attendances. The Act was to be enforced by the school boards, and where there were no boards, school attendance committees were to be set up with the duty of enforcement. School attendance committees were to be appointed annually by the councils of boroughs and by the Boards of Guardians of the Unions for each parish, while urban sanitary authorities within a Union might be authorized to set up their own in the same manner as boroughs if their population exceeded 5,000; the committees were to have at least six and not more than twelve members.

The Act of 1876 conferred on the new committees the same powers of making bye-laws for compulsory attendance as the school boards already possessed. Thus while the possibility of applying direct compulsion was extended to every district in the country, the government had still not gone so far as to bring in a system of universal direct compulsion. The Education Department was given authority to declare school attendance committees in default and to appoint a person to do their work for up to two years, charging the expenses of the substitute to the Council or Board of Guardians that elected the defaulting committee. School attendance committees were entirely dependent on the bodies appointing them for finance, they had no authority to raise a rate; this weakened their position considerably.

In 1877 the Education Department issued Revised Regulations for Certificates of Age, School Attendance and Proficiency[22] to enable both employers and those charged with enforcing the new law to determine whether or not a child was qualified to leave school and take employment. Certificates of age were to be obtained from the local registrar, of school attendance from the principal teacher of the school, and those of proficiency from Her Majesty's Inspector after he had completed his annual inspection. A 'Child's School Book' was recommended which combined all of these; it was said that it would 'serve as a pass to work, which may be shown to any person who may wish to take the child into his employment'.

The passing of the Act of 1876 and the creation of the new attendance committees did not settle the question of enforcing attendance although by 1880 about 73 per cent of the population was covered by bye-laws. In some areas, especially in the countryside, members of the committees showed a great lack of enthusiasm about school attendance and in 1880 Mundella's Act[23] finally dealt with the laggards by requiring all school boards and attendance committees which had not done so to pass bye-laws forthwith. This at least secured that children under the age of ten should attend school, but beyond that age the conditions for exemption continued to vary greatly from place to place.

The greatest amount of laxity in enforcing attendance even after it had become compulsory was in the rural areas and especially in the more remote. In July, 1881, the position in the Western part of Cornwall was such that the Education Department felt obliged to issue a special circular[24] addressed to local authorities in that area. This complained that the law was being very inefficiently administered, that the attendance of those children on school registers was very irregular, and that if all those who should have been on the registers were in fact inscribed there would not have been sufficient places. The Secretary concluded the circular 'I am directed to point out . . . that the Elementary Education Acts give the Department the power to declare in default any local authority that persistently neglects its duty and to appoint other persons to perform the duty, allocating such persons, if necessary, a remuneration out of the rates'.

In 1885 Cumin, then Secretary to the Education Department, told the Commons Select Committee on School Board Elections that '. . . from my experience I should not say that school attendance committees were so effective in enforcing the bye-laws as school boards'.[25] But three years later the Cross Commission found that the committees had administered 'the law of compulsion at least as well as rural school boards'.[26] The Commission felt that local authorities ought to render a more detailed account of their work in matters concerning attendance to the Education Department. It suggested that there should be regular returns of such statistics as the number of attendance officers employed, of meetings held, of parents interviewed, of summonses taken out and of convictions obtained. But machinery which consisted largely of local committees could only proceed at the pace permitted by local public opinion, and a couple of sentences from Cumin's evidence to the Commission were, perhaps, a fair indication of the state of the opinion of influential persons in some areas. '. . . although the school attendance committees and the boards may do all they can, of course it depends a good deal upon the magistrates, whether they will support the school attendance committees and the school boards; and I am bound to say that there are cases where, although the school attendance committee are very anxious to do their duty, and the school boards, too, they undoubtedly are rather hindered in their action by the magistrates. There is ample power in the Department to compel the school boards and the school attendance committees to do their duty, but there is no power in the Act of Parliament to compel the magistrates to do theirs.'[27]

Throughout the period of their existence school boards remained centres of controversy, supporters of voluntary schools carried on their bitter opposition to them, and fought for control of individual boards in each election, supporters of the boards sought to extend them to cover the whole country, the bigger boards were impelled by force of circumstances to extend the facilities they offered towards the field of secondary and technical education, thereby clashing after 1890 with the technical education committees and the county and county borough councils that appointed them, finally the steady increase in the school board precepts on the rating authority frequently led to local ill-feeling and jealousy.

It is against this background that complaints against the electoral system for boards should be considered. The complaints often centred on the effects of the cumulative vote and the expense of elections. There were two inquiries which produced a good deal of evidence concerning the electoral system, the first was that of the Select Committee of the Commons on School Board Elections in 1885, the second was that made by the Cross Commission in the course of its inquest concerning the whole field of elementary education. Sir Francis Sandford, who was Permanent Secretary to the Education Department from 1870 to 1884 and his successor, Patrick Cumin, both gave evidence to the Select Committee in favour of cumulative voting—as did W. E. Forster. This system whereby each elector could distribute as many votes as there were members of the board in the way he chose certainly ensured representation for minorities. In the first election in Sheffield, for example, the only Roman Catholic member came at the top of the poll with 17,057 votes, 13,485 of these were the result of 'plumping'—they represented the full fifteen votesthat an indiv idual elector might cast, and the *Sheffield Daily Telegraph* reported on 12 November, 1870, that the Roman Catholics of the borough had been instructed to give all their votes to the only candidate of their faith. The Roman Catholics of Sheffield continued to retain one member throughout the life of the school board, the first member, Ellison, retired in 1881, and was replaced by a priest who sat until 1899 when his place was taken by another priest.[28]

Both of the senior officials who had been connected with the working of the Act of 1870 felt that questions of compulsory attendance, and of school supply—the two main duties of the boards—would have been much more intractable without minority representation. In his evidence to the Select Committee, Sandford stated that the cumulative vote had made differences between the religious bodies much easier to overcome and pointed out how their representatives on the boards had been able to come together and agree on the need for the introduction of local bye-laws enforcing attendance. He believed that the various parties having been brought together in the school boards learned to work for the common good; many Roman Catholics who had been hostile to the school boards had become enthusiastic workers for them once they had attained membership, this had been especially noticeable at Liverpool. Sandford said that he had never heard of any prevailing wish among the constituents of school boards to get rid of the cumulative vote clause; the order of return by votes corresponded closely to what would have been the order of return by voters in most cases, the only exceptions to this were in some of the large boards when there were sometimes an exceptionally large number of candidates.[29] Apart from compulsion, on the other great duty of the boards—supply of places—Sandford said, 'It is certainly a great thing for the Department that questions relating to the situations in which board schools are to be erected, should be fought out as they are on the school boards, and not that the school board having settled on some abstract principle, as to the number of schools required, every decision of theirs with respect to the erection of individual schools should be made the subject of an appeal to the central office. They fight it out at the board and settle it, and they generally come to some compromise. We have had, as of course you know, and Mr. Forster knows, cases in which the decisions of the school boards have been challenged, and brought by the minority or by the inhabitants to the Department; we should have been overwhelmed by that work, I think, if the denominations had not been largely represented on the school board.'

Cumin, in his evidence, also dwelt on the practical value of a system of election which resulted in representation for minorities. He believed that if boards had been elected by single member constituencies they would probably have passed bye-laws, but they would not have succeeded in enforcing them on those minorities excluded from representation. 'If you took away the security which the minority, whether rightly or wrongly, consider that they now possess, you would raise up opposition to the enforcement of the bye-laws by a board elected simply by a majority.'[30] Apart from the question of cumulative voting, Cumin also expressed an interesting view on the direct election of local education authorities—something which official opinion in this country has been opposed to throughout the present century. '. . . there are many persons fond of education, and who take a great interest in it, who would be elected on the school board by the electors, and who would not probably or possibly be elected by the town council, and school boards having, besides compulsion, many other duties, I think that representatives elected directly by the parents for educational purposes are very superior to any committee appointed by the town council.'[31]

The difficulties which arose under the system of cumulative voting seem to have been due often to mis-calculations on the part of denominational or party managers concerning their likely voting strength. The best-known instance of this is, perhaps, the Birmingham election of 1870 where fifteen members were to be elected. Birmingham was the city of Chamberlain, Dixon and the Radical Education League. The Liberals nominated fifteen candidates for the school board election and were confident of winning a majority; the Tories, who might have expected to be a minority, realized the use that could be made of the cumulative system, nominated only eight candidates and urged their supporters to share all their fifteen votes among these eight. The Roman Catholics put forward one candidate. The outcome of the election was that the new board consisted of one Roman Catholic, eight Tories and six Liberals, thus thanks to their superior tactics, the minority had won control.

Occasionally one very popular candidate might receive five or six times as many votes as were necessary to secure his election to a board, and a complaint of 'wasted' votes (as they were called) was put forward as a criticism of the system. In their recommendations, the members of the Cross Commission suggested that cumulative voting should be replaced by the single transferable vote for they believed that this would preserve proportional representation and yet eliminate anomalies and wasted votes.[32]

Another fertile source of complaint about school board elections especially in earlier years was their expense. The actual expense to be met by candidates in attempting to secure their election naturally varied according to the size of the district. In small rural districts it was usually nothing, in London the Cross Commission estimated the expense of being a candidate at about £700, while in a large provincial city, such as Leeds, £60 would have been a usual sum to have to find.[33] The expenses to be met from public funds for organizing elections was initially so high that steps had to be taken by the government to control the situation. Many public authorities were as surprised as Sheffield's

Finance Committee when they received from their town clerk his account for conducting the first election. The total cost to the rates of the election in Sheffield was £732 10s. 3d., the return included one item of £150 which appeared to be a fee to the town clerk for the bother of running an election. A deputation from the Finance Committee visited the town clerk to ask for an explanation of the £150, the members of the deputation reported later that they 'had been unable to obtain from him any explanation'.[34]

It was against a background of circumstances such as these that the government decided to take power to control election expenses in the Elementary Education Act of 1873.[35] This Act authorized the Education Department to specify the duties, remuneration and so forth of election officials, and this had the effect of reducing the expenses to some extent. The complaints, however, continued and the Department did not find it an easy task to control these expenses as closely as it would have liked. In 1886, as a result of a further bout of complaints, it issued a circular laying down a scale of maximum charges and fees which officials might make.[36] The personal fee for the returning officer was to be £5 5s. for an uncontested election, £10 10s. for a contested election if there was only one polling station in use or, if more than one, not more than £5 5s. per polling station after the first, and in any case not more than a total of £105. In an effort to prevent returning officers multiplying their fees by multiplying polling stations, in boroughs there was not to be more than one station in each ward, while in parishes there was not to be more than one per 1,000 inhabitants. The fees for presiding officers, clerks, counters, etc., were prescribed in detail and the counting of votes after 9 p.m. at special rates of pay was forbidden.

As we have seen[37] the original proposal to permit school boards to aid voluntary schools from the rates met with such a hostile reception that it was withdrawn by Gladstone, but Section 25 of the Act of 1870 gave boards not only the power to remit the fees from indigent parents in their own schools, but also to pay such fees in voluntary schools. In the earlier years of their existence this power led to a stormy passage for a number of school boards. If the Liberal-Nonconformist faction was in control and refused to pay such fees for children in voluntary schools, the Church faction was aggrieved and campaigned against the board's policy; if the Church faction was in control and paid the fees, then their opponents felt that they were being forced to support Church schools when they paid their rates. In the early years when there were few board schools most of the money made available under Section 25 must of necessity have gone to the denominational schools. This was the situation in Manchester where the board paid the fees of necessitous children for a number of years before it actually opened any schools of its own. In Birmingham where the Church Party managed to gain control of the school board, the town council was firmly under the control of the Liberals, and refused initially to honour a school board precept that made provision for the payment of fees in voluntary schools; however, the precept had eventually to be accepted. The acrimony surrounding this issue was such that the Education Act of 1876 imposed on Guardians of the Poor the duty of paying the fees of indigent parents who were not actually paupers, and left the school boards to remit such fees in their own schools if they felt so inclined. In 1877 the Local Government Board issued a General Order authorizing the appointment of special relief committees by Boards of Guardians to deal with applications for the payment of school fees.[38] A later order authorized the Guardians to pay such fees by way of a loan to the parents: the offering of relief by loan rather than by grant wherever possible had been a standard recommendation of the Poor Law Board for many years since the Board believed that this encouraged a greater sense of responsibility among the poor.

Section 18 of the Act of 1870 provided another fertile source of criticism and controversy throughout the period of the existence of school boards and played its part in leading to the supercession of the boards by all purpose local authorities as Professor Eaglesham has shown.[39] According to this Section, it was the duty of the school board 'from time to time to provide such additional school accommodation as is, in their opinion, necessary in order to supply a sufficient amount of public school accommodation for their district'. In this way the school boards were made judges in their own case whenever they came into dispute with the denominations as to who should provide any additional school places that were necessary. At a time when the population was growing fairly rapidly there was bound to be frequently a need to increase the school provision of many districts; under this Section it was soon clear that the school boards had a prior right to provide all the extra accommodation needed, and that any additional accommodation provided by the denominations could only be by grace of the local school board. The Cross Commission found that the Education Department was very reluctant to interfere in such questions and let the localities fight out these battles for themselves so far as possible. If it had to intervene it was only able to do so by threatening to refuse to pay grants to schools which it deemed to be unnecessary.

The most widely publicized clash between a school board and Church authorities over the right to provide a new school arose in the case of the Dan-y-Graig school at Swansea. From 1880 to 1883 there had existed a board school but no Catholic school in a district containing ninety Catholic children, fifty-five of whom were compelled to attend the board school under the local bye-laws. The Catholic Church set about building a school at the end of 1883, and wrote to the Education Department seeking its recognition at the beginning of the next year. The Department examined the detailed plans for a school with 195 places, and wrote to Swansea School Board in February asking the Board whether it acquiesced in the provision of a school by the Church authorities, or whether it intended to exercise its prior right to supply the accommodation. The Board promptly took steps to enlarge its existing school, submitted plans for this purpose in June, and eventually answered the Education Department's letter of February in October, stating that it was taking steps to meet the deficiency in the supply of places itself. Consequently the Education Department felt obliged to refuse any grant to the Church school which was found by the local H.M.I. to be efficient, and which had 184 pupils by the end of 1884. Although the Department twice wrote to the Board in 1885 asking it if it would change its attitude, the majority of members refused to do so since they objected to public money going to denominational schools. Cumin was examined in detail on this case by Cardinal Manning before the Cross Commission, and he made it clear that the Department felt itself powerless to over-rule a school board in such circumstances.[40]

In some districts school boards seemed to site their schools in such a way as to deliberately incite children attending Church schools to attend the new school and then to claim that the accommodation offered by the Church school could not be described as 'suitable' because the parents clearly wanted undenominational instruction for their children. In these circumstances the denominationalists in a district could only really feel safe if they themselves managed to get a majority of their party on the school board, consequently the issue of denominational versus unsectarian education tended to be fought again and again at every school board election. The supporters of Church schools could never really be expected to view the school boards simply as agents with the duty of supplementing their own efforts when they found them armed with such powers as Section 18 conferred; these were obviously secular rivals, seeking to undermine the Church's position in education. Thus the school boards could never really be accepted by that considerable section of the population which still believed in denominational education.

The financial arrangements laid down in the Education Act of 1870 were both the source of strength and of the eventual downfall of the school boards. They were a source of strength in that the boards enjoyed unlimited access to the rates; they led in a sense to the downfall of the boards because of a lack of definition of the purposes for which boards might spend their money which led in its turn to the Cockerton judgment. Moreover, the unlimited access to the rates itself attracted the hostility both of some town councils which had the task of actually levying a rate over the spending of which they had no control, and of the denominationalists who found in the board schools with their resources pace-setters completely outclassing the voluntary schools dependent upon gifts and endowments.

The principles of school board finance were apparently straight-forward. 'The expenses of the school board under this Act shall be paid out of a fund called the school fund. There shall be carried to the school fund all moneys received as fees from scholars, or out of moneys provided by Parliament, or raised by way of loan, or in any manner whatsoever received by the school board, and any deficiency shall be raised by the school board as provided by this Act.

'Any sum required to meet any deficiency in the school fund . . . shall be paid by the rating authority out of the local rate.

'The school board may serve their precept on the rating authority, requiring such authority to pay the amount specified therein to the treasurer of the school board out of the local rate. . . .'[41]

When he introduced the Education Bill into the House of Commons, Forster said that the financial proposals would keep the existing proportions so far as school costs were concerned for about one-third would still be raised from parents in fees, about one-third would come from the Treasury, and the final third from local funds. 'Where local funds are not raised by voluntary subscriptions the rates will come into action.'[42] Since all moneys received had to pass through its school fund, a board would be able to assess its necessary call on the rates simply and accurately and the checking of finances by the auditors would be straightforward. Initially the position was fairly simple since the 'moneys provided by Parliament' really only amounted to the grant for elementary schools administered on the system of payment by results by the Education Department, but by the 1890s the position had become much more complicated in the case of the larger boards which had come to run various unusual types of elementary schools in answer to local demand. In the 1890s the main government grants which the London School Board received numbered six; the Education Department grant for elementary day schools, the fee grant (from 1891 to replace fees), Science and Art Department grants, Home Office grant for industrial schools, grants for schools for blind, deaf and defective children, and grants for evening continuation work.[43] The simple but rather vague phrase 'moneys provided by Parliament' in the Act of 1870 meant that the school fund could legitimately receive grants in respect of forms of education which the Parliamentarians of 1870 would probably not have regarded as elementary.[44]

By the last decade of the nineteenth century Forster's apportionment of the burden of school costs had been left a long way behind. When fees were abolished in 1891 the government paid a grant to replace them of ten shillings per pupil per year in average attendance. This was welcomed by many of the school boards, for they had often been receiving less than this by way of fees—the fee income per child in average attendance in London Board Schools was only seven shillings in 1890—but the voluntary schools usually charged higher fees and relied more heavily on them. Presumably on Forster's reckoning, after the abolition of fees the Government grants should have amounted to two-thirds of the total cost of running elementary schools with one-third coming from the locality. The position was very different in fact. The total income of board schools in England (excluding loans for Capital works) for the year to 29th September, 1898, amounted to £8,152,744; 40·6 per cent of this came from Government grants, 1·0 per cent from the sale of books and evening class fees, 1·8 per cent from other sources, and no less than 56·6 per cent from local rates.[45] With higher standards of teaching and of equipment the cost of elementary education had increased much more rapidly than had Government grants, in the case of the board schools the rates had been used to bear an ever-increasing burden.[46] The denominational schools, trying to manage on Government grants and such gifts as they could attract, were in an increasingly desperate plight in the years immediately before 1902 and the bitterness of their supporters at the privileged position of the board schools increased accordingly. In this connection it might be noted that 960 Church of England Schools had been transferred to school boards by 1899—presumably in most cases for financial reasons.[47]

Capital expenditure was nearly always met by raising loans repayable over a period of fifty years. School boards could only borrow after obtaining the agreement of the Education Department. If a board was seeking to borrow money on the open market, only formal consent was needed and the Department normally gave this at once. If a board wished to borrow from the Public Works Loans Board

Table to show total sums sanctioned for loans to school boards in England and Wales by the Education Department from the passing of the Education Acts in 1870 to 1899.[50]

For period or year ending	Total sanctioned, £
31st May, 1872	353,726
,, 1873	950,344
,, 1874	1,460,264
,, 1875	1,246,984
31st March, 1876	1,660,324
,, 1877	1,004,924
,, 1878	1,661,552
,, 1879	1,179,419
,, 1880	1,067,433
,, 1881	1,082,381
,, 1882	1,086,583
,, 1883	949,758
,, 1884	1,316,801
,, 1885	1,325,637
,, 1886	1,096,859
,, 1887	732,155
,, 1888	724,160
,, 1889	779,558
,, 1890	818,594
,, 1891	1,033,905
,, 1892	1,343,301
,, 1893	1,315,365
,, 1894	1,939,318
,, 1895	2,530,797
,, 1896	2,213,436
,, 1897	1,636,922
,, 1898	1,680,732
,, 1899	2,065,728

as permitted by the Act of 1870, then a recommendation was needed from the Education Department, mere consent was not enough. In order to obtain such a recommendation a school board had to prove a general deficiency of school supply in the district in which it was proposing to build a new school, the size and cost of the site, plans, specifications and cost of the premises all had to be calculated and submitted to the Department.[48] Initially school boards were able to borrow from the Public Works Loans Board at the favourable fixed rate of $3\frac{1}{2}$ per cent per annum, but from 1879 the Board began to vary the rates at which it offered money, and some school boards found that they could borrow more cheaply elsewhere. In 1881, for instance, Sheffield School Board raised the loan finance it then required from Leeds Savings Bank at $\frac{1}{4}$ per cent per annum below the rate the Public Works Loans Board was asking—4 per cent instead of $4\frac{1}{4}$ per cent— the saving to the ratepayers of Sheffield amounting to £1,150 over the period of the loan.[49]

School boards were obliged to keep their accounts in a manner prescribed in detail by the Education Department and Local Government Board. The books had to be made up and balanced for audit twice yearly, on 25th March and 29th September. It was the duty of the Local Government auditor to disallow any item of expenditure which was not clearly permitted by Act of Parliament, and to surcharge any person who had authorized such a payment.[51] The auditors were given very little discretion in the discharge of their duties, the whole aim was to make the audit rigid and inflexible so as to ensure that any dishonesty or shady dealing on the part of local authorities should not escape retribution. Any school board officer or member who was surcharged could always challenge the action of the auditor in the courts, but this course was expensive and usually less satisfactory than an appeal to the Local Government Board which had the power to remit the surcharge even where it continued to uphold the auditor's decision as to the illegality of a payment. There were a large number of surcharges and disallowances each year, most of them arising out of inadvertence, not from dishonesty; one consequence of excessive rigidity at the audit and the subsequent frequency of disallowances was that they came almost to be accepted as a normal feature of the school board scene. From time to time auditors challenged expenditure on the grounds that it was for some form of education that could not be described as 'elementary'; since this term had not been defined by Parliament, there was always some difficulty in interpreting it. It was out of such a challenge that the Cockerton Case of 1901 arose which provided the enemies of the school boards with the opportunity for which they had been seeking to overthrow the whole system established in 1870.

The weakest administrative organism created by the Act of 1870 was certainly the small rural school board. In villages where enthusiasm for education was so lacking that no voluntary school had been established, the local ratepayers found themselves reluctantly obliged to elect a board and take steps to provide a school. In some villages it was difficult to find five people in any way suitable to sit on a school board. The Education Department's analysis of the size of districts under school boards showed that in 1890, about a quarter of school boards were in districts with a population of less than 500 while about half of the boards served districts with populations of less than 1,000.[52] Such boards had the same legal powers and duties as those established for cities with half a million inhabitants. The grouping of small rural boards was urged on the Cross Commission, but while the Commission described them as 'notoriously weak as education authorities' it made no recommendation for action in view of the then existing uncertainty as to the future of county government.[53]

Yet whatever the weakness of the school boards and however bitter the hostility that their existence aroused, there can be no doubt as to the magnitude of the achievement of these first local elementary education authorities. They built and maintained schools in areas where others were either unable or unwilling to do so, and they made universal elementary education possible in this country. The larger school boards did a good deal to raise standards of teaching and their schools became pace-setters for the elementary schools of the country generally. The salaries and conditions of employment they offered to teachers compared very favourably with those offered by the impoverished voluntary schools which repeatedly found themselves obliged to improve salaries and conditions in order to keep their staffs. That the smaller school boards were very weak, that the boards only covered part of the country and that for various reasons they were centres of acute political and religious controversy all helped to make a review of local educational organization necessary towards the end of the nineteenth century, but these factors should not obscure the great deal of good that there was in the school board system.

REFERENCES

[1] Return-Schools for Poorer Classes in Birmingham, Leeds, Liverpool and Manchester, 1870.

[2] Ibid., pp. 111, 150, 164.

[3] Ibid., p. 78.

[4] Report of Committee of Council for 1870–71, p. ix.

[5] Ibid., p. xi.

[6] P.R.O., Ed. 24/2, 21/10/69.

[7] Hansard, LXCIX, 3rd series, 17/2/70.

[8] Ibid.

[9] P.R.O., Ed. 24/2, 21/10/69.

[10] 33 & 34 Vict., c. 75.

[11] Select Committee on School Board Elections (Voting) 1885. The controversy is discussed below, pp. 225–7.

[12] Report of Committee of Council for 1870–71, p. xvi.

[13] Select Committee on School Board Elections (Voting) 1885, Q 521. Evidence of P. Cumin.

[14] T. A. Spalding, The Work of the London School Board, 1900, p. 40.

[15] J. H. Bingham, The Period of the Sheffield School Board, 1949, pp. 1–10.

[16] Cross Cssn., Final Report, 1888, p. 68.

[17] Quoted in Spalding, op. cit., p. 112.

[18] Ibid., p. 111.

[19] Cross Cssn., Final Report, 1888, p. 69.

[20] Borough of Liverpool, Bye-laws of Liverpool School Board, Printed in Report of the Committee of Council for 1870–71, pp. xci–xcvi.

[21] 39 & 40 Vict., c. 79.

[22] Report of the Committee of Council for 1877–78, p. 358.

[23] 43 & 44 Vict., c. 23.

[24] Report of Committee of Council for 1881–82, p. 104.

[25] Select Committee on School Board Elections (Voting), 1885, Q 548. Evidence of Cumin.

[26] Cross Cssn., Final Report, 1888, p. 203.

[27] Cross Cssn., First Report, 1886, vol. I, Q 853. Evidence of Cumin.

[28] Bingham, op. cit., pp. 2, 3, 310–72.

[29] Select Committee on School Board Elections (Voting) 1885 QQ 7–32. Evidence of F. Sandford.

[30] Ibid., QQ 562–3. Evidence of Cumin.

[31] Ibid., Q 696.

[32] Cross Cssn., Final Report, 1888, p. 201.

[33] Ibid., p. 202.

[34] Bingham, op. cit., p. 4.

[35] 36 & 37 Vict., c. 86.

[36] Report of Committee of Council for 1885–86, p. 103.

[37] Supra, p. 132.

[38] Report of Committee of Council for 1877–78, p. 278.

[39] E. Eaglesham, From School Board to Local Authority, 1956, p. 11 ' . . . much of the vehement hostility which finally brought about the destruction of the school boards and some of their best work may be traced to the operation of this provision'.

[40] Cross Cssn., First Report, 1886, QQ 2,048–2,073. Evidence of Cumin.

[41] 33 & 34 Vict., c. 75, S 53 and 54.

[42] Hansard, CXCIX, 3rd Series, 17th February, 1870.

[43] Spalding, op. cit., p. 149.

[44] Eaglesham, op. cit., p. 15.

[45] Report of Committee of Council for 1898–99, p. xxxiii.

[46] There can be no doubt of the increasing burden that was falling on the rates. The average amount raised per scholar by school boards from the rates increased from 10s. $0\frac{3}{4}d.$ in 1872 to 21s. 2d. in 1896 (Report of Committee of Council for 1896–97, p. v). The increase in the total sum required was, of course, much more than doubled over these years because of the increase in the number of children in board schools. The London

L

School Board in 1871 needed an average rate of 0·48d. from the various authorities within its district, in 1899 the average rate it required reached 12·37d. in spite of the fact that the rateable value of London had increased considerably in the intervening years.

[47] Report of Committee of Council for 1898–99, p. xv.
[48] Report of Committee of Council, 1871–72, p. xxix, Circular to School Boards as to assistance available for providing school accommodation.
[49] Bingham, op. cit., p. 264.
[50] Statistics from Reports of Committee of Council, 1872–99.
[51] 33 & 34 Vict., c. 75, S 59 and 60.
[52] Report of Committee of Council for 1889–90, p. xxxvii.
[53] Cross Cssn., Final Report, 1888, p. 204.

CHAPTER 8

TECHNICAL INSTRUCTION COMMITTEES, 1889–1903

A SECOND system of local authorities dealing with educational matters was created alongside the school boards from 1889. In 1888 county councils had been established and their existence enabled some effect to be given to the recommendations of the Royal Commission on Technical Education which had reported in 1884. The strong movement that developed in support of technical education in the 1880s and to which the foundation of the National Association for the Promotion of Technical and Secondary Education bore witness led the government to pass the Technical Instruction Act in 1889.[1] This measure permitted county, borough and urban sanitary authorities to raise a rate of not more than a penny in the pound for the purpose of supplying or aiding the supply of technical instruction; they were also permitted to appoint a committee wholly or partly chosen from their own members to carry out their functions under the act, except the power of raising a rate or borrowing money. The act specified certain other conditions within which authorities were obliged to work, they were permitted neither to give aid to public elementary schools nor to an institution which did not accept a conscience clause, and they had to appoint one or more representatives to the management body of each school or institute receiving aid. The Department of Science and Art was made the central authority to settle any disputes which might arise on such matters as the distribution of grants and representation on governing bodies.

The 'technical instruction' which could be aided was defined as 'instruction in the principles of science and art to specific industries or employments. It shall not include teaching the practice of any trade or industry or employment, but, save as aforesaid, shall include instruction in the branches of science and art with respect to which grants are for the time being made by the Department of Science and Art, and any other form of instruction (including modern languages and commercial and agricultural subjects), which may for the time being be sanctioned by that Department by a Minute laid before Parliament and made on the representation of a local authority that such a form of instruction is required by the circumstances of the district.'[2]

The Act of 1889 was a weak measure and entirely permissive, no attempt was made to compel any authority to aid technical education; even so, in its passage through the Commons it encountered much opposition because it excluded school boards from the field of technical instruction. The Liberal opposition, as champions of nonconformity and of the school boards, managed to get an amendment incorporated in the measure requiring a conscience clause, but the amendment which would have given school boards the right to demand a share of the technical education rate was rejected by the government. During the year following the passing of the Act its adoption by local authorities was not very rapid.[3] In those areas where the school boards and their supporters were influential the measure was naturally not welcomed while few authorities showed much enthusiasm to increase the local rate burden.

The arrangements for helping technical education locally only really came to life with the passage of the Local Taxation (Customs and Excise) Act of 1890[4] for this offered non-rate aid. The original aim of this measure had been to raise duty on beer and spirits and to divide the total sum into three parts, £300,000 for police pensions, £350,000 for extinction of liquor licences and the residue (about £400,000) to be distributed to county councils in England and Wales in proportion to their rateable value. On the second reading of the bill, Acland moved an amendment to direct the compensation for the extinction of liquor licences to technical education, this was rejected at the time, but the licensing provisions in the bill were later dropped and a further attempt was then made to get the money for education. The Chancellor of the Exchequer, Goschen, announced that in England the money would be 'placed at the disposal of the County Councils, but an intimation will be given them which may guide them, so that they may not spend it in a manner which would seem to stereotype in any way that payment to them. It will be pointed out to them that charges may in the future be put upon them in regard to intermediate education.' Following this statement, Acland moved an amendment designed to make it explicit that the money should be used for technical education. The more emphatic section of this amendment was not acceptable to the Government, but it did accept part of it, viz. 'The Council of any such county borough or county may contribute any sum received by such Council in respect of the residue under this section . . .

for the purposes of Technical (including Agriculture and Commercial) Education within the meaning of the Technical Instruction Act, 1889, and may make such contribution over and above any sum that may be raised under that Act'. Thus the authorities received a sum in the first year of £743,000 in England and Wales, but they were not obliged to spend it on technical education, they could, if they so wished, devote the whole sum to the relief of rates.

The two immediate difficulties were, firstly, that the machinery so far created under the Technical Instruction Act was not adequate to bear the weight of so great a measure of expansion, secondly the new money seemed to some to be a temporary windfall and this then naturally had an effect on the willingness of authorities to commit themselves to continuing expenditure.[5] The National Association for the Promotion of Technical and Secondary Education was anxious to obtain some assurance as to the permanence of the grant from the Government and on its behalf, Lord Hartington asked the Chancellor of the Exchequer on 4th December, 1890, 'whether, in view of the fact that many of the county councils of England are setting apart sums of money under the Local Taxation Act, 1890, for important educational purposes . . . he can give an assurance that these grants are not about to be applied to some other purpose, but will continue to be available for intermediate, technical and agricultural education'. Goschen replied, 'I do not consider that I am in a position to give any formal or official assurance, but I may say that there are no suggestions before me for applying these grants to some other purpose, and I may add as my personal opinion that if county councils set themselves heartily to work, as in many places they appear to be doing, to utilize the grants for important educational purposes it would probably be difficult for any minister to persuade Parliament to divert them, even if he desired to do so'.[6]

Certain other minor difficulties arising from the existing legislation were removed by the Technical Instruction Act of 1891.[7] Frequently the most suitable technical institutions for the use of counties were situated in county boroughs and thus excluded from County aid. The councils of the three Yorkshire Ridings were anxious to aid the establishment of a Department of Agriculture in the University of Leeds, but the law prevented them from doing so; at the same time Leeds Corporation was unwilling to spend money on a form of instruction which could be of little immediate benefit to the inhabitants of the borough itself. The Act of 1891 accordingly permitted an authority to give aid to institutions outside its own area; it also stated explicitly that an authority could offer scholarships for attendance at institutions outside of its area, thus clearing up another difficulty.

Against this legislative background and with the 'whisky money' to encourage them, many of the authorities set about drafting schemes, appointing committees and officers. In most cases one of the earliest steps was the appointment of a county technical instruction committee. These committees usually consisted entirely of members of the county council, the only exceptions to this were Devon, Essex, Gloucestershire, Somerset, Wiltshire and the West Riding, all of which—along with the London County Council—appointed additional members who had special experience or knowledge of educational matters and often some representative capacity also. The Somerset Technical Instruction Committee consisted of fifteen members of the County Council and eight co-opted members, there was also a representative from any urban authority which raised a rate of not less than a halfpenny in the pound for technical instruction.[8] In the West Riding twenty-four members of the Committee were drawn from the County Council, while five members were co-opted 'almost entirely for special knowledge; sometimes they might incidentally be considered as having a representative quality, but still the main consideration would be their special knowledge'.[9]

The membership scheme for the London Technical Instruction Committee was designed to give representation to the various bodies interested in the field of secondary and technical education. It had thirty-five members in all, of whom twenty were drawn from the County Council, thirteen were appointed annually by the L.C.C. on the nomination of other bodies, and two were selected and appointed by the County Council. The other bodies which nominated members were the London School Board (three), the Trustees of the London Parochial Charities (two), the City and Gilds of London Institute (three), London Trades Council (three), Incorporated Association of Headmasters (one), and National Union of Teachers (one).[10] . . . About half of the county boroughs co-opted non-members to their technical instruction committees. The co-opted members included representatives of local technical institutions and frequently of the local school board.[11]

The form of organization set up by each technical education committee varied according to the problems and resources of the area which it administered. One of the most highly developed systems of sub-committees was that created by the London Technical Instruction Committee—or Technical Education Board as it was called. At the Board's first meeting Sidney Webb was elected as chairman and a special sub-committee was set up to consider the future organization and procedure of the Board, this body decided that all business should be handled through a series of sub-committees which would report to the Board. There were at once created a standing Finance and General Purposes sub-committee and two special sub-committees, one to prepare standing orders and the other to consider procedure and the appointment of staff. By the end of its first year, the Technical Education Board had ten sub-committees, they were Finance and General Purposes, Science Classes, Art and Technology, Domestic Economy, Scholarships, Secondary Schools, Polytechnics, Higher Education, Bethnal Green Museum and Aske's School, Hoxton.[12] The Bryce Commission found the London Technical Education Board 'of special interest as being the only example at present existing in England of a systematic local organization for the control of Technical and Secondary Education'.[13]

A complete contrast with this strong and centralized piece of committee administration was the system adopted in Dorset. In that county it was the duty of the technical instruction committee to formulate schemes, receive reports and generally control urban and rural work, but the power to take the initiative and control of much of the finance available was passed on to local committees, the main aim apparently being to see that each part of the county got its fair share of whatever money was available. Four Divisional Committees were appointed—one for each Parliamentary Division of the County—consisting of the chairman and vice-chairman of the council, the chairman and vice-chairman of the technical instruction committee along with the county aldermen and county councillors for the electoral divisions within the Parliamentary constituency. The task of these Divisional Committees was to appoint a local committee for each county electoral division and to receive applications and reports from such local committees. The local committees consisted of the county councillor, any resident county alderman and twelve local persons. It was with these committees for small areas that the initiative in developing some sort of technical education service rested. The committees for boroughs and urban districts were appointed by local councils and the county simply passed on to them their share of the money available for technical education.[14] The weakness of this system soon became apparent for in the small rural areas there was neither the knowledge nor the initiative necessary to accomplish the difficult and expert task of building up technical and secondary education. The system was severely criticized by the newly appointed Organizing Secretary in a Report to the Technical Instruction Committee in November, 1894. He wrote that 'The three main points which appear to me to debar the future progress of the work in this county are: (1) the distinction drawn between urban and rural districts; (2) the smallness of the areas entrusted to the local committees; (3) the absence of scholarships and aid to secondary schools'. He argued that good secondary education was essential if people were to be in a position to take advantage of higher specialized technical education and that the separation of rural and urban districts was a 'fatal impediment' since the country towns were the natural centres for the villages around them. He suggested that there should only be one local committee for each poor law union, thus reducing their number from fifty-three to twelve and that a secondary school should be built up in each union.[15] This Report bore little fruit at the time, but some reform was attempted two years later when the number of local committees was reduced from fifty-three to forty.

The amount of autonomy in the exercise of powers granted to their technical instruction committees by county and county borough councils varied considerably from those which virtually handed over all executive power to those which maintained very close control and gave their committee little more than the right to advise. London may be taken as an example of the former, and Manchester as an example of the latter practice. Sydney Webb in his evidence to the Bryce Commission as Chairman of the Technical Education Board explained that the London County Council had divested itself of all the powers which it had in this field except those which it could not delegate which only amounted to the power to raise a rate; within its annual appropriation the Technical Education Board had full financial discretion.[16] The Chairman of Manchester Technical Instruction Committee told the Commission that his Committee had far less power than the London Board. 'The money passes through the corporation, and everything we do requires to be submitted to it; and the recommendations of the committee are not effectual until after they have received the sanction of the council at its monthly meeting.' On being further questioned, he admitted that 'As Chairman of a committee which finds some little trouble occasionally in getting some of its items through the council, I should be disposed to fall in with the method adopted by the London County Council. . . .'[17] In general, the practice of most authorities seems to have been nearer to that of Manchester than that of London.

Apart from the membership of technical instruction committees and the powers entrusted to them, the calibre of the officials appointed to carry out the work of the authorities was of crucial importance. In its fifth Annual Report the National Association for the Promotion of Technical Education listed thirty-nine counties which had appointed directors or secretaries of technical instruction and remarked that the practice of appointing an expert permanent official was less common in county boroughs; it went on to point out that 'It need hardly be said that the future development of technical and secondary education throughout the country will very largely depend on the gentlemen who have been selected for these important posts. It may not be out of place in this connection to impress on County Councils which have not yet made their appointments the wisdom and ultimate economy of offering such salaries as will attract first-rate candidates. Where the administration of a fund averaging £12,000 is in question, the difference between a first- and second-rate organizer will save the difference in salary many times over.'[18]

A meeting of directors and secretaries was arranged by the National Association on 3rd July, 1891, to promote common action and to enable an interchange of views to take place; the most important consequence of this meeting was to initiate a train of events that was to lead to the formation of the 'Association of Organizing Secretaries and Directors'. The Organizing Secretary for Surrey, Macan, became the first convener, and the object of the Association was set out as 'to confer on matters relating to Technical and Secondary Education with a view to the members and the Committees they represent, having the benefit of the practice and procedure of other committees in matters of difficulty and doubt, as well as on the general administration of the Technical Instruction Acts and the various questions arising therefrom'.[19] By July, 1893, sixty counties and county boroughs had appointed full-time education officers and fifty-one of these had joined the Association of Directors and Organizing Secretaries.

There were considerable variations from place to place in the schemes of technical instruction undertaken by the different authorities. Initially a number of counties and county boroughs tended to interpret aid to technical education in the narrow sense of providing instruction directly related to the requirements of local industries. In Dorset, for example, the main effort initially lay in providing lectures in various aspects of husbandry, cooking, dairy-management and the like. Some of these courses were at quite an advanced level, and were given by lecturers from the universities. Of a total estimate of about £15,000 for the years 1892–95, Dorset proposed to spend £3,000 on the provision of lectures by the University of Oxford on such subjects as agricultural chemistry. Experience soon showed that a great deal of technical instruction in the narrow sense was wasted when those for whom it was intended lacked the background of general education essential for the comprehension of the more advanced courses. This led authorities such as Dorset, which had tended to make something of a false start, to turn their attention increasingly in the direction of providing increased assistance for secondary school work. According to that county's revised scheme issued in 1896 'in order to introduce an additional element of permanence into the work of technical instruction, it is desirable to bring it into connection with the educational institutions which the County already possesses, in the form of endowed secondary schools'; the new scheme provided for small annual grants and some aid by way of capital grants for schools which met certain conditions.[20]

London Technical Education Board was more fortunate in its earlier work. It was largely guided by a Report on the London area and its needs drawn up by Llewellyn Smith. The general policy followed by the Board was outlined in this resolution approved by the London County Council in 1893, 'That, without committing itself to details, the Council considers that every district of London ought to be adequately provided with technical education of every grade, rising from the school to the workshop and the university, and appropriate to the chief occupations of its inhabitants; that existing institutions of each grade should be systematically co-ordinated to avoid overlapping and to provide for continuous education; and that early provision should be made, in whatever manner may be found expedient, for supplying the gaps at present existing; that the most pressing want is further inducements and facilities for the poorest parents to keep their children at some secondary or continuation school after leaving the elementary school; that the Council therefore instructs the Technical Education Board to provide, as its first duty, considerable further facilities for practical and technical education in the poorer and manufacturing districts of London, provided that no scholarship be given of a less value than £10 per annum; and that the Council, recognizing the value of the comprehensive report prepared by Mr. Lewellyn Smith, refers it for the information of the Technical Education Board'.[21]

Thus from the beginning an attempt was made in London to build on existing institutions, to strengthen them and to weld them into a system; this involved giving a good deal of aid to secondary schools. The Chairman of the Board explained to the Bryce Commission that 'We accepted from the beginning that a large proportion of the work of technical education was the promotion of the teaching of those subjects which fall within the definition in secondary schools. We said it was not to be excluded from technical education merely because it was being taught in secondary schools. Consequently from the beginning we regarded the secondary schools of London as a very important factor in the technical education of London; and we received applications for aid from a great number of them. Ultimately, for the first year we awarded £12,215 to some thirty-seven secondary schools in London, . . . it may be looked upon in some sense as a large addition to the endowment of secondary schools in London.'[22] The money was intended to cover maintenance and improved equipment. Grants were made after the circumstances of each school were considered individually and were usually conditional on the acceptance of conditions laid down by the Board, and intended to raise the efficiency of the schools. The schools also had to accept a certain number of scholarship winners selected by the Board on the results of an annual examination. One of the major achievements of the Technical Education Board was to build up a county scholarship system at the Junior, Intermediate and Senior levels which could take a child through both the secondary school and the university; by 1901 there were ten holders of senior county awards at the universities.[23] In the more narrowly technical field, London made considerable progress in strengthening its system of polytechnics, technical institutes and schools of art.

The aim in London of strengthening secondary education found a parallel in many other counties and county boroughs and became of increasing importance in the years following the publication of the Bryce Report. Apart from London, Surrey and the West Riding were both noted for their wide interpretation of technical education. The county boroughs appear to have been more reluctant initially to extend their efforts beyond technical instruction in the stricter sense of the word. The Bryce Commission remarked that 'Unlike the county councils the county boroughs have given comparatively little so far to schools professedly secondary'.[24] In the year 1893–94 only fourteen out of sixty-one county boroughs made grants in aid of a total of twenty secondary schools, they tended to concentrate their resources on aiding technical institutes, schools of art, books and apparatus for libraries and museums. Some of them handed over considerable sums of money to the school board for the support of higher grade elementary schools and evening classes, in Leeds about half of the total sum available under the Technical Instruction Acts was paid to the school board, £3,000 out of £6,045 in 1892–93. The practice of regarding the school board as in some way responsible for education beyond the elementary level in some cities is understandable when the extent to which they had developed their higher grade education is considered, and since the school board and county borough areas were coterminous it was perfectly feasible for county boroughs to discharge some part of their responsibilities for technical instruction in this way. In Leeds the city council was represented on the expenditure committee of the school board, in some towns the school boards submitted schemes annually to the town council for technical instruction projects while in other towns grants were paid unconditionally to school boards without any very definite provision for the supervision of expenditure by borough councils.

The technical instruction authorities were encouraged to take a wide view of the scope of their activities by the willingness of the Science and Art Department to add to the list of subjects which it was prepared to sanction under the Technical Instruction Act. In 1894 the Department sent a circular to all counties and county boroughs offering them extracts from the reports of the Science and Art inspectors when they related to schools or classes receiving aid from local authorities. During the following year extracts from about 850 reports of the Inspectors were forwarded to local authorities.[25] In addition the advice of the Department was sought and given in a multitude of administrative matters arising out of offers of or requests for aid to schools by technical instruction committees.

Against this background of steady development, expenditure on technical education increased gradually. In the year 1892–93 the local authorities assigned £472,560 of the residue to technical education while in 1900–01 they assigned £863,847; in the first of these years they raised £12,762 from the rates for this purpose and in the last year £106,209.[26] At the time of the passing of the 1902 Act, forty-two out of forty-nine county councils in England were giving all of the residue grant to education, the seven which were not doing so were Gloucester, Hereford, Isle of Ely, Lincolnshire (Holland), London, Rutland and the Soke of Peterborough; by this time only three county boroughs were diverting part of the residue grant to the relief of rates, Gateshead, Grimsby and Preston. The following table gives some idea of the position in the counties and county boroughs in the six years preceding the 1902 Act.[27]

	1896	1897	1898	1899	1900	1901
Devoting all (a) Counties of the grant	40	41	38	39	39	42
to education (b) County Boroughs	55	55	56	56	61	63
Devoting part (a) Counties of the grant	9	8	11	10	10	7
to education (b) County Boroughs	5	6	5	5	3	3
County borough devoting whole grant to relief of the rates .	1	—	—	—	—	—
Total number of Counties and County Boroughs in England . . .	110	110	110	110	113	115

By this time, seventeen county boroughs were raising the full penny rate permitted, but only two county councils had levied a rate for technical instruction over the whole of their administrative areas, Surrey and the West Riding of Yorkshire.

The Technical Instruction Act of 1889 foreshadowed the educational organization of to-day in that it recognized county councils as local authorities in education for the first time. The field in which they were recognized appeared to be very limited, but by the end of the century many of them had become authorities not merely for technical but also for secondary education. Through offering scholarships to attend secondary schools, and through offering financial aid to such schools, the county authorities became increasingly involved in the administration of the schools themselves. The Technical Instruction Acts required that an authority offering aid should be represented on the governing body of the school aided; it became usual for the authority to lay down some rules concerning the subjects of instruction and for inspection and examination.

The degree of control which authorities exercised varied a great deal. In the West Riding the Council required a list of the teaching staff, their qualifications and remuneration and the Councils' approval of the teaching staff was a condition of grant aid. The subjects of instruction of a school had to be approved by the Technical Instruction Committee and the school had to be open at all times to inspection by any person authorized by the County Council. The grants offered were dependent on the number of children in attendance, the number of technical subjects taken, the suitability of the school fees and the general efficiency of the school.[28] Surrey County Council created a similarly centralized pattern of secondary organization. The Assistant Commissioner of the Bryce Commission concluded his Report on Surrey thus: 'The Council are attempting to put within the reach of all students in the county secondary education, either by means of schools or classes, and, hampered as they are by legal restrictions, they are rapidly succeeding in their endeavour. The way in which they have used their money goes, I think, a long way towards justifying their claim to be recognized as the local authority for secondary education. I started my inquiry with a strong prejudice against the educational work of the county councils; my experience here has shown me that, in one case at any rate, the prejudice was unjustified, and I feel sure that anyone else who examined the work closely would form a similarly high opinion of it.'[29] The steady enlargement of the field of the county education authorities within the framework of the Technical Instruction Acts pointed towards the administrative settlement of the 1902 Act. As early as 1894 in giving his evidence to the Bryce Commission Sydney Webb put the position clearly: 'Either the powers which are now granted to the County Council under the definition of technical education must be withdrawn or limited, or they must be expanded. It is inconceivable that you can have two bodies offering aid, as we are, to secondary schools, and directing and criticizing the action of secondary schools, within one area.'[30]

REFERENCES

[1] 52 & 53 Vict., c 76.
[2] Ibid., S 8.
[3] 3rd Annual Report of the National Association for the Promotion of Technical and Secondary Education, July, 1890.
[4] 53 & 54 Vict., c 60.
[5] 4th Annual Report of the National Association for the Promotion of Technical and Secondary Education, July 1891, p. 6.
[6] Ibid., p. 9.
[7] 54 & 55 Vict., c 4.

[8] Bryce Cssn., 1895, Minutes of Evidence, Q 3278.

[9] Ibid., Q 14420.

[10] L.C.C. Report of the Technical Education Board for the year 1893–94.

[11] Bryce Cssn., 1895, Report, p. 38.

[12] L.C.C. Report of the Technical Education Board for the year 1893–94.

[13] Bryce Cssn., 1895, Report, p. 37.

[14] Scheme under the Technical Instruction Acts, 1889–91, accepted by Dorset County Council, 7th November, 1891.

[15] Report presented to Dorset County Technical Instruction Committee, 10/11/94.

[16] Bryce Cssn., 1895, Minutes of Evidence, QQ 2547–2552.

[17] Ibid., QQ 3345–3347.

[18] 5th Annual Report of the National Association for the Promotion of Technical and Secondary Education, July, 1892.

[19] Ibid.

[20] Dorset County Council Technical Instruction Committee. Revised Scheme for the Year 1896.

[21] L.C.C. Report of Technical Education Board, 1902–03.

[22] Bryce Cssn., 1895, Minutes of Evidence, Q 2736.

[23] L.C.C. Report of Technical Education Board, 1902–03.

[24] Bryce Cssn., 1895, Report, p. 38.

[25] 43rd Report of the Department of Science and Art, 1896, p. lxv.

[26] House of Commons Paper No. 225, 1902, p. vi.

[27] 14th Annual Report of the National Association for the Promotion of Technical and Secondary Education, July, 1903.

[28] Bryce Cssn., 1895, vol. VII. Report of Assistant Commissioner on the County of Yorkshire, p. 204.

[29] Ibid., Report of Assistant Commissioner on the County of Surrey, pp. 42–3.

[30] Ibid., Minutes of Evidence, Q 2650.

CHAPTER 9

THE CREATION OF LOCAL EDUCATION AUTHORITIES
IN 1902

I

As already noticed, proposals had been made from time to time
during the latter part of the nineteenth century for the creation or reorganization of local administrative machinery for education. The
Newcastle Commission on Popular Education in 1861 had recommended that in every county or part of a county a local board of education
should be appointed and that every town of more than 40,000 inhabitants should appoint a borough board.[1] A quarter of a century later,
the Cross Commission inquired into the working of the Elementary
Education Acts; since Parliament was then considering the question
of county government, the Commissioners abstained from making any
definite recommendations as to the nature and powers of any new
local education authorities, but they did print an interesting memorandum drawn up by one of their members, Sir Francis Sandford, on
the reorganization of local educational administration. The proposals
contained in this document pointed unmistakably towards the ultimate
settlement of 1902 for the new county councils were to act as the
educational authorities for their counties, and were to appoint
education committees to carry out their functions in this field, certain
grants were to be made available to all elementary schools from the
county rate while school boards and attendance committees were to be
abolished.[2]

In the sphere of secondary education also, both the Schools Inquiry
Commission and the Bryce Commission had recommended the creation
of an efficient local administration. The Schools Inquiry Commissioners recommended the creation of county or provincial authorities
for secondary education. They made it clear that they would prefer
to see a board in every county but, before the days of county councils,
they felt unable to recommend compulsion in this matter, and suggested
that counties should be enabled to choose to have a board as an alternative to participating in a provincial organization. The actual form that
the board should take was that two-thirds of its members were, for

preference, to be directly elected by the rate payers while the other third should be nominated by the Crown; if such direct elections were not acceptable, then the chairmen of boards of Guardians might serve in place of the elected members. As a less desirable alternative, the Commission suggested the formation of provincial local authorities, based upon the Registrar-General's divisions; in each division there should be a board consisting of an Official District Commissioner appointed by the Charity Commission and six or eight unpaid district commissioners appointed by the Crown from among local residents.[3] The failure of the Government of the day to act on any of these suggestions and the difficulties which arose for the Endowed Schools Commissioners as a consequence of the absence of any local authority for secondary education has been shown above.[4]

Although by the time the Bryce Commission reported, various local agencies had begun to administer aid to some form or aspect of secondary education, each had a strictly limited province and their efforts were not co-ordinated. The Commission found that 'Councils of counties and boroughs can aid secondary education only within the terms of the Technical Instruction Acts. They are further hampered by various doubts as (e.g.) whether such a council, acting alone, can found a general secondary school; at what kind of school scholarships are tenable, etc. Then, within the same town or district, the local power over secondary education may be shared between a county or borough council, a school board, various governing bodies, managing committees of proprietary schools, local committees under the Science and Art Department, and managers of voluntary schools. Each of these unconnected local agencies must, or may, have relations with one, or two, or perhaps three central authorities, which are similarly independent of each other. It is not surprising that, under such conditions, ability, energy and a cordial desire for co-operation have not always availed to prevent waste of power, or one-sided developments of educational forces.'[5] The Commission concluded that there was an imperative need for representative local authorities to supervise the interests of secondary education as a whole.

Once the Commissioners had advanced their argument to this point, they were faced with two problems, firstly to decide the most suitable areas for local management, and secondly, to describe how the authorities for those areas should be constituted. They felt that recent legislation in other fields indicated that the proper rural area was the county and the proper urban area the county borough; towns with

M

population of less than 50,000 and therefore not county boroughs under the Act of 1888, were held not to be sufficiently large to be regarded as distinct areas for secondary education, they would gain more by forming part of the county in which they were situated.[6] The Commissioners made separate recommendations for the formation of authorities in counties and county boroughs because of the position created by the existence of school boards in most county boroughs. The county authority for secondary education should, it was recommended, have the majority of its members chosen by the council; of the remainder, about one-third (or one-sixth of the whole) should be nominated by the Education Minister after consultation with whatever university had connections with the area while the rest of the members should be co-opted by the members already chosen. By way of example, the Commission envisaged a typical county authority composed of sixteen members chosen by the county council, four by the Minister, and eight co-opted by the two groups already chosen. It was hoped that in this way a suitable blending of the representative element with those possessing expert knowledge would be obtained. In the case of county boroughs a broadly similar pattern was recommended except that half of the representative majority should be chosen by the county borough council, and half by the school board, since each of these bodies was said to have a claim, but neither an exclusive claim, to occupy the field of secondary education. An interesting suggestion put forward by the Commission in the case of county boroughs containing a university was that the one-sixth normally nominated by the Minister should be chosen by the university directly.[7]

Apart from the bewildering variety of local bodies exercising some sort of influence over secondary education described by the Bryce Commission, the elementary field was shared among the school boards, school attendance committees, managers of voluntary schools and the Voluntary Aid Associations. The very multiplicity of the bodies which had acquired some sort of standing in the local administration of education made reform much more difficult politically since any change in the direction of unification and simplification would be bound to offend some of the existing interests. Moreover, some of the existing bodies were not without hope of enlarging their spheres of interest at the expense of their rivals. The county and county borough councils clearly expected to extend their activities from the technical aspect to the whole field of secondary education; the school boards were steadily winning their fight with the voluntary bodies in the elementary schools, were well established with their higher grade schools in secondary education and had some claim to be regarded as the future authority at this higher level. By the end of the nineteenth century the educational case for administrative reorganization was—and had for some time been—convincing, but the political situation had never been favourable. The Liberals, who might possibly have attempted to build on the school boards and to extend their power and influence, were suffering during the later years of the nineteenth century from their divisions over the Irish question. The Conservatives were quite as much concerned with saving the Church elementary schools from insolvency as with those administrative reforms which were needed so desperately from the educational, economic and social points of view; indeed, it might justly be said that it was the financial plight of the voluntary elementary schools which forced the Government to turn its attention to educational reform.

Education had been one of the issues in the general election of 1895, which was won by Lord Salisbury and the Conservatives with the aid of the Liberal-Unionists. The aid of the Liberal-Unionists under Chamberlain complicated the position so far as the new ministry was concerned for these allies were predominantly nonconformist in sympathy and supporters of the school board system. Immediately after Salisbury's triumph in the election, the Archbishops of Canterbury and York drew up a memorial which was presented to the Government. This memorial asked for larger grants for voluntary schools, the right to give Church teaching to those pupils who sought it in the board schools and the right to establish new denominational schools where parents demanded them. The Archiepiscopal appeal was not likely to fall on deaf ears, for the new prime minister had himself addressed the National Society in these terms: 'It is your business to capture the Board schools—to capture them, in the first instance, under the existing law, and then . . . under a better law which shall place you under no religious disability. . . . And, intermediately, we must do all we can to strengthen the voluntary schools, and to swell the resources on which they rest. By all means let us get what we can out of increased contributions from the National Exchequer.'[8] Many Churchmen regarded the Cowper-Temple clause in the Act of 1870 as manifestly unjust, since it permitted only undenominational teaching in board schools, a situation which might suit the Nonconformists but which was unsatisfactory to both the Church of England and the

Church of Rome. The natural dislike which Churchmen felt for the board schools was strengthened by the 'unlimited wealth' at the command of the boards and the increasingly severe competition which they offered the voluntary schools.⁹

In 1896 the Government tried to meet the situation by introducing an Education Bill prepared by Sir John Gorst, which would have both reformed the local administrative arrangements and relieved the voluntary schools of their financial difficulties. The Bill proposed to make county and county borough councils the local education authorities controlling both elementary and secondary schools, to pay a special grant of 4s. per pupil to the new authorities for distribution to voluntary schools within their areas and to permit denominational religious instruction to be given in board schools to children whose parents desired it. The Bill came under attack from various directions, the school boards naturally opposed vigorously a measure which would have led to their demise; the nonconformists opposed any suggestion of denominational instruction in board schools and the creation of machinery which could have given rate aid to voluntary schools; the medium sized municipal boroughs opposed the measure because their claims to become education authorities were over-ruled in favour of the counties. It was mainly the opposition from even Unionist M.P.s representing medium-sized boroughs which led the Government to drop the Bill as it stood and to bring first aid to the voluntary schools through the Voluntary Schools Act which passed through Parliament in 1897.¹⁰ This Act paid an aid grant for voluntary schools at the rate of 5s. per pupil, the funds to be administered by newly-created Voluntary Aid Associations which usually operated on a diocesan basis. Another Act passed in the same year offered similar aid to the much smaller number of necessitous Board schools. Thus by the end of 1897 the attempt to simplify and reform the system of local educational administration had merely resulted in the addition of yet another local administrative agency for the distribution of yet another grant. At the time of the enactment of the Education Act in 1902, seventy-five of these Voluntary Associations had come into existence, forty-five Church of England, eleven Roman Catholic, six Wesleyan and thirteen British and other Associations.

The Act of 1897 brought no more than temporary relief to the voluntary schools, and the Government's return to the question of reforming the local administrative structure was largely the outcome of renewed financial stringency in the Church schools. A confidential

Board of Education Memorandum to Morant on the financial condition of 11,000 church schools for the twenty-one years preceding 1900 showed that their finances were sound until 1885 but that of the next fifteen years, eleven were lean and only four were fat. The total indebtedness accumulated by these schools stood at £450,000 by 31st August, 1900.[11] The aid grant amounted to about £600,000 each year, between 1897 and 1900 the total bill for salaries alone in schools receiving the grant had increased by £544,000, thus the grant had not brought stability.[12] On the other hand it had brought various non-financial benefits to the schools concerned; the Voluntary Associations formed in 1897 often secured such improvements as better management of the schools, improvement of average attendance, the establishment of Pupil-Teacher centres and Cookery Centres, etc.

Sir John Gorst expressed his views on the situation of the Church schools at the end of 1900 thus, ' . . . the voluntary schools are in the same difficulty now that they were in 1895. In rural districts these schools as a class have never been in imminent danger of extinction. . . . They do not come into competition with the board schools and the imposition of the school board system on a rural parish as the result of the collapse of the Voluntary school, is so disastrous financially that every effort is usually made to avoid the catastrophe. The rural schools, board and voluntary, are poor and isolated and many attempts which have been made to improve them have broken down because of the impossibility of imposing upon them any additional burden. . . .

'But in the towns, voluntary schools are not only in danger of extinction, but are being extinguished at a rapid and accelerating rate. Soon there will be few left to save. All expedients for saving these schools must fail, unless they result in providing them with a secure income, something like that of the board schools with which they have to compete. . . .'[13]

Churchmen were active throughout 1901 in urging the government to come to their aid and to rescue their schools from financial collapse. After the Cockerton Judgment, which was finally confirmed on appeal in March, 1901, it looked as though the government would attempt some reform of secondary education, the leaders of the Church were most anxious that this reform should also bring relief to their elementary schools. In the autumn of 1901 Churchmen of Leeds, Manchester and Birmingham met and urged the government to action. In reporting on the meeting the Archdeacon of Birmingham wrote to Gorst: 'I was desired by our Committee especially to urge their strong conviction that a measure dealing with both Primary and Secondary Education and removing the disabilities under which the voluntary schools lie to the detriment of national education would arouse enthusiasm, whereas a measure dealing with Secondary Education only arouses the antagonism of school boards and of many Governors of secondary schools without enlisting any compensating strength of public opinion in its favour'.[14] The future Archbishop of Canterbury, G. Cosmo Lang, then Bishop of Stepney, expressed the feelings of many of his fellows when he urged that the giving of rate aid to voluntary schools should be made compulsory on a national basis and should not be a matter for local option as some were suggesting.[15] The Bishop of Rochester wrote a strong letter to the Prime Minister appealing for early aid at the beginning of December, 1901. '. . . the palliative of 1897', he wrote, 'is exhausted (in many places), and the strain is now at *breaking point*. Putting it practically, I mean that, if the schools are not in some way relieved in this next session, many will go within the year—enough greatly to weaken the cause, and, by creating the impression that "the Game is up", to bring down others in increasing numbers and an accelerating rate. I am speaking of what I know.'[16]

It was against this background that the Cockerton affair arose in which the auditor of the Local Government Board, Cockerton, who dealt with the London School Board's accounts disallowed certain items of that Board's expenditure concerned with Higher Grade and Evening School work. The matter went before the courts and on 20th December, 1900, the verdict was given that all the work of the Board conducted under the regulations of the Science and Art Department was illegal, that the Board had no legal right to conduct evening classes for adults and that its powers were limited to giving instruction to children within the limitations set down by the Codes of the Education Department. This verdict was upheld by the Court of Appeal in a decision given on 1st April, 1901. The Government, for its own ends, stressed the limitations implied in the judgment rather than the remarkably wide interpretation which the courts in fact attached to the phrase 'elementary education'. Mr. Justice Wills in his judgment pointed out that 'The code (in 1870) provided for no grants for any instruction beyond what have been called the three "Rs". I cannot believe for a moment that it was ever intended that in board schools nothing beyond the very low standard to which alone elementary education, as then understood, had reached should be

aimed at by the board schools. . . . Elementary education is obviously
a term which may shift with the growth of general instruction and
attainment.' The limits imposed by the courts were that elementary
education must, firstly, be for children—probably up to the age of
16 or 17, and secondly that it must be that prescribed by the Code
from time to time in accordance with Section 97 of the Act of 1870.
Provided that the principal part of the instruction given was elementary
in this sense, there was nothing to prevent education other than elementary being given in a public elementary school. It has been said that the
'Cockerton Judgment' made a recasting of the system of educational
administration inevitable. Of itself the judgment did not do so, but
the government of the day regarded the situation that arose as creating
an opportunity and suitable occasion to attempt a settlement of the
educational issue.

While the Cockerton issue was still before the courts, Gorst wrote
to Devonshire, 'I have never regarded it as possible that School Boards
could be a permanent institution. Like Boards of Guardians they are
a modern anomaly in Local Government, which would never have
been created if County Councils had existed in 1870. There should be
one Administration for all local purposes, and one body having the
entire control of local finance, . . . the School Board of a town must
ultimately become a Committee appointed by the Municipal Council
and the School Fund be provided out of the ordinary town rate with
due regard to the requirements of other branches of municipal expenditure. . . .'[17] Gorst's intention remained that of replacing the
school boards at the earliest opportunity and the first legislative step
in that direction was taken when the so-called Cockerton Bill was
hurried through Parliament in 1901 to deal with the situation arising
out of the judgment on a short-term basis. This Act forced every
school board threatened with being surcharged for undertaking
illegal expenditure on higher education to make an arrangement
with its county or borough council to cover such expenditure for the
financial year beginning in 1901. Gorst refused to consider any such
simple expedient as a one-clause Bill authorizing the Board of Education to sanction such expenditure temporarily. He was determined
to show the school boards that outside the elementary sphere the
counties and boroughs were their masters. He explained his intentions
to Morant in this way 'According to my idea the procedure is simple
enough. The school board applies to the County or Borough Council.
The two bodies settle the terms and the sum, as in most cases they

would do without difficulty. If there is difference, they come to the Board of Education which should confine its action to conciliation and inquiry whether there is any ground to suspect *mala fides*. If the schools are finally discontinued, it is the Act of the representatives of the ratepayers not of the Board of Education. The only case I know of where such a conclusion of the matter is probable is London; where the evening schools of the London School Board are a discreditable imposture, and where the Technical Instruction Committee are ready and anxious to replace them by real educational institutions.

'The Board of Education is so notoriously under the influence of the teachers, whose financial interests are deeply involved in this matter, that the less it has to do with the arrangements, the better.'[18]

The attitude shown here by Gorst as the responsible minister for educational policy is worth commenting on. His over-riding aim was to use the situation to hit at the school boards regardless of the effect of this on the more advanced schools they were providing, even to the point of closure so long as that would appear to be 'the Act of the representatives of the ratepayers not of the Board of Education'. His view of his own Department some six years after he had taken it over also appears to have been odd. Professor Eaglesham has shown how the planning of the Act of 1902 was initially largely in the hands of Gorst and how from late in 1901 Morant came increasingly to take the initiative in the matter from Gorst. This change did not result in any softening of the government's intentions towards the school boards; on the contrary it was when Gorst began to have doubts as to the political wisdom of trying to abolish the boards in the large cities and of repealing the Cowper-Temple clause which prevented the teaching of denominational religion in board schools that the initiative began to pass from Gorst to Morant as the more faithful reflector of the Church and Conservative feeling that the time was opportune for radical change.[19] The minister with whom Morant dealt in the later stages of preparing the Bill and during its passage through the Commons was Balfour. In a sense the Education Act of 1902 was the result of the determination of the many Tories who sought as Gorst had done to help the denominational schools and to destroy their rivals the school boards coupled with the capacity of Morant who, alone it would seem of those concerned in planning the measure, could envisage a new form of organization which would both accomplish these ends and establish a sounder administrative system for primary and secondary education.

Morant sought to create a unified structure for local educational administration. He saw in the chaos of conflicting authorities a barrier to the growth and development of educational facilities generally, and believed that the administrative tangle must be dealt with if there was to be any hope of providing the country with the secondary schools it needed. A crucial question which faced anyone who was trying to overcome the administrative confusion was whether to build up an 'Ad Hoc' system dealing with education alone or whether to include education as one of the services to be provided by the general purposes local authority; in practice this meant choosing between building on the foundations offered by the school boards or turning to the county and borough councils. Morant showed his attitude to this fundamental issue in a paper he drew up under the heading 'Points against AD HOC'. He wrote:

'1. It is admittedly impossible to dispossess the Municipal Authorities of their Higher Education powers which they have exercised admirably for ten years. Hence to organize our Elementary Education on an Ad Hoc basis would necessitate separate authorities for Elementary and Higher Education in the large cities. No arrangement of composite committees would suffice to mitigate the evils of this division and competition of public authorities in regard to education.

'2. Moreover an Ad Hoc authority is in itself a mistake. By making Education a separate claim upon the town purse it becomes, in the eyes of town councillors, a rival and greedy swallower of the funds which the town councillor feels ought to be at his disposal for all the needs of the town. . . .

'3. There is further the waste of time and money and interest involved in the extra elections required in the town; a quite considerable item as regards expense and a very serious matter as regards the already too limited interest of the average townsman in the affairs and needs of his town and townsfolk.

'4. And especially there is the mistake of getting together a lot of people whose sole (or main) hobby is education and letting a body of such folk have the run of the public purse. It becomes a matter of "There's nothing like leather". Education lends itself particularly to the development of extravagances.

'Ordinary common sense restrictions, such as would be obvious to an ordinary person, are wholly overlooked; and so-called education fads and extravagances of all kinds and out of all proportion to the rateable capacity of the town and its useful needs in other directions, became the normal course of policy with school Board members.

'All this is avoided, without any real educational needs suffering at all, if all education is part of the ordinary municipal purse.'[20]

Morant worked towards making county and county borough councils alone authorities for elementary and higher education. He was certain that smaller towns could not stand outside of their counties for purposes of secondary education since it was their schools which naturally served the rural areas about them, and as small isolated authorities they were scarcely likely to show a sufficient breadth of vision to run secondary schools well. Many of the issues involved in such an administrative reconstruction as Morant was envisaging are listed in a memorandum entitled 'some questions to be considered before drafting Education Bill for 1902'.[21] The first question was whether to concentrate in the first place on secondary education only or whether to re-open the 'so-called settlement of 1870' in the elementary field and thus reorganizing the whole of the local administrative structure. Two consequences of following the latter course it was suggested might be 'to save for ever the Denominational Schools (which will otherwise be swept away inevitably by the next Radical Government) and to raise enthusiasm for our Bill'. Other important questions were the need for demarcation between elementary and higher education, whether education should be paid for on a parish or county rate assessment and the likely reactions of County Borough and County councils to the imposition on them of additional duties, for while Lancashire had welcomed the powers the abortive bill of 1896 would have conferred, the West Riding had deprecated the measure. On this last issue, the opinions of the inspectors of the Local Government Board were sought in strictest confidence. Their reports gave the impression that in England the County and County Borough councils would for the most part be prepared to take over; the small school boards were unpopular and often considered to be a failure; the non-county boroughs and urban districts would dislike education being run by the county and the school boards would, naturally, oppose any such change. In Wales the position was different; the County Councils were willing to take over secondary education although Cardiff, Newport and Swansea school boards were also anxious to do so, but the time was said to be not yet ripe to transfer elementary education to the counties, 'the school boards are very popular in Wales and the general feeling would probably be in favour of not interfering with them'.[22] The government was certainly warned of the difficulties it was later to encounter when it came to enforce the Education Act after 1902 in Wales.

A reasonably full summary of the structure Morant felt should be created by the 1902 Act was given for the first time in a memorandum from him to Balfour in the first days of January.[23] Primary and secondary education were to be dealt with together, and in all county boroughs and most of the county areas there would in future be only one authority. 'All this is our great line of defence for compulsorily *abolishing* the school boards. This is the *only* way of getting one authority.' So far as administrative areas were concerned, Morant foresaw no difficulties in the county boroughs where the limits of the school boards had been coterminous with those of the boroughs, nor would any problem arise in those non-county boroughs and urban districts large enough to administer their own elementary education for the same reason. In the smaller urban and all rural areas the county was to become the area for educational purposes 'as the obvious correlative of the county council as the authority'. This was an important departure from the settlement of 1870, for there would be an authority for every part of each county and not simply for those parts which could not supply sufficient school buildings from voluntary effort, 'the county councils become the education authority for the *county as a whole*, and not in respect of each parish separately'. Maintenance of the schools would be abolished from individual parish rates and laid squarely on the county rate, if this were not so, it would be difficult to justify the destruction of parish and smaller borough school boards. A county rate could only be defended if all parts of the county which were going to have to pay the rate would also receive benefit from it. 'This at once involves us in a scheme for financing voluntary schools out of the rates.' These wide financial responsibilities which the counties were to be given meant that they must also be given the right to fix the actual level of county educational expenditure, and therefore county educational policy, in every school maintained out of the county rate. 'We, in fact, place the County Council in exactly the same relation to *all* elementary schools in its area, rate-built or *not*, which it maintains, as is a school board now towards its board schools. In fact (subject only to compliance with the Whitehall Education Department minimum), the County Council will, by our scheme, lay down what is to be done in the elementary schools; and the managers of each school, rate-built *or not*, will merely carry on the schools under these instructions; in every point of educational efficiency, the county council, who finds (with the Exchequer) the money, will have absolute control. . . . We destroy the School Boards, but, in their place, we set up an authority with just as real power, but with far wider range, for it covers practically the whole country.' The new rating authority for education should not actually manage the schools itself, but should have managers under it who would carry out its instructions in individual schools. In the case of voluntary schools the existing bodies of managers might continue in office having representatives of the county added to their number.

It was the need to bring the fourteen thousand or so voluntary elementary schools within the new local rate-supported structure, while for political reasons preserving their denominational charac-teristics, that caused the Education Bill of 1902 to arouse so much fierce controversy for so long. In perspective, the Act of 1902 may be thought of as bringing about the structure of the educational system which this country still enjoys to-day: at the time the measure appeared to half of the nation as an attempt to make it pay through the rates for the propagation of religious views which were unacceptable. While the Bill was still being drafted, the government, fearing the conse-quences of compelling local authorities to give rate aid to denomina-tional schools, sought to find some workable scheme of local option: Morant argued successfully that there was no fair way of levying the rate needed for an optional aid scheme[24] even though its advocates within the Government included the influential leader of the Liberal Unionists, Joseph Chamberlain.

II

The new administrative arrangements envisaged by the government emerged virtually unscathed from the bitter Parliamentary conflict of 1902. School Boards and School Attendance Committees were abolished, their powers and duties under the various Elementary Education Acts from 1870 were transferred to the new local elementary education authority[25] as were their assets and liabilities.[26] The officers of the defunct bodies were transferred to the new authorities which had to pay them compensation if it abolished their posts. During the interim period between the passing of the Act and the 'Appointed Day' on which the new authorities were to take over, the existing members of school boards were to stay in office and were to furnish the future authority with any information which it might desire.

In establishing the new authorities, a clear distinction was introduced between the management and control of schools. A body which had only management was merely responsible for certain detailed administrative work, but the education authority with control was made responsible for the school; it was the duty of the authority to provide the funds needed, to settle questions of principle and to secure efficiency. The new local education authorities were to be the councils of counties and of county boroughs along with the councils of non-county boroughs with a population of over ten thousand people and the councils of urban districts with a population of over twenty thousand, the last two being authorities for elementary education only in terms of Part III of the Act.[27]* All non-county boroughs and all urban districts had power to spend up to the limit of a penny rate on 'supplying or aiding the supply of education other than elementary',[28] but the smaller boroughs and urban districts were not considered to be education authorities, they were not obliged to set up education committees and—since they were also rated for higher education by the county authority—few of them considered exercising these powers.

The creation of authorities for elementary education only meant that the argument advanced by Morant in memoranda for abolishing the school boards, viz. the difficulty and undesirability of trying to distinguish between elementary and other forms of education and the need for only one authority for all education in each area, appeared to be contradicted by the Act itself. The explanation of the concession of elementary powers to the larger non-county boroughs and urban districts lay in the anxiety of the government to secure the passage of the bill and not to stir the Parliamentary representatives of these towns into rejecting this measure as they had that introduced by Gorst in 1896 because that had tried to give the control of education in their towns to the county councils. The powers of Part III authorities were confined to 'the provision in a public elementary school of instruction given under the regulations of the Board of Education to scholars who, at the close of the school year, will not be more than sixteen years of age'.[29] In Part III areas the county council was made responsible not only for secondary school provision, but also for a number of

---

* There were 137 non-county boroughs and 64 urban districts whose councils qualified as authorities for Part III (elementary) purposes only. The population limit for qualification was that shown by the Census of 1901 (S 23 (8)) and the Act did not contain any provision for admitting boroughs or urban districts whose populations might later increase.

fields formerly occupied in some places by the school boards such as the training of teachers, higher grade schools, continuation schools and evening classes.

Before 1902 the Board of Education dealt directly not only with the school boards, but also with the bodies of managers of more than 14,000 voluntary elementary schools each of which was, to some extent, an authority itself since it possessed powers of control as well as of management and bore the ultimate financial responsibilities for its own school. The Act not merely removed powers of control from the managers of voluntary schools, it also set out the future constitution of bodies of managers for both non-provided (or voluntary) and provided (board or council) schools. All schools provided by a county council were to have managers, four of whom were to be appointed by the council and two by the minor local authority of the district; in the case of schools provided by county borough or Part III councils, managers could be appointed if the authority wished to do so. Non-provided schools in all areas were to have their own bodies of managers, normally consisting of four 'foundation' managers chosen in accordance with a school's trust deed along with two appointed by the education authority in a county borough or Part III area or, in a county area, one by the education authority and one by the minor district council.[30] In the vast majority of cases existing trust deeds did not require the appointment of the four foundation managers and one of the heaviest tasks which fell to the Board of Education in putting the Act of 1902 into effect was the revision of the trust deeds of voluntary schools to fit them to the requirements laid down for non-provided schools.

The powers of managers of provided schools were such as the local authority allowed them. The most important administrative function which managers of non-provided schools kept concerned the appointment of teachers, for within the establishment for the school set by the authority, the managers appointed the head teacher and assistant staff and could dismiss them. The authority could refuse to accept an appointment on the grounds that the nominee of the managers was educationally inefficient, in cases of dispute the matter was to be referred to the Board of Education. Managers could dismiss teachers on religious grounds, and in these circumstances there could be no appeal from their decision, but if they dismissed a teacher as educationally inefficient, then the agreement of the authority was necessary. The managers kept complete control over the religious teaching in their school which was to continue in accordance with the trust deed. It was the duty of the managers to provide the school building and to keep it in repair, undertaking any improvements 'reasonably required' by the authority; the local authority in its turn was to meet the cost of repairs made necessary by 'fair wear and tear'.[31] After 1902 control of salaries and finances generally, control over secular education, the curriculum and all other aspects of the administration of non-provided schools lay with the local authority.

These provisions had no close parallel in the arrangements made for secondary education. Here it was the duty of the local authority to consider the needs of the area and then 'to supply or aid the supply of education other than elementary, and to promote the general co-ordination of all forms of education'.[32] Where an authority decided to build a new school, then full management and control clearly lay in its hands, but in the case of existing schools there was no attempt in the Act to lay down general rules as to the constitution of their managing or governing bodies. Where local authorities gave aid to grammar schools they usually sought the right to appoint representatives to their governing bodies, but they were no longer obliged to do this as they had been under the Technical Instruction Act of 1889. Secondary education was still a voluntary matter, parents could not demand it as of right for their children and authorities were not obliged to spend even up to the limit of the twopenny rate on 'education other than elementary'. Moreover, the acute religious controversy which made necessary the imposition of a detailed settlement by Act of Parliament in the elementary field did not exist in the same way in secondary education.

The new local education authorities were to discharge their functions through education committees constituted in accordance with schemes approved by the Board of Education. 'All matters relating to the exercise by the council of their powers under this Act, except the power of raising a rate or borrowing money, shall stand referred to the education committee, and the council, before exercising any such powers, shall, unless in their opinion the matter is urgent, receive and consider the report of the education committee with respect to the matter in question.'[33] In practice the full powers of control, management and the sanctioning of expenditure raised devolved upon education committees while the parent body confined itself to levying rates and borrowing money.

Section 17 of the Act laid down that a council should appoint a majority of the members of its education committee (although in the case of counties these did not need to be members of the council); apart from this provision, the Act also required the appointment of persons of experience in education, of persons acquainted with the needs of various types of schools and of women as well as men as committee members. Early in 1903 Morant issued a Memorandum on Education Committees in which he suggested suitable ways of constituting these committees in some detail. This document suggested five interests that should always be represented:

> University education;
> Secondary education;
> Technical instruction and commercial and industrial education having special regard to local industries;
> The training of teachers;
> Elementary education in both council and voluntary schools.

One of the most important changes introduced in 1902 was the imposition on the new local authorities of financial responsibility for all elementary schools, whether voluntary or board. To meet this burden the authorities were to have up to eight sources of income apart from the local rate. These were:

(1) The Parliamentary grants payable in respect of public elementary schools under the Code.

(2) Fee grant (amounting to 10s. per child).

(3) Agriculture rating grant (a fixed sum).

(4) Proportion of any income arising out of school endowments.

(5) Charges for the letting of schoolrooms, sale of books and so forth.

(6) Proportion of school fees where these were still being charged.

(7) New grant of 4s. per child.

(8) Variable grant for poorer areas.

The two last grants were intended to replace the grants which had been paid under the Voluntary Schools Act of 1897, the variable grant being calculated in such a way as to be of special assistance to rural areas which were largely represented in the Commons by government supporters. The basis for calculating the variable grant was set out in the Act as 'an additional sum of three half-pence per scholar for every complete two-pence per scholar by which the amount which would be produced by a penny rate on the area of the authority falls short of ten shillings a scholar'.[34] Items 4, 5 and 6 in the list given above could not have been expected to produce very much. The difference between the amount receivable under these various headings and the actual cost of running the elementary school system was to be charged to the rates.

Some services which had previously been paid for by school boards from the funds for elementary education were specifically excluded from those moneys and made chargeable to higher education by the operation of the Act. Thus pupil teacher centres and teacher training generally, evening schools and higher grade board schools could hardly be disowned and left derelict, but had to be paid for out of the funds available for higher education. In some areas where County Technical Instruction Committees had made no attempt to use the rates to assist secondary and technical education and where even the 'whisky' money had been spent on relieving the general county rate instead of on education, a rate to pay for higher education had to be levied for the first time under the new Act. The revenue for supporting 'education other than elementary' was to come from three main sources:[35]

(1) Parliamentary grants for instruction in science and art paid through the Board of Education's branch at South Kensington.

(2) Revenue arising under the Local Taxation (Customs and Excise) Act of 1890.[36]

(3) The ability to levy a rate, unlimited in county boroughs but limited to 2d. in the £ in county areas.

It should, perhaps, be added that there was no limit on the amount which councils could borrow on the security of the rate to meet their items of capital expenditure, other than that which the Local Government Board might see fit to impose in exercising its discretion.

Morant was anxious that the new administrative system should begin to function as soon as possible. On 4th March, 1903, he wrote to the future authorities suggesting that 1st April would be 'widely adopted' as the appointed day for them to take up their new responsibilities; he added that if an authority requested a date later than 1st May, 1903, it was to 'furnish a statement showing fully the reasons which, in their opinion, render the postponement desirable'.[37] Even so, many authorities found themselves unable to complete the pre-

N

liminary arrangements rapidly enough to be ready to take over in the spring of 1903. However, by the autumn of that year Morant could write to Balfour that 'all the English authorities are administering the Act . . .';[38] the picture was very different in Wales, but the difference was not due to any administrative fault, it was due to political and religious feeling in that country.

REFERENCES

[1] Newcastle Cssn., 1861, Vol. I, pp. 333–40 and 204.
[2] Cross Cssn., 1888, Final Report, pp. 204–06.
[3] S.I.C. Report, pp. 639–43.
[4] Supra, pp. 63–4.
[5] Bryce Cssn., vol. I, 1895, p. 65.
[6] Ibid., p. 207.
[7] Ibid., pp. 267–70.
[8] *The Times*, 13th June, 1895, quoted by A. Rogers in an article 'Churches and Children —A Study in the Controversy over the 1902 Education Act', *B.J.E.S.*, vol. VIII, pp. 29–51, where there is a full discussion of the religious factors involved.
[9] Supra, pp. 147–8.
[10] 60 & 61 Vict., c 5.
[11] P.R.O. Ed. 24/19, 14/2/02, Kingsford to Morant.
[12] P.R.O., Ed. 24/20, 21/3/02, Note on Voluntary School Aid Grant.
[13] P.R.O., Ed. 24/29, 13/12/00, Gorst to Devonshire.
[14] P.R.O., Ed. 24/17, 2/11/01, Archdeacon of Birmingham to Gorst.
[15] Ibid., 28/11/61, Bishop of Stepney to Morant.
[16] Letter from Bishop of Rochester to Lord Salisbury, 4/12/01, quoted by B. M. Allen, *Sir Robert Morant*, p. 163.
[17] P.R.O. Ed. 24/29, 13/12/00, Gorst to Devonshire.
[18] P.R.O. Ed. 24/16, 23/6/01, Gorst to Morant.
[19] E. Eaglesham—Planning the Education Bill of 1902—*B.J.E.S.*, vol. IX, pp. 4 and 5.
[20] P.R.O. Ed. 24/14, points against *Ad Hoc* by R.L.M.
[21] P.R.O. Ed. 24/14, 1/8/01. Eaglesham attributes this unsigned Memorandum to Morant, *B.J.E.S.*, vol. IX, p. 9.
[22] P.R.O. Ed. 26/14, Oct. 1901, Precis of Inspectors (L.G.B.) Reports.
[23] P.R.O. Ed. 24/18, 3/1/02, Morant to Balfour.
[24] Ibid., 10/1/02, Memorandum by Morant on the Administrative Difficulties of Free Option in Rate Aid.
[25] 2 Edw. VII, c. 42, S 5.
[26] Ibid., Schedule II.
[27] Ibid., S 1.
[28] Ibid., S 3.
[29] Ibid., S 22.
[30] Ibid., S 6.
[31] Ibid., S 7.
[32] Ibid., S 2.
[33] Ibid., S 17 (2).
[34] 2 Edw. VII, c. 42, S 10 (1(b)).
[35] Board of Education, Circular No. 470, 1903.
[36] 53 & 54 Vict., c. 60.
[37] Board of Education, Circular No. 474, 1903.
[38] P.R.O. Ed. 24/14, Morant to Balfour, 28/10/03.

CHAPTER 10

LOCAL EDUCATION AUTHORITIES SINCE 1902

I

BEFORE the 'appointed day' when they began to exercise their educational duties, the local authorities needed to make themselves acquainted with the educational facilities of their districts. So far as elementary schools were concerned, the new Act required managers and school attendance committees to provide the new authorities with the information that they might 'reasonably require';[1] accordingly many councils set about issuing questionnaires to school board clerks and to correspondents asking for particulars of accommodation, average attendance, tenure of school buildings and the relationship between income and expenditure during the past year. Apart from this information which was essential to enable the new authorities to take over the 'board' schools and to extend rate-aid to 'voluntary' schools on the appointed day, the new authorities also needed to prepare lists of suitable persons willing to accept appointment as managers in provided and non-provided schools. Immediately the schools were taken over the existing managers went out of office and newly constituted bodies had to be installed. So far as the administration of higher education was concerned, much less preparation of this sort was needed for most counties and county boroughs were already well aware of the existing situation in this field through exercising powers under the Technical Instruction Acts. The only exceptions to this were the higher grade 'board' schools and the pupil teacher centres of both the school boards and the diocesan bodies, both of these now became part of higher education, and the Part II authorities needed to obtain particulars of them in order to arrange for their maintenance.

The establishment of an education committee by the appointed day did not, generally speaking, cause much difficulty. Morant set out the requirements of the Act clearly in a Board of Education circular to the new authorities[2] and the Board was able to give its approval without delay to the great majority of draft schemes for education committees submitted. In the case of the counties, the new committees were often seen as remodelled versions of the technical instruction committees and the technical instruction committees or their chairmen usually advised on—and were sometimes given the task of preparing—the new schemes. In Staffordshire, for example, the chairman of the technical instruction committee prepared the draft scheme by which the County Council delegated all its powers under the Act of 1902 to the education committee with the exception of those of appointing members to the committee, raising a rate and borrowing money.

While the composition of education committees followed the lines laid down by the Act and the Board's circular, there was considerable local variation in their size and in the proportion of co-opted members. A typical committee in a rural county was that for West Suffolk with thirty-two members, chosen thus:

24 members from the county council, including the chairman, the chairman of the finance committee and four members of school boards,

2 members appointed by the county council to be women experienced in the education of girls,

1 member appointed by the county council on the nomination of Cambridge University,

2 members appointed by the county council, one of whom was to be experienced in secondary and one in technical education,

3 members appointed by the county council, one of whom was to be from West Suffolk N.U.T., one from Sudbury Voluntary Schools Association, and one from the Free Church Federation.[3]

The more populous and industrialized county of Stafford had a larger education committee, and included representatives of the main industries. This committee had 52 members including the chairman and vice-chairman of the council, 34 members of the county council including 2 representatives each for agriculture, metallurgy, mining and pottery, 2 women of experience in education, one member to be nominated by the University of Birmingham, 3 persons with special knowledge of secondary and 2 with special knowledge of elementary schools, 2 secondary and 2 elementary teachers and 4 representatives of the voluntary schools including 2 from the Church Schools Association, 1 from Birmingham Roman Catholic Diocesan Association and 1 from the Wesleyan and British Associations.[4]

The co-opted members in counties and county boroughs tended to constitute about one-third of the total membership of the education committees; in Liverpool the committee consisted of 34 members of the council and 18 co-opted members, while in Manchester from 1906 the committee of 33 included 13 co-opted members. This proportion of co-opted members was not found on all education committees in the years following 1902, one of the largest authorities to make little use of co-optation almost from the start was Leeds. The original scheme for the constitution of the education committee provided for 22 members of the city council and 14 co-opted members. When the first committee retired after the municipal elections in the autumn of 1904, 'the committee was reconstructed on lines laid down by the City Council, all members being members of the City Council with the exception of two ladies specially co-opted for the purposes of the Act'.[5] This tradition has persisted in educational administration in Leeds and sixty years later the education committee has only 3 co-opted members.

The many duties of the new education committees made it essential for them to divide their work among sub-committees. Generally speaking, the larger authorities tended to appoint more sub-committees; an urban district with powers under Part III of the Act dealing only with elementary education clearly needed a less elaborate sub-committee system than a county or large county borough charged with the administration of education at different levels. Under the Local Authorities (Admission of Press to Meetings) Act, 1908, representatives of the press gained the right to be present at meetings of the local education authority. When education committees dealt with business that did not require the later approval of the Council, the press could claim admission. Consequently, it was convenient always to arrange that at least one sub-committee included all members of the education committee so that as and when the need arose it was possible to refer potentially difficult topics to that sub-committee where every member could take part in a discussion in 'sub-committee' and speak quite freely. Without this device it could happen that some members might only be able to make their views heard at the public meeting with the press in attendance. The name given to this sub-committee of all the members varied, but it was frequently the finance and general purposes sub-committee.

In small Part III authorities, it was often found adequate to appoint only three sub-committees, those for finance and general purposes, for attendance and for elementary education—the latter being sometimes known as the school management sub-committee. In a few towns, the sub-committee system seems to have been more or less consciously based on the organization originally used by the school board. This happened in Leeds where the clerk to the Leeds School Board became the chief officer of the new education committee, and his advice might well have been influential in this matter.

Leeds School Board Committees in 1900[6]	Sub-committees of Leeds Education Committee in 1904[7]
Education and Management	Elementary Education
Technical Instruction, Higher Grade and Evening Schools	Higher Education
School Attendance	School Attendance
Finance and General Purposes	Education Finance
Sites and Buildings	Sites and Buildings
Industrial Schools	Industrial Schools
Blind and Deaf Schools	Special Schools

The main sub-committee structure remained unchanged in Leeds for some years with only minor variations, for instance, the Higher Education sub-committee became the Higher Education and Training College sub-committee after the establishment of the City of Leeds Training College.

Possibly one of the few general remarks which can truthfully be made about sub-committee organization is that it varied greatly from place to place depending on the work to be done and local tradition. West Suffolk, a county authority with a population less than half that of Leeds had an apparently more elaborate sub-committee structure in the years before 1914. It had nine main sub-committees as well as five Joint Higher Sub-Committees to deal with higher education in the boroughs of Bury St. Edmunds and Sudbury, and in the urban districts of Haverhill, Hadleigh and Newmarket.[8]

The sub-committee arrangements of most authorities indicate the much greater importance of questions connected with attendance sixty years ago. Most of the central government's grants were made to hinge in some way on attendance, consequently at a time when attendance at school was far from popular in many areas local authorities made great efforts to ensure regular attendance. In Stafford-shire 'a firm and uniform administration of the bye-laws' had led to an increase from a percentage attendance of 88·7 in 1904 to 91·4 in 1912.

'This improvement represents an approximate saving to the county rates of £48,000 in the last eight years.'[9] The difficulty inherent in trying to enforce attendance directly through a central office in a large county was one of the main reasons why a number of counties established district committees with the important duty of maintaining regular attendance as well as advising the county authorities on local needs and providing a means of co-operation with minor local authorities. In many cases the secretary to such a committee would be the local attendance officer. These local committees would report direct to the education committee or through a sub-committee, often the attendance sub-committee.

The expansion of the education service to include medical inspection, the provision of school meals, juvenile employment bureaux and similar supplementary services before and after the First World War led to the establishment by many authorities of more sub-committees to manage the additional services. There was always the danger that if an authority set up too many sub-committees there would be difficulty in arranging times for meetings without clashing dates; especially was this so in the case of council members of education committees who had to fit in their attendances with engagements in connection with their work on other committees of the council. On the other hand, too few sub-committees could lead to very long meetings if the business was to be adequately dealt with. Authorities had, therefore, to maintain a balance between these conflicting require-ments. The further delegation of work by the sub-committees them-selves helped to overcome these difficulties provided that members of the superior body abstained from frequently re-arguing matters when the smaller group reported its findings. The careful definition of the duties of each sub-committee to avoid over-lapping also helped to make the system work more smoothly.[10]

Perhaps the most important single factor in the successful administra-tion of the schools by the local education authorities after 1902 was the appointment of knowledgeable experts as their officers. Most of the counties and some county boroughs already had suitable men working for their technical instruction committees and the director of or secretary for technical education often found himself translated to be director of or secretary for education. In some county boroughs and in many of the boroughs and urban districts administering elementary education only, the clerk to the school board became the Chief Officer of the new education authority; this tended to occur only in the towns because the area administered by the former school board and that administered by the new authority was usually the same. In Manchester the authority appointed Reynolds, the former Director of Technical Education as Director of Higher Education and Wyatt, the former Secretary to the School Board as Director of Elementary Education. The two sections of the city's education department did not come under the control of one official until 1911 when Reynolds retired and Wyatt became simply Director of Education.[11] In different authorities the post of the head of the education office was described by a variety of terms Clerk, Secretary, Director or Chief Officer—but the variation in titular description did not indicate any general difference of functions. The post in all cases carried with it responsibility for the proper working of the education department and for the efficient discharge of their duties by the officers working under him. In some of the smaller Part III authorities the Clerk to the Council acted as Director of Education, in others the full-time Director or Secretary might well have only one clerical assistant by way of office staff.

In the larger authorities a much more elaborate arrangement was necessary. In Staffordshire in 1912 the education department staff included an Assistant Secretary for Elementary Education, an Assistant Secretary for Higher Education, a Senior Medical Inspector and four assistant inspectors, a School Architect, an Accounts Clerk, a School Attendance Superintendent and a clerical staff. The appointment of separate assistant education officers to be responsible for elementary and higher education was usual among the larger county borough and county authorities. The different codes and grant regulations for elementary and higher education made it convenient to divide the work of a department in this way. Just as the growth of supplementary services often led to some extension of the sub-committee system, so it also led to an increase in the number of officers that the larger authorities needed to appoint. Before the First World War it became necessary to appoint a school medical officer; in the 1920s those authorities which took over Juvenile Employment Exchanges from the Ministry of Labour—mainly county boroughs—usually appointed a Juvenile Employment Officer.

II

The main weakness in the local administrative arrangements enacted in 1902 arose where the government of the day had been obliged to retreat from Morant's proposals to have only one authority responsible for all forms of education in each area. The need to appease government supporters from non-county boroughs and urban districts by offering those areas powers over elementary education under Part III of the Act led to difficulties in some places between the authorities for higher and those for elementary education. The distribution of local authorities for elementary education only was dependent upon population distribution and the legal standing of townships in 1901, and there was no provision either to give powers of higher education to those places which grew or to take powers of elementary education away from towns whose populations diminished. It so happened that in 1901 the greatest concentrations of towns able to claim this status were in the northern industrial counties of Lancashire and the West Riding, and in Middlesex. The actual distribution was summarized in the Hadow Report thus:[12]

England.   6 counties contained no autonomous areas;
             16 counties contained one each;
             8 counties contained two each;
             8 counties contained three each;

the remaining 10 counties contained respectively 4, 5, 6, 7, 8, 9, 12, 13, 16 and 27 autonomous areas.

Wales.   8 contained no autonomous areas;
           2 contained two each;
           2 contained three each;
           1 contained seven.

The 1902 local administrative arrangements for counties appear in general to have worked most smoothly in counties which contained no autonomous areas, and in some of those which contained most, for in the former no friction could arise while in the latter— such as Lancashire—the possible difficulties would have been so overwhelming that attempts had to be made to devise reasonable working arrangements.

The triumph of the Liberal Party in the general election of 1906 gave those opposed to the religious settlement of 1902 an opportunity to try to reverse it; many of these opponents also lamented the passing of the school boards and their replacement by an allegedly remote county administration which was said to lack the boards' understanding of local conditions. Consequently, the Education Bill introduced by Birrell proposed to grant autonomy for all forms of education to boroughs and urban districts with populations of 50,000 or above and to compel counties with populations in excess of 65,000 to prepare schemes for delegating their functions to district authorities or to local bodies elected especially for this purpose on the lines of the former school boards. None of this Liberal Government's attempts to revise the Act of 1902 were to find favour with the House of Lords, consequently these administrative proposals came to nothing.

The Government did start an inquiry into the extent and desirability of devolution of powers by county councils to local district committees and the Report of the Consultative Committee was issued in 1908.[13] Most of the arguments advanced since 1944 for and against the system of divisional administration were put forward to the Committee in the course of its inquiry. Under the Act of 1902 education committees had the power to appoint sub-committees and these could be concerned only with certain parts of the county, they would be district committees and would report to the county education committee just in the way that any other sub-committee would do. Where they were established, these district committees usually consisted of some members of the education committee along with nominees of the district councils. The Consultative Committee found that most counties had not set up district sub-committees; their reasons for not doing so can be grouped under three main headings:

(1) Economy of administration; district sub-committees led inevitably to an increase in the number of officials and correspondence and proved incompatible with the economies possible under a centralized system:

(2) Educational efficiency; educational progress was more likely to be secured by the central body of a large area than by a more limited and local body, only large areas could afford highly trained and efficient staff with a wide outlook:

(3) Administrative efficiency; the multiplication of committees involved delay in administration, moreover such local committees were bound to limit the scope for managers. In two-thirds of the counties objections to any scheme for local devolution had been such that it had not been thought wise to adopt such district sub-committee schemes, while of the twenty counties that had tried the system, it was

reported to be giving general satisfaction in about eleven. District sub-committees—unlike school managers—could be given delegated powers to initiate prosecutions for failure to attend school and in some counties the local bodies were acting mainly as local attendance committees.

The Consultative Committee was unable to make any very positive recommendations. It commented that if the system was to work, districts would have to be given real executive powers and that it was possible to combine this with retention by education committees of the ultimate control of their sub-committees' proceedings. In those counties where district committees were most used, the business devolved to some extent included attendance, accommodation, repairs and school supplies. 'The Committee, however, consider—and this is the point upon which they wish to lay especial stress—that in view of the widely differing circumstances of the various counties, it would be difficult, if not impossible to devise any uniform system which would give general satisfaction throughout the country. . . . [The reasons for this included social and industrial conditions and also] that the personnel and the educational history and traditions of a county often have nearly as close a bearing upon its educational organization as have its geographical or industrial conditions.' The Report of the Consultative Committee had little effect save to confirm the situation as it already existed.

A further attempt to enact legislation that could have affected the position of the Part III authorities was made when Fisher was President of the Board of Education. He proposed that as part of the educational reconstruction to be based on his Act of 1918 the Board should be given power to deprive any Part III authority of its powers if it appeared to be inefficient and that where this happened the administration of elementary schools should be taken over by the county council. This proposal evoked defensive action among the Part III authorities and a group of those in the West Riding called a meeting at which resolutions opposing Fisher's proposal were adopted. The Association of Education Committees showed itself sympathetic to these resolutions and Fisher dropped his proposal.

So far as autonomous areas for elementary education were concerned, the steady growth of county secondary (grammar) schools in their areas often led to difficult practical problems. The organization of the scholarship examinations at the age of eleven could lead to difficulties. In some places a joint committee of the county and the Part III authority made the necessary arrangements, but in others there was disagreement and failure to co-operate. Some Part III authorities set up central schools under the elementary code in an effort to provide their own form of secondary education in competition with that provided by the county; where the county and local school years did not coincide it happened that children might win a scholarship to a central school and take it up there in April, only to be offered a scholarship later to go to the county grammar school in the following September so that their places in the central school would then have to be filled by another reshuffle in the elementary schools after only one term. Evening classes also grew in number and importance, these were run by the county, often in Part III elementary day school buildings using Part III equipment and Part III day-time employees as teachers; thus these evening classes were, in a sense, being provided by the Part III authority and 'hired out' to the county which simply financed them. The Hadow Committee was forced to face the problem of autonomous areas for elementary education only in view of the nature of its proposals for the future education of those over the age of eleven. 'As the law now stands', the Committee commented, 'authorities for elementary education administer only Elementary Schools which include, however, in view of Section 20 of the Education Act of 1921, a large portion of post-primary schools (e.g. Central Schools and Classes, Senior Schools, Senior Departments and Higher Tops), which we, in common with many of our witnesses, regard as belonging properly to the secondary grade of education. Will it be possible in the future for the country to acquiesce permanently in the division of part of the secondary grade of education between two separate authorities in the same area, with the result that an authority for elementary education only may start a Modern School or Senior Class when neighbouring "Secondary" Schools under the administration of the authority for higher education are not fully used?'[14] The full adoption of the Hadow Report in the existing administrative structure would presumably have meant that those who failed to win scholarships would have continued under the elementary code in their post-primary schools which would have had a less well-paid staff, less apparatus and equipment and fewer books than the post-primary schools run by the county authority under the secondary code. The Part III administrative arrangements stemming from the Act of 1902 did constitute one of the barriers to a parity of treatment of the different types of post-primary schools in the 1930s. The Hadow Committee recommended that as a medium-term solution legislation should be introduced to abolish the elementary education authorities as such, giving to those of them which attained a minimum standard of population full powers in respect of higher education also, while those which did not reach the minimum standard should have their existing elementary powers transferred to the county authorities. The Committee suggested that the long-term solution to the question would be to institute provincial authorities for education 'in which the authorities for Elementary Education only and the Authorities for Higher Education shall both be ultimately merged'.[15]

The Board of Education submitted evidence to the Royal Commission on Local Government in 1927 explaining that the development of 'central' or 'modern' schools on the lines suggested by the Hadow Report as a separate and individual contribution to the supply of post-primary education could be unfavourably affected by their administrative segregation from other forms of post-primary school.[16] For economic reasons, the May Committee on National Expenditure found that in the interests of efficient administration the number of authorities should be reduced by the concentration of local educational work in the hands of the County and County Borough Councils.[17] The final recommendation on this subject to appear in a government report before the Second World War was that of the Spens Committee. This recommended that the problem of Part III authorities should be remitted to a Departmental or Inter-Departmental Committee which would investigate the circumstances of individual areas and then suggest a solution.[18] The Spens Committee recorded in their Report that they had been informed that Lancashire had found a measure of devolution of higher education powers to be a workable scheme.

The certainty of encountering political trouble as well as administrative inertia prevented the central government from taking any steps to resolve this issue between the wars. However, the Second World War brought with it a measure of educational upheaval and produced a widespread desire for reform in most fields of political and social activity. The Board of Education set out some ideas on post-war educational reconstruction in its Green Book of 1941, a 'confidential' document, and in this the Board looked forward to a reduction in the number of local education authorities and a more unified national system. These suggestions stirred the Part III authorities and their representatives in national political life to activity. Dr. P. G. Richards has commented 'So the story of 1896 began to be repeated in 1943, and finally Mr. Butler introduced proposals for divisional administration to reduce difficulties in the passage of the Bill'.[19]

III

The attempt made in the Education Act of 1944 to deal with the Part III problem was the most important innovation which it introduced in the local administrative structure.[20] The White Paper on Educational Reconstruction[21] stated that there were two serious objections to the existing system, firstly the division of responsibility for education in some areas between two authorities, secondly the incongruities which had arisen from determining elementary education authorities on the basis of population figures in the 1901 census. This latter provision had led to Harrow Urban District with a population of 183,000 in 1938, but of recent growth having no educational powers, while the Borough of Tiverton, with fewer than 10,000 inhabitants, was an elementary education authority because its population exceeded that figure in 1901. The White Paper suggested that all local education authorities should be charged with all educational functions and that there should be 'arrangements for preserving and stimulating local interest in education'. It proposed that these principles should be carried out by regarding only councils of counties and county boroughs as local education authorities and, so that local interest was maintained, proposed to require county authorities to set up district committees. These committees were to have the general duty of keeping educational provision under review and making the district's wishes known to the county. The counties could also delegate other functions to district committees which were to have a right of appeal to the Board if they were dissatisfied with the extent of delegation proposed by the county.

The Part III interests were unwilling to accept these proposals which seemed to envisage nothing more at the district level than the committees which some counties had set up under the Act of 1902. The government retreated on this issue to the extent that the district education committees proposed were to be guaranteed some executive functions, and county authorities would not be able to treat them simply as advisory committees. The provisions of the Education Act relating to divisional executives were set out in Part III of the First Schedule. This required county education authorities to review the circumstances of each part of their areas and to make schemes for the establishment and operation of divisional executives as seemed most expedient. The Minister had power to exempt the area of any local education authority if he considered it to be unnecessary for it to introduce a scheme of divisional administration.[22] Boroughs and urban districts with a population in 1939 of at least 60,000 or with at least 7,000 children on the elementary school registers, had the right to claim to be excepted from any scheme of divisional administration; the Minister could also direct that in special circumstances small boroughs and urban districts should also be excepted. The council of any town whose claim to excepted district status was found to be acceptable then drew up its own scheme of divisional administration which it submitted to the county to be forwarded to the Minister.

The selection of geographical areas, the constitution and the functions of divisional executives were all treated in a Ministry circular on Schemes of Divisional Administration issued for the guidance of those concerned.[23] The circular indicated that some areas were not suited to divisional administration; areas that were selected to become divisions should have a population not far short of 60,000, the inhabitants should have a community of interest and there should be a convenient administrative centre. The size of population in the various divisions set up varied greatly, ranging from about 22,000 to well over 200,000. Local conditions varied a great deal, and different counties took different lines of approach to the question. In some counties the main concern was to base divisions on the most suitable catchment areas for educational purposes. This was the line taken in Surrey where five towns which fulfilled the conditions required for excepted district status abandoned their claims and merged with the remainder of the county to form nine divisions whose populations ranged from 80,000 to about 210,000. Other counties basing their divisions mainly on educational considerations included Derbyshire and Kent. At the other extreme some counties fitted their divisions into the existing pattern of local administration, foremost among these was Lancashire. The former district committees in this county had been linked to the district councils and the divisional executives largely replaced them, thus the county had no less than 37 divisions including two excepted districts and the smallest of these had a population of only 22,000. Two unfortunate consequences of this arrangement were that the cost of administering education in Lancashire was heavy and some divisions were too small to make reasonable arrangements for the more specialized forms of secondary education. In many counties the divisions were based partly on educational functions and partly on the local government framework.

The constitution of the executives followed the advice given in Circular No. 5; normally they consisted of representatives of the local education authority, nominees of the district councils and other persons of experience in education. In excepted districts, the town council became the divisional executive and in such divisions a committee for education consisting of members of the council and co-opted educationalists was set up. The circular pointed out that in preparing schemes of divisional administration, a local education authority 'cannot divest itself of its statutory responsibility for finance, or for ensuring that an adequate standard of educational provision is maintained throughout its area'. Even on many matters that were delegated, such as school meals, the county might need to issue regulations from time to time to ensure that there was a reasonable measure of uniformity throughout its area. Apart from powers which the authority itself needed to keep, certain powers were reserved to the governors and managers of schools. Most administrative matters left after these reservations could be delegated and the Circular listed them:

(1) Assessment of the educational needs of the divisional area and advising the authority on the need for new schools and extensions;

(2) Care and use of school premises, repairs and lettings;

(3) School supplies—under arrangements agreed with the local authority;

(4) In connection with the work of the schools, to consider inspector's reports and to arrange out-of-school visits;

(5) School attendance, and, subject to the authority's regulations, to arrange school holidays, admissions, transfer and transport;

(6) Welfare of pupils, subject to the authority's regulations, to administer milk and meals and to arrange medical inspections.

Since schemes required Ministry approval, it is not surprising that the functions delegated to the divisions followed closely those listed in the circular; in very few cases were further education functions delegated, the Ministry stated that the delegation of an authority's functions in respect of technical colleges and the like would not be appropriate 'in view of the wide area and varied interests normally served by such institutions'.

Of rather more than 200 divisional executives which were set up under the Act of 1944, nearly a quarter—forty-four—possessed excepted district status. Under the Act, an excepted district is a divisional executive with certain special features of its own, but in practice there are differences in the way an excepted district administers its affairs which are of some importance. In the first place, the members of the executive are accustomed to working together in fields other than education, they are not a gathering of nominees from various separate district councils. They find it easier to attain a measure of unity since they do not feel—as members of more widely scattered executives sometimes do—that they must press the claims of their particular district against the representatives of some other district within the same division. Secondly, an excepted district usually makes use of its own local officials instead of relying upon those provided by the county council, thus some of the financial and legal work arising in the course of administering the schools is undertaken by the relevant departments of the local civic organization. Thirdly, excepted districts tend to have rather more widely drawn schemes of divisional administration than do the other executives since they alone were given the right to draw up their own schemes of delegation, after consulting the county authority, for submission to the Minister.[24]

In an excepted district, the divisional education officer is frequently regarded as head of one of the main departments of the civic organization, on a par with the borough engineer or borough treasurer, in fact, in common with all other divisional education officers and their staffs, he is an employee of the county. The qualifications, salary and terms of appointment of divisional officers are decided by the county authorities, but divisional executives are often consulted on these matters, and they can make any representations they wish to their authority. The salaries offered to and the qualifications sought in divisional officers vary widely, they varied even more in the years immediately after divisional administration was introduced. Some counties which had had district committees served by a clerk stationed in the district thought in terms of the post of divisional education officer being filled by men with the background of section clerks, men who had left school and gone straight into an office without either higher education or teaching experience.[25] On the other hand some counties from the beginning sought to appoint as divisional officers men who had a degree and some teaching or administrative

O

experience. In more recent years authorities generally have come to adopt a policy of appointing men of the latter type.

The duties of divisional officers were set out in Circular 5, and the statement of duties in most schemes of divisional administration followed the circular closely. Briefly the officers have to act as chief executive officers to the divisional executives, give them such advice as they may require and carry out the executives' instructions on matters delegated to them; at the same time the officers as local representatives of the counties have to serve as agents for the authorities in respect of matters that have not been delegated. There is no doubt that their responsibility to two masters has placed officers in a difficult position when the relations between the division and the county have been poor. Where tensions of this sort exist, the situation demands great tact on the part of divisional officers; their position is such that they can at times of difficulty act as most valuable intermediaries, ensuring that both county and division see the other man's point of view.

Since both division and county are trying to share between them the task of administering the education system at a local level, there are almost endless opportunities for discord and bad feeling if the will to co-operate is lacking. Probably the most vital field is that of finance for here while 'ultimate financial responsibility must rest with the local education authority, to whom the power to borrow money or to raise a rate is specifically reserved, schemes may provide for the delegation of financial responsibility in varying degrees'.[26] The way in which a county authority exercises its financial responsibility and the closeness of its control over expenditure must affect every branch of a divisional executive's work; even in the case of services entirely delegated to a division, the authority can bring about any curtailment of an activity by removing items from a division's estimates. The procedure of preparing estimates in divisions and getting them accepted by the county education and finance committees itself contains plenty of opportunities for difficulties to arise. Once estimates have been approved, the usual arrangement is that within the estimates expenditure may be incurred up to a certain limit without prior approval for individual items.

Apart from finance, the normal procedure of committee government does itself lead to delay and frustration. A major proposal for an alteration to the structure of a school may well have to go before the school's governors, a sub-committee of the divisional executive, the executive itself, a sub-committee of the county education committee and the finance committee. It is very improbable that the meetings of all these bodies will be arranged in such a way that the proposal passes from one stage to the next without delay. If at some stage an important modification is made in the original proposal, the whole procedure may need to be repeated or lengthy negotiations may have to be undertaken between the various committees involved. Moreover, a major proposal will often involve other departments of the county council as well as the education department, the county architect's or the clerk's departments may well become involved and in some cases their attitudes to the wishes of divisional executives may be less liberal than that of the education department. Thus quite apart from questions of policy or finance, the structure of the administrative machinery may itself cause ill-feeling and conflicts between a county and its divisions.

The Act of 1944 required that every scheme of divisional administration should provide for the Minister to determine any disputes between the local education authority and any divisional executive. The Minister has, in fact, interpreted his power to determine disputes in a very narrow way; differences as to the wisdom or expediency of exercising powers in a particular way when the scheme provides for the authority of the division to do so lawfully are considered to be beyond the scope of adjudication by the Minister. He is only prepared to give decisions where one party claims that the other has failed to comply with the scheme or where the scheme in force does not make any provision for the matter in dispute. Thus appeals to the Minister have been much less frequent than they might have been, and disputes have generally had to be resolved at the local level.

It may be true to say that in general terms relations today between counties and divisions are much better than they were in the years immediately following 1945. The bad feeling that had existed in some places between Part III authorities and the county administrations offered an unpromising beginning. Largely as a defensive mechanism, the National Association of Divisional Executives for Education was formed in 1947, and most excepted districts and divisional executives joined it. This body has done a great deal to help the executives to work together to find solutions to their problems; it holds an annual conference and circulates a journal containing articles of a general nature on education as well as on specific problems concerned with divisional administration.

In the third year of its existence, the National Association found itself involved in an effort to prevent what might have become a considerable reduction in the number of divisional executives. In October, 1949, the Ministry of Education suggested in a circular that schemes of divisional administration might be reviewed in an effort to secure economies in administrative costs. This led a number of counties to propose to reduce or abolish their divisional executives. In order to achieve any change in the existing system, the Minister must agree to the making of a new scheme, statutory notices are then published, objections made are considered by the Minister and eventually he approves, disapproves or alters the Scheme as he thinks fit. Somerset proposed to abolish its divisional executives, four in number, so as to save £29,000 per annum, and to enlarge the powers of managers and governors so as to ensure adequate local contact. Devon proposed to abolish three divisional executives and thereby save £12,000. The Minister rejected both of these proposals at the first stage, i.e. without even permittting new schemes to be submitted, on the grounds that they ran counter to the will of Parliament as expressed in the Education Act which had upheld the principle of divisional administration. Dorset had only one divisional executive, the Weymouth area, apart from the excepted district of Poole, and this it proposed to abolish on the grounds that as its population was only 47,000, it was too small to be an effective unit of administration; it estimated that a financial saving of £3,500 per annum would result. The Minister in this case permitted an amended scheme to be made and submitted, but then refused to approve it. Buckinghamshire proposed to reduce its six divisional executives to four so as to save £7,000 per annum, but abandoned these proposals in the face of strong opposition from the district councils involved. The only county in which any drastic reform took place at this time was Lancashire, which had an amended scheme under consideration before the circular was issued. Many of the Lancashire divisions were too small for educational purposes, nineteen had populations of fewer than 50,000; accordingly the county proposed that in place of the existing thirty-seven divisions there should in future be twenty-seven larger divisions. The Lancashire proposals met with general acceptance and received Ministerial approval.

From the reforms in Lancashire until the Local Government Act of 1958 there were very few changes in the map of divisional administration. After the issue of Circular 210 in 1949 the National Association set on foot an inquiry into the relative cost of administration in counties with and without divisional executives. The report of this investigation seemed to show that the rate of administrative expenditure did not vary appreciably with the number of divisional executives or because there was or was not divisional administration. When another Ministry circular appeared calling for administrative economies, it made no mention of divisional administration.[27]

The consequences flowing from the Local Government Act of 1958,[28] the work of the Royal Commission on London's Government, and that of the Local Government Commission in various parts of the country, will affect the future size and shape of local education authorities as well as divisional executives. So far as the latter are concerned, the reorganization of local government in the London area has led to the disappearance of twenty or so excepted districts. Outside the London area a few of the larger excepted districts may become county boroughs and acquire the status of education authorities; some of the smaller county boroughs may well become excepted districts on losing their county borough status, Burton, Worcester and Wakefield, for instance. The Act of 1958 provided for the creation of new excepted districts as of right in towns the populations of which had grown to 60,000, and in special circumstances in smaller towns.[29] Six towns claimed excepted district status as of right within the period allowed, and were granted the status automatically, they were Colchester, Basildon, Gosport, Hove, Slough, and Huyton-with-Roby. Thirty-nine more towns based claims to excepted district status on special circumstances, but the Minister only approved eight of these:[30]

five boroughs—Bedford, Scunthorpe, Crosby, Middleton, Sutton Coldfield;

two urban districts—Havant and Waterloo, Woking;

one rural district—Easington.

The process of negotiating schemes between the counties, the ministry and the new excepted districts proved to be very lengthy.

One of the most difficult problems in the organization of local educational administration during this century has been that of reconciling the strong desire evinced by civic leaders of medium-sized towns to control their own educational service with the increasing demand for more specialized techniques and functional efficiency which only large authorities can supply economically. The attempt in 1902 to solve this problem by hiving off elementary education led to increasing complications as post-primary education gained in importance. The solution of divisional administration incorporated in the Act of 1944 led initially to a good deal of friction in some areas such as Middlesex, but over the greater part of the country sound working relationships have come to be established between county and divisional levels. There can be little doubt that the 1944 solution represents a great advance over that of 1902, but the present system does exact its toll in the shape of an elaboration of committee work and of the bureaucracy.

The toll exacted by divisional administration may be illustrated from the situation in the West Riding, a county where a mixed local system prevails, divisional executives having only been set up in those parts of the county where the locality sought them.[31] Before the last war, Selby's elementary schools were managed by a district sub-committee working in direct relationship with the county; the High School and Technical and Art School had their own governors who were also responsible directly to the county. Thus a two-tier system might be said to have existed, and since no divisional executive was established in 1945 the system remained unchanged save that governors were appointed for new secondary schools. In Rothwell, on the other hand, a divisional executive was established in a mid-way position between the grouped school managers and the county committee. The county's report commented that 'it is difficult to escape the conclusion that if education in the two-tier area of Selby is as effective as it is in the three-tier area of Rothwell, more time and energy are being expended to achieve the same result in the latter than in the former'.[32]

The system of divisional executives has certainly enabled a variety of arrangements to be made within the same county in accordance with the wishes of the local community in such a controversial field as the organization of secondary education, and this is no small advantage. At the same time it has introduced another tier into the administration which results in delay on occasion, complicates the structure of local educational government and offers many more opportunities for friction. There is some truth in the conclusion of an American investigator that much of the criticism of divisional administration is directed towards the system as it has operated rather than towards the theory, while favourable comment seems to be based upon the system's theoretical possibilities rather than on its practical achievements.[33]

IV

A second reform in the structure of local educational administration introduced by the Act of 1944 was the requirement that all maintained primary and secondary schools should have bodies of managers or governors.[34] Before 1944 the only provided elementary schools required by law to have bodies of managers were those in county areas; in boroughs and urban districts the local authority could decide whether or not its provided elementary schools should have managers. Non-provided elementary schools in all areas naturally had bodies of managers. Not more than four of the managers of a provided school in a county area were to be appointed by the county while up to two could be appointed by the minor authority; in other areas the local education authority appointed the managers. In a non-provided school the foundation appointed up to four managers and the education authority two—or in a county area, the county authority appointed one and the minor authority one. The managers of a provided elementary school had such powers and dealt only with such matters as the local education authority determined. Thus in some parts of the country the managers of these schools enjoyed considerable powers while in other parts they fulfilled almost no functions. The managers of non-provided schools had the considerable powers left to them by the Education Acts of 1902 and 1921 which included the right to appoint and to dismiss teachers within the limits as to numbers and qualifications laid down by the local authority.

Secondary schools provided by local authorities usually had governing bodies although they often had little power and in some boroughs a sub-committee of the education committee sometimes acted as the governing body for all secondary schools. Secondary schools not provided by local authorities normally worked under schemes drawn up in accordance with the Endowed Schools Acts and these invariably set out the composition of the governing body that administered the school.

The reconsideration of the principles of financial support for voluntary schools led to a re-casting of the constitution and powers of their managing and governing bodies so as to reflect the greater financial responsibility that the public authorities were to undertake. The legal obligation to set up bodies of managers and governors in provided schools appears to have arisen from the desire to establish a common administrative framework for all schools maintained by local authorities, whatever their origins. So far as secondary schools were concerned this was connected with the desire to ensure parity of esteem for new schools with those of earlier foundation. If voluntary secondary schools continued to have governing bodies of their own—and they could hardly be deprived of them—while the newer council foundations did not do so, this would have meant in many places that the grammar school kept its governors while the modern schools had none and were simply 'run by the office'. As the white paper of 1943 explained, 'It is desirable that any legislation should prescribe the status of the Local Education Authority in relation to all types of secondary schools—and that steps should be taken to give authoritative definition of the status and powers of the Governing Body'.[35]

The Education Act stated that there should be an instrument of management for every primary school and an instrument of government for every secondary school which would provide for the constitution of a body of managers or governors.[36] These instruments were to be made by the local authority in the case of provided schools and by an order of the Minister in the case of voluntary schools. Primary schools were to be conducted in accordance with rules of management made by an order of the local authority, county (i.e. provided) secondary schools in accordance with articles of government made by an order of the local authority and approved by the Minister, and voluntary secondary schools in accordance with articles made by an order of the Minister. Before making any order under this Section of the Act, the Minister had to give an opportunity for interested parties to make their views known to him and he was required to 'have regard to the manner in which the school has been conducted theretofore'. It was hoped that this provision would enable the very different traditions of the various schools that were to be known as maintained to be taken fully into account,

Section 18 of the Act set out the principles to be followed in constituting bodies of managers for primary schools. In the case of county schools, the local education authority should appoint all the managers— six being the minimum number—except that where there were minor authorities, they could appoint one-third. Voluntary primary schools were also to have bodies of at least six managers; in aided schools two-thirds of these were to be appointed by the foundation and one-third by the public authority, in controlled schools only one-third were to be foundation managers.[37] Section 19 laid down similar provisions for constituting the governing bodies of secondary schools save that there was no requirement for the appointment of representatives of minor authorities. The Act permitted local authorities to group any number of schools, primary or secondary, under one governing body,[38] but no voluntary school could be grouped without the consent of its managers or governors.

Many of the older secondary schools were alarmed in 1944 at the prospect of being administered directly by local authorities and losing the measure of independence that they had in the past maintained; consequently they sought strong governing bodies as some protection against such a development. Largely because of pressure from this quarter, the Board of Education issued a white paper on the Principles of Government in Maintained Secondary Schools.[39] This document gave these as the main functions of governing bodies:

(a) finance,

(b) appointment and dismissal of staff,

(c) internal organization and curriculum,

(d) admission of pupils.

It qualified each of these functions in such a way as to make it clear that in exercising them a governing body was usually to be subject to the over-riding authority of the county or county borough maintaining the school. Under the heading 'internal organization and curriculum' for instance, it was explained that the local education authority would have the right to settle the general character of the school and its place in the local system, while the headmaster would control the internal organization, management and discipline of the school; presumably whatever was left after the claims of the authority and the head had been staked might be left to the governors. Again, on school holidays the White Paper said that 'in order to secure the necessary uniformity it will no doubt be necessary that the local education authority should fix the school terms, but the governors should be empowered to grant a limited number of occasional holidays at their discretion'. Some governing bodies may well have had cause to feel that the keynote of this document lay in the equivocal sentence that 'Independence implies, not freedom from proper control, but freedom to exercise legitimate and appropriate functions', which may be interpreted by the more cynically inclined as freedom to do only what Authority wants.

The number of administrative duties to be performed in running schools are, of necessity, limited. Thus the attempt to find room in some areas for the ministry, the local authority, the divisional executive, the governing body and the head teacher all to have a share in the work must often occasion a certain amount of overlapping. In some districts the governing bodies have been reduced to ineffective cyphers by the local authorities and have either been edged out of exercising any effective powers or have never been permitted to do so. There is little doubt but that a group of interested governors can be of considerable assistance to a school. The very fact that a school has a governing body containing men known in the district as people of worth wins for it greater respect in the eyes of the community which it serves. From the wider point of view it is important that schools should be encouraged to develop in an individual way, and one method of forwarding this is to give them independent-minded governors, prepared to take an interest in their school and to do their utmost to see that its needs are not overlooked. It is sometimes said to be difficult to find enough suitable people willing to serve on governing bodies, but authorities that are prepared to leave a reasonable amount of worthwhile activity to their school governors seem able to find sufficient candidates.

v

The principal direct change made by the Education Act of 1944 in the position of the county councils was to give them overall responsibility for elementary education in those parts of the county which had hitherto been autonomous; the county boroughs remained unchanged as local education authorities. The main effect of the Act on these local authorities was to cause them to extend and, to some degree, to remodel the administrative structures which they had built up before the Second World War. The reorganization of schools and of codes in accordance with the conception of education in three successive stages, primary, secondary and further, led to a reorganization of the committee structure and of the duties of officers. Thus the separate sub-committees for elementary and higher education, which had been a usual feature of committee arrangements, now disappeared and were often replaced by a schools sub-committee for primary and secondary education, and by a further education sub-committee dealing with technical colleges, evening institutes and other educational activities which were beyond the orbit of the schools. The separate branches of education departments dealing with elementary and higher education had likewise to be reorganized. The organization of sub-committees and of administrative work was a matter for each authority, but confronted with similar needs and problems, the sort of solutions arrived at often followed a broad pattern. The changes made in the sub-committee organization of the West Riding, as set out in *Ten Years of Change*, were as follows:[40]

I. Before the Act of 1944 there were fifteen standing and other sub-committees:

Finance and General Purposes,
Endowments,
Child Welfare,
School Canteen,
Elementary Education,
Staffing,
*Joint Buildings,
*Joint School Supplies,
Higher Education,
Staffing and Salaries,
Bingley (T. C.) Visiting,
Adult Education,
*Joint Buildings   ⎫
*Joint School Supplies ⎬ 'Joint' with Elementary Education,
Post-War Education,   ⎭
County Library,
Agriculture.

II. After the Act twenty were set up, of which six were standing sub-committees and ten were governing or visiting sub-committees for special schools and residential establishments:

Policy and Finance,
Sites and Buildings,
Property,
School Management,
Staffing and Salaries,
Appeals,
Further Education,
Governing sub-committees for the four training colleges, for Grantly Adult College and Woolley Hall Refresher Course College,

Special Services,
Four Visiting sub-committees for residential special schools,
County Library,
Agricultural Education.

At the very time when the educational work of the local authorities was expanding rapidly under the influence of post-war reconstruction, they found their functions in certain other directions diminished or at an end. The establishment of the National Assistance Board and of the National Health Service and the nationalization of the electricity supply industry all had the effect of transferring work from local to central government. One consequence of these developments was that education became the principal function of county and county borough councils accounting for a far larger proportion of budgeted expenditure than any other department and in some cases for more than half of the total expenditure of a council. All this has tended to make the education committee a popular committee in the sense that more members of a council often wish to serve on it than there are places for. It has also served to strengthen political interest in education in many localities. As Dr. Lawrence has pointed out, the extent to which discussion in education committees 'follows political lines varies greatly from one authority to another; it tends to be greater in the presence of representatives of the press and its extent has certainly increased during the last ten years'.[41] Education has also come to play a larger part in the work of other main committees of a county or borough council such as the establishments committee and the finance committee; if an education committee is not to be frustrated, it must ensure that its needs are fully understood in other committees, and one way in which this has been achieved is through the council members of education committees also serving on other committees.

Possible difficulties between the various committees of a council can often be avoided by co-operation between an authority's chief officers. The large school building programmes which have followed the Second World War have brought the chief education officer into frequent contact with the authority's architect and if the two can work well together, clearly obstacles can be prevented from arising. Sir Arthur Binns, for many years Chief Education Officer for Lancashire has written that sometimes it is necessary to criticize the architect's efforts 'and some architects don't like that. . . . The treasurer to the authority has to find the money which, as he would put it, the Education Officer spends, and sometimes the treasurer tries to dictate how much shall be spent and for what purpose it shall be spent.' The growing importance of education has also led to great interest in the education department from the town or county clerk and this has at times led to difficulties in the relationship between the clerk and the education officer. 'Chief Education Officers recognize that each council must have a chief officer to co-ordinate the work of the departments with each other, and with the general policy of the council. This Chief Officer or Clerk should be the legal adviser of all departments and the adviser on matters of procedure. He is entitled to be consulted by the Chief Education Officer on all such matters and is also entitled to be kept informed on all matters of general policy so that he can fulfil his prime function of co-ordination.'[42]

Before 1944 there was no legal obligation on authorities to appoint an education officer, although it was, in fact, customary to do so. The Education Act then passed imposed a duty of appointing a chief education officer and required authorities to consult with the Minister before making an appointment by submitting to him the names, qualifications and experience of those from whom they proposed to choose. The Minister was given power to prohibit the appointment of anyone he might consider not to be suitable. A high proportion of chief education officers have been appointed from among 'sitting deputies', that is to say the deputy for an area has succeeded his chief; three-quarters of the vacancies for chief education officers were filled in this way between 1950 and 1956.[43] There can be no doubt that those who sit on public appointing committees have a duty to appoint always the best man, but it may be doubted whether the best man was in so many cases already occupying the post of deputy when his chief left. From time to time the deputy may well be the best person available, but it can hardly be a good thing for deputies to form the habit of waiting for their chief's post instead of seeking promotion on the basis of their merit in other places.

Chief education officers and their senior assistants are usually selected from those who have had experience both in teaching and in educational administration. They therefore bring to their work qualifications and experience which are almost always lacking in senior officials of the Department of Education and Science. The latter are members of the general adminstrative class of the civil service and their stay at the Department is only part of a career which takes them round various ministries. Thus a man might easily be appointed even as Permanent Under-Secretary of the Department with no experience of administering education or of teaching or of schools since the day he ceased from being a pupil in one. These senior officials of the central government have to obtain guidance in educational matters from the inspectorate or advisory bodies. This situation is quite unlike that which obtained as recently as Morant's day when senior officers were recruited as 'assistant examiners' and made their careers in the service of the Board of Education. One consequence of the present arrangements for staffing the Department is that a heavier burden of responsibility for the well-being of the schools now falls upon local education officers whose training and experience enable them to comprehend much more readily than the Department's officials the needs of pupils, teachers and schools.

VI

The only major change in the structure of local educational administration since the settlement of 1944 has been that in the Greater London area following from the general reorganization of London local government. The problems arising from the rapid expansion of the population of the London suburban areas and the absence of any local authority which could take a view of the needs of the area as a whole led to the appointment of a Royal Commission on London Government to study the situation and to make recommendations. The Report of the Commission recommended that the London County Council and the Middlesex County Council should be abolished, that a Greater London Council should be set up to cover London and Middlesex counties along with much of suburban Surrey, Kent, and Essex; the whole area was also to be divided into a number of much smaller districts each with its own borough council and all local government work should be divided between these two tiers.

The Commissioners suggested that responsibility for education should be divided between the Greater London Council and the boroughs and that the role of each should be defined by statute. It pointed out that the boroughs would be large and could claim to be full local education authorities, but the L.C.C. had accorded to parents a considerable freedom of choice of school in the central area and 'we attach great importance to the maintenance of this policy and its full application to the wider area of Greater London. The powers [in education] cannot be concurrent nor can there be a clear-cut division between different aspects of education. The broad division should be that the Council should be responsible for the provision of a statutory standard of education throughout the area and that the boroughs should be responsible for the discharge of the executive work subject to the budgetary and other controls by the Council referred to hereafter. We think that the cost of education should be the responsibility of the Council and be met by precept by the Council upon the boroughs as rating authorities.'[44] The Report made specific and detailed proposals for a statutory division of functions which might prove to be of interest if any form of regional government came to be adopted in this country.[45]

These proposals met with little favour in the Ministry since they appeared to depart from the principle achieved in 1944 of only one statutory local education authority entirely responsible for all educational services within its area. The government favoured giving full educational powers to each of the new boroughs and this was the solution eventually accepted for most of the London area. The boroughs created by the London Government Act of 1963 have populations of 200,000 or 300,000, and would be considered quite capable of standing alone educationally in the provinces. At the same time there was much pressure on the government to preserve the existing education service for central London operated by the L.C.C. and having a continuous history of successful administration back through the days of the London School Board.

The outcome is that twenty of the outer London boroughs, those outside the former L.C.C. area[46] have become full local education authorities exercising the powers conferred on L.E.A.s by the Education Acts 1944–62. In central London there is now a single purpose authority dealing with education only for the first time since the London School Board was abolished in favour of the multi-purpose local authority at the beginning of this century. This central zone, to be known as the Inner London Education Area, has a special committee of the G.L.C. to exercise the powers of an L.E.A. This special committee consists of

'(a) such councillors of the G.L.C. as have been elected by local government electors for an inner London borough or the City;

(b) one representative of each inner London borough council appointed by the borough council from among the members thereof;

(c) one representative of the Common Council appointed by the Common Council from among the members thereof'.[47]

The Special Committee itself has power to precept upon rating authorities of the Inner London Education Area in respect of educational expenditure as well as power to borrow. These arrangements for central London have been introduced initially for a period of five years. The Secretary of State for Education is obliged to review the situation and report to Parliament before 31st March, 1970, as to whether the present I.L.E.A. should continue or whether its functions should be transferred to the inner London boroughs. At the time of writing it is much too soon to make any appraisal of the degree of success likely to attend the new form of organization for local educational administration in the London area.

REFERENCES

[1] 2 Edw. 7, c. 42. Schedule II (15).
[2] Board of Education Circular No. 470 of 1903.
[3] The Work of Education, 1903–14. Report by F. R. Hughes, Secretary to West Suffolk Education Committee, 1914, pp. 9, 10.
[4] G. Balfour, Ten Years of Staffordshire Education, 1903–13, p. 113.
[5] City of Leeds. Report of the Education Committee to the City Council for the year ending 31st March, 1905. Women were not eligible to serve on municipal councils until 1907—hence the special provision requiring the co-option of at least two women to each education committee.
[6] Leeds School Board, Tenth Triennial Report, 1900.
[7] City of Leeds, Report of the Education Committee to the City Council for the year ending 31st March, 1905.
[8] F. R. Hughes, op. cit., p. 14.
[9] G. Balfour, op. cit., p. 108.
[10] The authority given to chairmen of sub-committees to make provisional decisions (subject to later confirmation) also enabled urgent matters to be dealt with more expeditiously.
[11] S. D. Simon, A Century of City Government, p. 262.
[12] Report on the Education of the Adolescent, 1927, p. 161.
[13] Report on the question of Devolution by County Education Authorities, Cd. 3952, 1908.
[14] Report on the Education of the Adolescent, 1927, p. 163.
[15] Ibid., p. 182.
[16] Royal Commission on Local Government, 1927, App. CVII, p. 1867, Memorandum of Evidence submitted on behalf of the Board of Education.
[17] Report of the Committee on the Nations Expenditure, Cmd. 3920, para. 503.
[18] Report on Secondary Education, 1938, p. 318.
[19] P. G. Richards, Delegation in Local Government, 1956, p. 66.
[20] 7 & 8 Geo. 6, c. 31.
[21] Educational Reconstruction, 1943, Cmd. 6458.
[22] The Minister exempted 13 English and 9 Welsh counties.
[23] Ministry of Education Circular, No. 5, September, 1944.
[24] Dr. P. G. Richards discussed this matter fully in an address on Divisional Administration which he gave to the National Association of Divisional Executives, 10th Annual Conference—N.A.D.E.E. Report of 10th Annual Conference, 1956.
[25] E. W. Cohen, Autonomy and Delegation in County Government, n.d., p. 37.
[26] Ministry of Education, Circular No. 210, para. 4, October, 1949.

[27] Ministry of Education, Circular No. 242, November, 1951.

[28] 6 & 7 Eliz. 2, c 55.

[29] Ibid., S 52.

[30] N.A.D.E.E. Report of 15th Annual Conference, 1961.

[31] These illustrations are drawn from *Ten Years of Change*, published by the West Riding Education Committee in 1953.

[32] Ibid., p. 139.

[33] T. L. Reller, *Divisional Administration in English Education*, 1959, p. 204.

[34] 7 & 8 Geo. 6, c 31, S 17.

[35] Educational Reconstruction, 1943, Cmd. 6458, para. 61.

[36] 7 & 8 Geo. 6, c 31, S 17.

[37] The managers (or governors) of voluntary schools had to decide whether to apply for 'aided' or 'controlled' status under the Act. In the case of the former they had to be willing, and show the Minister that they were able, to meet half of the cost of any necessary alterations, improvements and repairs. If they lacked the resources or were unwilling to meet the expenditure required for 'aided' status, their schools became 'controlled'. The small group of 'special agreement' schools, whose origin lay in the Education Act of 1936, were treated similarly to 'aided' schools in this respect.

[38] 7 & 8 Geo. 6, c 31, S 20.

[39] Principles of Government in Maintained Secondary Schools, 1944, Cmd. 6523.

[40] *Ten Years of Change*, West Riding Education Committee, 1953.

[41] B. E. Lawrence, 'The Work and Spirit of a Local Education Authority', *Adult Education*, vol. XXXI, pp. 87–99.

[42] A. L. Binns, 'The Chief Education Officer and His Task', *Journal of Education*, April, 1957.

[43] Norman Fisher, 'Training for Chief Education Officers?' *Journal of Education*, June, 1957.

[44] Report of R.C. on Local Government in Greater London, 1960, para. 800.

[45] Ibid., para. 829.

[46] The twenty London boroughs are Barking, Barnet, Bexley, Brent, Bromley, Croydon, Ealing, Enfield, Haringey, Harrow, Havering, Hillingdon, Hounslow, Kingston-on-Thames, Merton, Newham, Redbridge, Richmond, Sutton, Waltham Forest.

[47] 11 & 12 Eliz. 2, c 33, S 30.

P

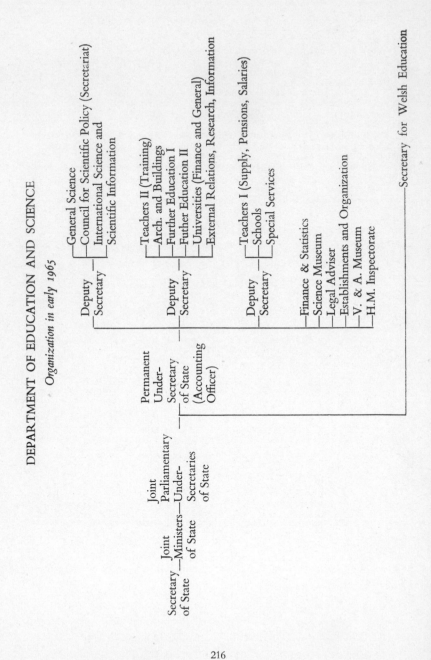

DEPARTMENT OF EDUCATION AND SCIENCE

Organization in early 1965

Secretary of State — Joint Ministers of State — Joint Parliamentary Under-Secretaries of State — Permanent Under-Secretary of State (Accounting Officer)

Deputy Secretary
- General Science
- Council for Scientific Policy (Secretariat)
- International Science and Scientific Information

Deputy Secretary
- Teachers II (Training)
- Arch. and Buildings
- Further Education I
- Futher Education II
- Universities (Finance and General)
- External Relations, Research, Information

Deputy Secretary
- Teachers I (Supply, Pensions, Salaries)
- Schools
- Special Services

- Finance & Statistics
- Science Museum
- Legal Adviser
- Establishments and Organization
- V. & A. Museum
- H.M. Inspectorate

Secretary for Welsh Education

216

CONCLUSION

THE rearrangement of the central government's educational administration during recent months may be viewed as a continuation of the process of unifying and rationalizing which has been going on since the setting up of the Board of Education in the late nineteenth century. The expansion of the universities and their increasing cost to the nation inevitably raised the question of whether the arrangement whereby they received grants from public funds on the advice of the University Grants Committee working directly with the Treasury was any longer adequate. The Robbins Report recommended that a Ministry of Arts and Science should be established to care for the needs of the universities and the various research bodies. The existing Ministry of Education did not appear to members of the Royal Commission to be a suitable agency to preside over higher education.

The view of the Commissioners was widely supported inside the universities, especially among scientists, but outside the universities and the world of science there was much general support for school education and higher education being the responsibility of one minister, that is for a return to the situation which had prevailed during the second decade of this century. In order to attempt to compromise between these two views, a Secretary of State for Education and Science was appointed from 1st April, 1964.[1] To the new Secretary of State were transferred all the functions of the Minister of Education and all the functions of the Minister for Science. The Lord President of the Council and Minister for Science, Mr. Hogg, became the new Secretary of State, and he explained the new arrangements to the House of Commons in this way: '. . . the new Department for Education and Science will consist of two administrative units, one of these will deal with the universities and civil science and the other with schools and other forms of education in England and Wales. Each unit will be associated with one of the two Ministers of State. . . . There will be two Permanent Under-Secretaries who will be accounting for the two units.'[2] Mr. Hogg added that the principle was 'that the handling of universities, and of new technological universities in particular, cannot be separated from the handling of research. The function of a university is not simply to teach. It is, and must be, equally to consolidate and advance the frontiers of knowledge. Part of the value of

217

a university education to an undergraduate lies in the exposure of his mind to teachers who are doing precisely this. From this point of view the treatment of the universities must be associated with the treatment of research in other areas.'[3]

The arrangement described by Mr. Hogg did last for a few months, but by the beginning of 1965 the universities and civil science no longer had their own accounting officer, but had been put under the accounting officer for the former Ministry of Education. Moreover, Universities (Finance and General) were no longer administered along with civil science but had been handed over to the deputy secretary in charge of teacher training, technical colleges and non-vocational further education as may be seen from the plan on p. 216. The University Grants Committee continued to act as a buffer between the universities and the Department.

The division of work among the political appointees in 1965 did still reflect to some extent the federal arrangement of the two units established the previous year. One Minister of State dealt with science, the universities and liaised with the Ministry of Technology, while the other Minister of State dealt with schools, teacher training and special services. The Secretary of State kept in his own hands business connected with the reorganization of secondary education, teacher supply and the general question of the future control of the training colleges; possibly these latter might have been considered the most delicate fields politically. The Parliamentary Under Secretaries dealt with technical, commercial, adult and art education as well as sport, the youth services and libraries.

These developments have strengthened further the administrative authority of the Secretary of State for Education and Science. In 1944 Parliament gave his predecessor, the Minister of Education, more power than had been entrusted to the President of the Board of Education—largely at the expense of the local authorities, with the aim of bringing about a greater equality of educational opportunity in different parts of the country. Since then various factors have led to the increase in the authority of the central government in education, factors which are often not educational.

One of the most important is the ever increasing role of the state in the economic life of the nation. The concept which prevailed before the First World War of the state only being concerned with balancing governmental income and expenditure in an annual budget has long since been set aside. The amount of the nation's resources which can

be devoted to education at any time can really only be decided by
the central government. The importance attached to education by
local communities in recent years has been such that most local
authorities appear to have been willing to spend more on new developments
than the state has been able to permit. A consequence of this
has been the very close control which the former Ministry and present
Department has maintained over local authority building programmes.
To some extent it was also this factor which led the then Minister of
Education to seek to take part at an early stage in the Burnham
negotiations. The total amount which the nation can afford to spend
on teachers' salaries is obviously of vital concern to the government,
and the government also naturally wishes to see that the money
available will be disbursed in such a way as to obtain the maximum
advantage for the community.

The increasing weight of the demands education is making on the
resources of the nation is illustrated by the following figures comparing
the latest year for which particulars are available with ten years
earlier.[4]

Expenditure on education (excluding milk and meals):

	1953–54	1963–64
(a) England and Wales .	£405,100,000	£1,166,800,000
(b) United Kingdom .	£470,200,000	£1,354,100,000

Expenditure as a percentage of the Gross National Product of the United Kingdom

	1953–54	1963–64
(a) Education . .	3·1	5·0
(b) Milk and Meals .	0·3	0·3
(c) Total .	3·4	5·3

Another factor which has served to strengthen the position of the
central authority is the extent to which the community's political
and social ideas have changed during the last half-century. Individuals
expect far more services from the state than their grandparents, or
perhaps even their parents, did. Thus it is no longer enough for the
central government to ensure that a basic, elementary education is
provided free of charge for all, it must now attempt to ensure that
every sort of educational service is available to all who need it in any
area. This concern has now been made to extend to the form which
secondary provision should take for the central authority has now

come to insist on a number of prescribed varieties of non-selective schooling.

While the centre has come to strengthen its administrative and financial control over education, there has been a strong tendency through most of the present century to leave more and more of the questions concerning the content of education to local authorities, schools, training colleges, area training organizations and the like. The amount of devolution of authority from the centre that has taken place here is not always sufficiently recognized. In the late nineteenth century the Education Department still concerned itself with prescribing the studies of every elementary school child and examined him annually. By the middle of the twentieth century the Ministry had even passed over to the training colleges, acting through area training organizations, the right to recommend students for recognition as qualified teachers without further examination.

Throughout the period with which this book is concerned, the successful administration of the schools has depended upon a measure of co-operation between the localities and the central government agencies. At no time has the centre been able to ignore local feeling and regard local authorities or managers as mere local agents to carry out orders; in this respect the system in this country has differed from that to be found in most continental countries where highly centralized forms of organization with little or no reliance upon local initiative have been typical. Perhaps there are two main advantages to this system of sharing authority between the centre and the localities which has evolved here, in the first place there has been an opportunity for a locality to experiment or to meet a special local need, secondly it has also made it possible to build up a national system with reasonably even provision for educational needs in all parts of the country.

REFERENCES

[1] Statutory Instrument, No. 490, dated 26th March, 1964.
[2] Hansard, 1963–64, vol. 691, cols. 570–1.
[3] Ibid., col. 576.
[4] 1964 Statistics of Education, Part I, 1965. Table 29.

INDEX

Aberdeen, 45
Abney, W., 92, 93, 94
Acland, A. H. D., 154
Adderley, J. A., 25, 38, 46
Administrative Class Civil Service Examination, 108
Adult Education Committee, 118
Archbishop of Canterbury, 169
Archbishop of York, 169
Area Training Organizations, 119
Army Schools, 8, 9
Arnold, Matthew, 23
Assistant Mistresses Association, 123
Association of Education Committees, 119, 123, 193
Association of Municipal Corporations, 119, 123
Association of Organizing Secretaries and Directors, 159
Association of Principals of Technical Institutions, 119
Association of Teachers in Colleges and Departments of Education, 119
Association of Teachers in Technical Institutions, 119, 123
Association of Technical Institutions, 119
Association of University Teachers, 119
Attendance, compulsory, 137–9

Balfour, A. J., 177, 184
Basildon, 203
Bedford, 203
Bethnal Green Museum, 49
Birmingham, 43, 45, 127, 133, 135, 142, 144, 171
Birmingham, Archdeacon of, 171
Birmingham Church Schools Association, 186
Birmingham Roman Catholic Diocesan Association, 186
Birmingham University, 186
Birrell, A., 192
Board of Education, 2, 27, 39, 44, 217; Chapter 5 passim; early organization and functions, 91–8; staffing, 105–8, 212; post-war organization, 108–12; Welsh difficulties, 113–15; advisory committees, 188 ff.; Cockerton affair, 173–4; 1902 Act, 179–83; Part III authorities, 193, 195; governing bodies, 207
Board of Education Act, 1899, 88, 90, 92, 93, 112
Boards of Guardians, 7, 138, 144, 167
Board of Trade, 8, 39, 43, 44, 45, 52
Bournemouth, 112
Boy clerks, 31–2
Bradford, 135
Bradford Grammar School, 49
Brecon, 113
Bristol, 45
British and Foreign School Society, 1, 6, 10, 186
British Medical Journal, 104
Bruce, H. A., 26, 34
Bryce Commission, 52, 55, 70, 77–81, 83–4, 84–6, 94, 157, 158, 162, 164, 166, 167–8
Bryce, James, 90
Buckinghamshire, 202
Burnham Committees, 118, 122–4
Burnham, Lord, 118, 122
Burton, 203
Butler, R. A., 196

221